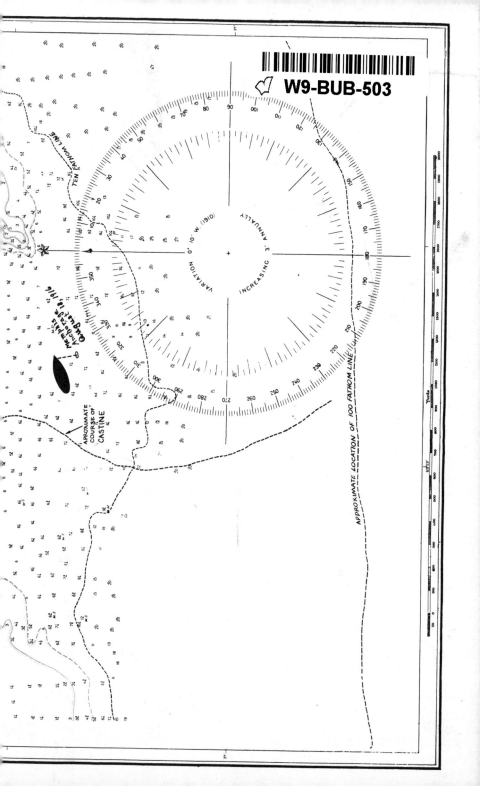

W9-BUB-503

The Wreck of the Memphis

Captain Edward L. Beach

UNITED STATES NAVY

Holt, Rinehart and Winston

New York   Chicago   San Francisco

Books by Edward L. Beach

The Wreck of the Memphis
Around the World Submerged
Run Silent, Run Deep
Submarine!

THE WRECK OF THE MEMPHIS

Copyright © 1966 by Edward L. Beach

All rights reserved, including the right to reproduce
this book or portions thereof in any form.

Published simultaneously in Canada by Holt, Rinehart
and Winston of Canada, Ltd.

Library of Congress Catalog Card Number: 66-13207

First Edition

80850-0516
Printed in the United States of America

To the officers and men of the USS *Memphis*

Contents

Foreword   3

1   Whence Came USS *Memphis*   9
2   Tuesday, Aug. 29, 1916, at Santo Domingo—
    Until Midafternoon   31
3   Engine Rooms and Firerooms, from 3:30 to 4:35   53
4   *Castine*—to 4:06 P.M. 29 Aug., 1916   77
5   *Memphis,* Topside During the Critical Hour
    3:35 to 4:35 P.M.   86
6   The Marines at Fort Ozama 3:30 P.M. to 4:30   116
7   The Recreation Party   126
8   *Castine*—4:06 P.M. and Afterward   132
9   The Starboard Engine Room of *Memphis,* After 4:35   149
10   The Firerooms After 4:35   161
11   The Port Engine Room from 4:30   173
12   Topside—4:35 and After   184
13   As Seen from the Shore   211
14   Abandon Ship   227
15   The Boats   249
16   The End of the *Memphis*   260
17   A Board of Inquest, Two Courts of Inquiry,
    and a General Court-Martial   270
18   Vindication   297
    Acknowledgments   303

The Wreck of the Memphis

Foreword

This is the story of a ship of the United States Navy, and her people, as told by her commander and his son, and by the members of the ship's company who served in her on the twenty-ninth of August, 1916.

My father graduated from the U.S. Naval Academy in 1888 with the rank of "Passed Midshipman." In those days the new graduates were given two years of sea duty before being brought back to the Academy for a final examination and determination as to which of the basic branches of the Navy each should go into. Father, who had always liked and understood the operation of the new high-pressure engines with which ships of the new modern Navy were being fitted, applied for the Engineer Corps. In due course he became a "Passed Assistant Engineer."

The new machinery was all wonderfully interesting to the enthusiastic young engineer, but during the next ten years he came to realize that the system of having two separate subdivisions of the Navy on board a single ship, with the engineers essentially independent even of the captain, simply could not work. He had discovered, besides, that there was a lot more to the Navy than operating the engines. Most of the young members of the Engineer Corps thought as he did, and they heartily approved when it was combined with the Line of the Navy in 1900.

Dad was a part of the Navy during the creation of the new modern fleet, its trial of strength in the Spanish-American War and its burgeoning development afterward. It was one of the exciting periods. In 1914 he became a captain, and he retired in 1922 to help bring up the three young children of his second marriage. He died in 1943.

3

I graduated from the Naval Academy in 1939 and now also hold the rank of Captain, USN. Father wrote a number of books about the Navy, including several which have not been published, and naturally I have inherited all his papers. Much of what is contained in the pages to follow has come from his unpublished autobiography and from his other written descriptions of the events related. The remainder is from the personal recollections of members of the *Memphis* ship's company who are still alive and who meet annually, on the anniversary of the disaster which this book describes.

The story of a shipwreck which brought death or injury to so many people, and in which my father figured so prominently, cannot but be a very personal one from my point of view. Consequently, the reader will probably detect a certain amount of transmigration of personality in the story which follows, and for this I beg his understanding in advance. Of course, it must also be clearly stated that, although the events here described actually occurred and have been retold as accurately as is possible these fifty years later, all opinions expressed or inferred are strictly my own and all errors of fact must be laid at the door of the son, not the father.

This is the story of the United States Ship *Memphis,* which was christened *Tennessee* in 1904 and died as *Memphis* in 1916. There are those who would hold that a ship has no personality and no soul, and that therefore a ship can have no character. With this idea, sailors will never agree. There are authors, likewise, who hold that the development of character is the only true purpose of authorship, and that the ship can never be more than a locale, the scenery around which character is built.

With this theory, I emphatically do not hold; there are as many valid objectives of the writer as there are writers, and not only is the environment part of the man—he is part of the environment.

In the environment on board ship men are particularly changed from any resemblance to their characters as seen on the streets of a large foreign city, at home, or in any other situation of life. It might take a psychiatrist to explain why this must be, but men who have been at sea in U. S. men-of-war, who have spent long hours on watch with nothing to see but the horizon, the ceaselessly moving machinery of the ship, or the crammed innards of a submarine, know that this is true. Perhaps we even have a hint of why—an inkling of the deep underlying traditions of our military men of the sea, their dedication to excellence, their devotion to their ships, which causes them more often than not to think of these huge, mobile, water-borne fortresses in a completely personal way.

All this is not to infer that these men are not individuals. Within the framework of the environment which must condition their primary reactions, there is ample room for the specialized individual reaction which is the product of each separate personality. Thus, every society, or sub-society, has its own rules; and it is only those with deep psychological inhibitions who do not soon find themselves living within the group mores encompassed by their ship.

As a child I never wearied of Father's stories about our Navy: his service in sailing ships or in the old monitors *Puritan* and *Nevada*, his command of the battleship *New York* at the German surrender in 1918 and, of course, the disaster which overtook the *Memphis* (which he always called *Tennessee*). I can particularly recall one day when the Pacific Battle Fleet came into San Francisco Harbor and he took me to visit her twin, the *Washington*, which he had also commanded. She was by this time known as *Seattle*, but she was the flagship of the Commander-in-Chief of our fleet, all the same. I was impressed with *Seattle*'s four tall smokestacks ("pipes," as her crew called them), and especially with her trim gray lines and her immaculate condition. Her name had been changed from *Washington* to *Seattle*, just as that of the *Tennessee* had been changed to *Memphis*, in order to release the state name for a new superdreadnaught then under construction. This new *Washington*, it might be mentioned in passing, was launched but never finished. She was sunk as a target by the U. S. battle fleet, a casualty of the London Naval Treaty of 1920, when she was about 75 per cent complete. The battleship *Washington* which fought in World War II was built in 1940.

In 1955, I received a letter from a Mr. Leslie B. Kidwell of Chicago, asking if I were related to his old skipper of 1916; and as a result of the acquaintanceship here begun, in 1959 I was present at a Philadelphia reunion of the men who had served with Father in the *Memphis*. At this time the Society of the Survivors of the United States Armored Cruiser *Memphis* was formed. I was shown the colors which had been flying when the ship was destroyed and was told the story of how they had been quietly preserved all these years. I was given one of a pair of cut-glass wine decanters—mementos of a day before our Navy went dry—which had been rescued from the officers' wardroom of the *Memphis*. This has been proudly restored to its original use, though not aboard ship.

In February of 1960, I wrote to Mr. Sam Worth of Cleveland, Ohio, custodian of the flag, and asked him if he would send it to me as a matter of great urgency. It arrived immediately by special delivery, and so it was that we were able to carry it with us in USS *Triton* when that vessel, a nuclear-powered submarine, made the first entirely submerged circumnavigation of the world. Upon our return to port in May, 1960, we flew it from the highest part of the ship—an extended periscope—in double symbolism.

This was fitting; for though our Navy is composed of ships and aircraft and the equipment necessary for them to function effectively, it also is composed of people—and people are the most important part. Ships, indeed, have souls, but the soul of a ship is the composite soul of all the people who make up her complement, to whom must be added those who helped design her, build her, place her in the water, and bind her to her mission—in short, the soul of a ship is the synergism of the souls of all the persons who create her, both past and present. Without people, a ship is nothing. With her people, a ship is a living entity, possessed of a will and a drive and a fortune of her own. Thus, by logical if poorly understood transliteration of personality into the sexless fabric of its structure, the sailor frequently refers to a ship as "she."

She, the ship, consequently has a personality. A modern aircraft carrier, which may hold as many as six thousand people, is a fantastic conglomerate of activity; yet her entire purpose may be epitomized in a single objective toward which everything else is directed.

All of this is done by people. But time progresses, and people progress with the times. It has been said that we are in the midst of a technological revolution. It would be hard to refute this, but if so, then people too must change—in their capabilities, their education, their relationships with each other. Though the essence of their personalities may not be particularly changed by their developing environment, the expression thereof cannot help but be affected. This adaptability is among the most important of human characteristics.

The forces of social or economic or technological revolution need a balance wheel; for without some relationship to reality, there would be danger inherent in the rapid changes taking place today. It is an awareness of this danger which has given rise to many despairing books about the latent possibilities of the future. The psychological premise of all such stories is that man, in his continual need to fit himself to the technological explosion now taking place, will somehow lose his hold upon reality and become an amoral mechanical being.

Had this been a real danger, it would have been apparent long since; so might George Washington have thought at predictions of jet aircraft flying at Mach 3; private carriages going seventy-five miles in an hour without horses; everyday conversations between individuals miles apart; light or darkness available at the flick of a finger; artificial heat, artificial cooling, and even artificial atmosphere available upon request; and a peripatetic way of life which has uprooted all of us from the solidity of old ways and old places and put us, instead, on wheels and highways.

The answer, of course, is that our hold on reality has not been lost, and will not be. There is a balance wheel: our regard for the inherent values. This awareness permits us to recognize these changes as being only peripheral. We have evolved, perhaps, but we have not changed our values. So is it with our Navy.

While holding firmly to those time-proved traditions of worth and integrity which have supported it these many years since it was founded, the United States Navy sets its face firmly toward the future and keeps pace with the development of science and progress. It was our Navy, for instance, which developed nuclear power. It was the U. S. Navy which invented a new type of capital ship, the aircraft carrier, to go along with the rapidly developing capabilities of the modern airplane. It was our Navy which built the true submarine, and demonstrated what it could do; and it was the U. S. Navy which merged the nuclear bomb, the long-range rocket, and the nuclear submarine to produce an invulnerable deterrent system for the maintenance of peace and security on this troubled globe.

Our country has always drawn much of its strength,—and, in its infant days, protection—from the great waters surrounding it. Now these same seas have given us the means to project our influence for stability and national probity to the far reaches of the world. As these words are written, this has again been proved in Cuba and in Santo Domingo, as it was a little earlier in Lebanon; and the decision in South Vietnam will, in the largest sense, have also come from the sea.

Chapter 1

One of the things which our Navy learned from the Spanish-American War was that a cruiser, if fast enough and properly handled, might be as effective as a battleship. The Spanish-American War, so far as both navies were concerned, was pretty much a cruiser war. The Battle of Manila Bay was fought entirely by cruisers on both sides. In the other great sea battle, the Battle of Santiago, there were several battleships on the American side, but the Spanish fleet was made up entirely of cruisers. Aside from the magnificently steaming *Oregon,* the two ships of greatest significance to the United States Navy were the big, fast armored cruisers *New York* and *Brooklyn,* the respective flagships of Admiral Sampson and Commodore Schley, second in command.

This "splendid little war," as it has been called in some quarters, lasted only for a few months during the year 1898, not long enough for any of the real problems of operating a navy in a lengthy sea campaign to be recognized. It did, however, produce a wave of new ideas.

One of these was connected with the design of ships, and another one related to the size and accuracy of guns. Someone made a compilation which purported to prove that of several thousand shells fired by Dewey and Sampson in these two sea fights, less than three hundred had actually hit anything; another calculation was that none of the great thirteen-inch projectiles—and only forty-two of eight-inch or larger—fired off Santiago struck their targets. The only shots that counted were the shots that hit; ergo the most effective ships were those whose guns hit most often. And if it was necessary to sacrifice a little in terms of the size of guns in order to get more accuracy and greater rapidity of firing, this would also enable the ship to have bigger engines. The reduction in size of guns could easily be made up by higher quality and a ship of greater speed.

To naval officers who were beginning to feel the impact of Mahan, the teacher, Isherwood, the engineer, and Stephen B. Luce, the schoolmaster, it was evident that had the 21-knot *Brooklyn* and *New York* not been present at Santiago, our 16-knot battleships (with the possible exception of the *Oregon*) would have been left far in the rear of the flying Spanish cruisers. So far as the *Oregon* was concerned, it was recognized that the extraordinary accomplishments of her engineering department had pushed her at speeds beyond those for which she was designed and thus had enabled her to stay in the fight when the rest of the battleships had dropped behind, unable to keep up. And it was a matter of pride that one of *Oregon*'s big thirteen-inch shells, splashing over and beyond the *Cristobal Colon* (but not hitting), became the final factor in the Spanish Captain's decision to give up the fight.

But this was not battleship work, and *Oregon*'s remarkable performance only bolstered the arguments of the cruisers' proponents. Among the latter there was also a running argument between advocates of the "armored" cruisers—so named because, like battleships, their vital spaces were protected by both an armor belt on the side and an armored deck overhead—and the "protected" cruisers, designed primarily for commerce raiding, which had only the curved "protective deck."

Stripped to its essence, the argument was really over what percentage of a warship should be given over to each of the basic components: machinery, armor, and armament. Within a given state of the art, or a given amount of expenditure, an increase in one led inevitably to a decrease in one of the others. The battleship was theoretically the most powerful ship afloat, though what good did that do if it was not fast enough to bring an enemy to grips? Supporters of the battleship argued that so long as it remained in the way, the enemy would be forced to come to grips at some time or other, at which point the battleship's superior armor and heavier guns would carry the day.

These discussions went on in many quarters—in the halls of the Naval War College at Newport, Rhode Island; at the headquarters of the Navy Department in Washington, D. C.; and in Congress. Aided by the results of the war with Spain, proponents of cruisers were able to convince Congress to authorize the construction of a great squadron of armored cruisers of a type similar but greatly superior to the Navy's favorite ship of that time, Admiral Sampson's flagship, the *New York*. These new ships were to have the most powerful engines yet installed in ships of war, and were designed with exceptionally fine lines in order to realize the maximum benefits in terms of speed. The armor belt was of an improved type, giving greater protection with less weight, and the guns likewise were of a lighter design. The result was a group of ships considerably bigger than the battleships then being built, and considerably faster. Their advocates proudly claimed they could defeat any ship fast enough to keep up with them, and show their heels to any carrying more protection or bigger guns. They were, in fact, the prototypes of the battle cruisers which won fame (and a degree of infamy) during World War I.

Not satisfied, however, the Navy pressed Congress even further, with resultant authorization, in 1902, for the construction of two armored cruisers of a new and yet improved class, to mount four of the newest and largest guns in centerline turrets, to have even bigger engines, and to combine all these with an armor belt equal in size but superior in hardness to any save that of the newest battleships. The first of the new ships was to be named after the state of Tennessee, and it was boasted that in a fair trial she could both catch and defeat any battleship in existence.

On the third of December, 1904, the partially completed hull of the *Tennessee* was ready for launching at the Cramp ship-building yard in Philadelphia. Miss Anne Keith Frazier, fifteen-year-old daughter of the Governor of Tennessee, had been selected to be the sponsor of the ship. Despite the rain and sleet of a rather dismal Tuesday morning, she stood happily on the launching platform, clutching a bouquet of American Beauty roses. Attached to the bouquet by a long ribbon was a bottle of champagne, brought from Tennessee for the occasion by her father, and high above the launching party towered the mighty bulk of the new ship.

As she lay on the ways, ready to taste the water, *Tennessee* reflected two shades of red. That portion of her soon to be submerged had recently been given the prescribed two coats of anti-corrosive paint and one of anti-fouling paint. The final coating, applied only hours earlier, had a metallic, dark bronze sheen, almost as if it had been designed to match the actual bronze coloring of the propellers at the stern of the ship. The above-water portion of the ship's hull was a brighter, mottled red, showing the patchwork effect of sporadic painting for utilitarian preservation only.

The officials of Cramp shipyard had one problem. The Delaware River, into which the *Tennessee* was soon to be launched, had been experiencing a low water level because of a steady westerly wind during recent weeks. It was necessary that there be at least six feet of water over the end of the ways which projected into the river, in order that there not be too precipitant a drop at the critical moment when the bulk of the ship passed from support of the ways to support of the water. Launching had been set for eleven o'clock in the morning. The day before there had been some southerly winds which gave considerable encouragement, but on this particular day winds had backed around again to the west and the water level was dropping fast. A hasty consultation was held with Governor Frazier with the result that, ten minutes before the appointed hour, the signal was given to commence launching procedures.

Keith Frazier had said she was not nervous, but some nervousness she could not prevent, as she stood at the top of the launching platform with her bottle of champagne. All supporting structure and other paraphernalia had been knocked away. The ship rested entirely upon the launching blocks, four great structures of wood attached to the underwater body of the ship, two near the bow and two near the stern; they would support it during the slide down the greased runway into the water. The ship was held fast by only a single large wooden beam attached to a steel-and-concrete anchoring structure under the ceremonial platform. Upon a second utilitarian platform, built several feet below that for the launching dignitaries, stood two specially selected workmen with a large, recently sharpened, double-ended saw. They were ready to cut the wooden beam asunder.

Calculations had shown that about three-quarters of the timber would have to be sawed through before the weight of the ship, tugging at it, would break the remaining fibers of the wood and release the entire mass. But these things are difficult to judge so precisely. The movement of approximately nine thousand tones of steel depended upon the correctness of the calculated strength of this single piece of wood. A slight increase in the lubrication quotient of the beeswax with which the launching ways had been coated—unpredicted and unknown—might cause a little more strain upon the timber, possibly enough to break it in twain prior to the appointed time; or, in embarrassing contrast, the lubricating quality might be insufficient; or some other unanticipated impediment, such as freezing weather after a light rain—as was actually the case—might prevent the ship from moving at all even after the timber had been sawed completely in two. Ships had been known to remain poised in this precarious situation for days, until the builders were able, by either stratagem or brute force, to overcome the resistance and start them on their way into the water. More than one ship in this situation had toppled over when a strong wind blew.

But these considerations, since she had not been told of them, had nothing to do with Keith Frazier's nervousness. She was only concerned that she do a proper job of breaking the bottle of champagne. The few tentative practice sessions she had held with her friends at The Castle School, Tarrytown, New York, had only served to bring home to her that it took more than ordinary courage deliberately to smash a bottle filled with frothy liquid bound to splatter all over her nice dress. Also there was a possibility of hurting herself or someone else on a splinter of glass.

Still worse, however, was the horrifying thought that the ship might move too soon and leave her standing ignominiously at the top of the platform with a virginal bottle of champagne in her outstretched hand, having failed in her duty to her father, embarrassed the United States Navy, and doomed the ship to bad luck the rest of its time at sea. Worst of all—and this was entirely subconscious, though somehow she felt the emotion deep inside—it would be a symbolical failure in her first effort at the most significant of womanly duties, that of giving birth.

Keith Frazier minded the cold not at all, though she wore only a little fur stole about her shoulders. She shivered nervously and deliciously at the thought of all the terrible things that might happen if she failed to smash the bottle of champagne; and she laid down the roses, gripped the neck of the bottle with both hands, and prepared to do her duty. Mr. Grove, president of the Cramp Shipbuilding Company, and her father, the Governor, had a hurried conversation.

"I'll tell you when your daughter should smash the bottle," she thought she heard the shipyard official say. Then Mr. Grove stepped to the edge of the platform, signaled to the workmen down below.

The two men with the saw bent to their task. "Let's go," said one as they began to saw.

Keith Frazier waited not one second longer. "Go" to her at this moment meant only one thing. Gripping the wickerwork-and-ribbon-covered bottle of Tennessee champagne, she slipped by her father and Mr. Grove to the edge of the platform and swung the bottle as hard as she could against the steel prow of the ship. Froth and champagne spurted everywhere. People nearby who had been preparing to duck out of the way, anticipating, as Keith had, the problem of cleaning their clothing if it were caught in the champagne froth, were taken entirely unawares and deluged in the spray.

But the ship had not yet started to move. Keith drew back to try a second time. It wasn't so bad after all, she thought, and anyway she was already pretty well splashed. With time for a second blow she would do a really good job!

"All right, Keith," she heard Mr. Grove whisper, "she'll be starting to move in a moment. Get yourself all set and hit her hard just as soon as you see this distance get a little greater." He indicated the space—hardly six inches—between the massive bow of the ship and the bunting-draped rail of the launching platform at her waist.

Far below, the two men with the saw worked industriously. Somehow events had moved a little faster than they had anticipated. They increased the rapidity of their saw strokes. The hissing, reciprocating, sawing noise seemed to be louder than a moment before. Suddenly there was a sharp crack. The sawing noise stopped. Nothing happened for almost a second, and then Keith noticed that the space between the bow of the ship and the rail in front of her had widened to almost a foot.

She swung the bottle with both her arms and all her strength, struck the receding bow fair—it really was receding from her now—smashed the bottom half of the bottle entirely into little pieces within its wicker basket. Both her arms, now covered with froth to the elbows, tingled pleasantly as the countless tiny bubbles of golden-white liquid formed, broke, and formed again on her smooth skin.

"I christen thee *Tennessee*," said Keith Frazier, "and bid thee good luck and godspeed." This was the speech the officials had told her she should make, which she had been rehearsing in her mind ever since she had been informed of the honor in store for her. She had meant to say it loudly and well, but she had not been prepared for the nearly total silence on the launching platform at just this moment. Her voice rang out clearly in the silence, almost startlingly loud, with just a hint of girlish tremulousness. Instantly there was a tremendous hubbub, and then nobody could hear anything. But it didn't matter, and she turned—jumping and bubbling with excitement, clutching the neck of the broken bottle in its wicker cover, her arms and the front of her dress splattered with the wine—to embrace her anxious parents.

It was as though the launching platform itself were receding from the hull of the ship. Somewhere a whistle blew, and then another and yet another, until a very respectable din was created through which the giant red hull swiftly skidded backward into the water. News accounts of the event noted that the new warship dipped a curtsy to her sponsors as her bow slid off the

end of the ways and the burden of her hull was fully taken up by
the water. More prosaically, this was the result of the low water
level in the Delaware River.

The ease with which rapid motion can be imparted to such a
large structure as a ship has never failed to startle and impress
onlookers at a launching. Man is so small and himself so frail
that he can only attempt to direct, or influence, the tremendous
forces with which he is everywhere surrounded. The movement
of a great mass of steel—the hull of a ship—from the land into
the sea thereby takes on a significance far in excess of the homely
fact that similar ceremonies have been going forward for thousands of years.

Someone—Mr. Grove—took the broken neck of the champagne bottle from Keith Frazier's hand with promise to return
her souvenir later on, and the entire party of official guests went
to lunch in the Mold Loft of the yard. So much for the newspaper accounts of the ceremonies.

That the new, heavy, fast armored cruisers would be a great
success was evident even before they were completed, and Congress in 1904 appropriated additional funds for two more identical ships. Thus there were in all four ships of this type built: the
Tennessee, Washington, North Carolina and *Montana.* With the
exception that the last two lacked accomodations and office space
for a fleet commander and his staff, all four were exactly alike.

The immediate service to which *Tennessee* was put bore out
the promise of her design. Bigger and faster than the battleships,
she was immediately in demand as fleet flagship, and was so assigned. During the next few years she hung up records for target
practice, engineering efficiency, and general effectiveness in all
departments. The *Washington,* completed a few months later,
was for a time the only ship able to compete with her, and the
two vied for the Navy Battle Efficiency pennant.

When all four ships of the type were completed, they were
organized into a crack cruiser squadron, which was for a time the
most desired command of all admirals as, indeed, the ships themselves were the most desired by all captains. A well-known song
of the Navy of this period, since parodied into numerous additional versions, was orginally composed in tribute to them and

still may be heard at an occasional nostalgic gathering of old timers:

The *Washington* and *Tennessee,*
The finest ships that sailed the sea,
They came around the Horn to be
In the Armored Cruiser Squadron.

So, here's to the cruisers of the fleet,
So gol-durned fast they're hard to beat.
The battleships they may be fine—
But me for a cruiser every time!

Because of the four big cruisers' very high speed—23 knots, with everything wide open—their unusually long cruising range, and the extraordinary effectiveness of their gun batteries, they quickly became the Navy Department's favorites for special and unusual duties. This was particularly true of the two original ships of the class, whose special accommodations made them extremely useful for missions involving diplomatic personages or other high-level groups.

Tennessee's first such mission was to pave the way for the fleet's Around-the-World voyage in 1908. She completed a major portion of this trip the year previous, making arrangements for diplomatic receptions at each major port, and for coaling stations, reprovisioning, and target practice during the long voyage.

This period just prior to the outbreak of World War I was one of upheaval in many areas, most particularly in the Middle East, and *Tennessee*'s history shows her twice involved in humanitarian expeditions to render assistance to the unfortunate victims of persecution in those far-off and chaotic lands. Literally thousands of Armenians, survivors of one of the most brutal pogroms of which the world has record, owe their lives and their decisions to become United States citizens to the intervention of this determined, yet gentle-handed, warship and her crew. When the war in Europe broke out in 1914, thousands of Americans suddenly found themselves caught in the confusion, some unable to obtain funds, many with plans for returning home completely disrupted. All looked to the Navy to solve their dilemma, and again, the ship-of-war, which had so far been mostly a ship-of-peace, loaded her hospitable decks with displaced tourists and brought them to places of safety.

Not known at the time to most of those on board, or to the world at large until many years had passed, was the fact that, when the *Tennessee* returned to the United States in 1915, her magazines held something far more valuable than merely ammunition. The gold bullion of the Bank of England was also there, safely stowed under charge of a chief gunner's mate, on the first leg of its transfer to the comparative safety of Canadian banks.

For the first few years of her career, like all the ships of our Navy at that time, *Tennessee* sported a strikingly attractive white, buff, and black color scheme. Her hull was white up to the main deck; her upper works and masts were buff; her guns, standing starkly in their white or buff-colored stations, were a deadly, glistening black. Surmounting her prow, or stem, was a gilded scrollwork directly descended from the golden cutwater and carved figureheads with which all ships used to be fitted—and which was considered as necessary as any of the other important accouterments of a man-of-war. Immediately below the scroll and slightly aft on both sides were located four massive hawse-pipes for her anchors.

At the after end of the forecastle, in dominating position snug against the base structure of the foremast, was located one of the two major reasons for the ship's existence: the fore-turret, commanding a total arc of rotation of three-quarters of a circle. Its twin correspondingly overlooked the after portion of the main deck, the quarter-deck. Through the slanted steel face plate of each turret protruded the muzzles of two late model ten-inch guns, by far the heaviest guns mounted on any cruiser, able, at the time the ship was built, to outrange and outshoot the turret guns of any battleship then in commission. *Tennessee* was entirely flush-decked; that is, she had a single main deck extending her whole length, with a slight rise at bow and stern for increased seaworthiness. In the central portion, spanning the entire space between the turrets and comprising half of the length of the ship, her sides were extended upward one deck space so that the main deck between the turrets was enclosed. This superstructure, or casemate, provided an armored, weatherproof house for its four six-inch and ten three-inch guns, whose muzzles protruded ominously through gun ports in the side plating. Each gun commanded an arch of train from ahead to astern, and when in action, or in port in warm weather, the heavy steel shutters which could close off the necessary openings were removed. At all times at sea, except in the imminence of battle, the shutters—steel plates several feet in cross section and weighing more than a hundred pounds—were bolted in place so that the entire opening around each gun was sealed; this left protruding only a few feet of the barrel around which the shutters were tightly fitted.

The deck below, the gun deck, carried twelve more six-inch and twelve more three-inch guns, and was similarly fitted with gun ports and shutters. Since the entire length of this deck was enclosed, however, its guns were not confined to the space between the turrets and ranged, instead, the length of the ship.

The exposed deck above the superstructure, known as the boat deck, supported four tall ramrod-straight stacks, a mast at either end, two tall power-operated cranes and ten great rabbit-ear venilators through which air was sucked for the firerooms and engine rooms in the bowels of the ship directly below. Nested in chocks under the cranes and covered with canvas for protection while *Tennessee* was under way were her two steam launches, her four gasoline motor launches, the Captain's gig and the Admiral's barge, and several smaller boats. Low on the deck between the number one and number two stacks was a squat flat-roofed structure with long dimension athwartships. This, the ship-fitter's shop, had a door in either end and was primarily employed in repairing topside equipment associated with the anchors, the boat cranes, or the boats themselves. It was from its preoccupation with the ship's boats that the boat deck got its name, for with the exception of the two lifeboats, which swung from davits on either side of the main deck just clear of the firing arc of the after turret, all boats were handled from here.

The stacks occupied the forward two-thirds of the boat deck and each was directly connected with the four boilers in the pair of firerooms which it served. The empty space between the fourth stack and the mainmast, being directly above the main engines, contained only one pair of ventilator "ears" symmetrically placed on either side; between them, exactly on the center line and surmounting a low boxlike foundation, was a set of

hatches made of relatively light steel and arranged like a skylight
—which they were in fact intended to be, for each contained a
glass insert to admit additional light into the engine rooms
below. The hatches served a dual purpose, for they too could be
reached, their centers plumbed, by the boat cranes, which could
be swung into position over the cavity to hoist, or sometimes only
lift a few inches, a piece of heavy machinery. In tropical climate,
when the atmosphere in the engine rooms became too oppressive,
the hatches could be left open to provide an escape route for
the oil-and-steam-laden air.

Tennessee's foremast was of the "cage" type, resembling an
elongated, inverted wastebasket whose spidery construction, from
a moderate distance, took on an unsubstantial aery quality giving no hint of the interlocking strength of its steel tracery.
Wrapped around the forward side of the foremast and actually
built into it was the bridge, the ship's main control station while
under way. From here she was steered, and from here voice tubes
led to the other stations of most importance: the conning tower,
the Captain's cabin—aft, under the quarterdeck—and the engine
rooms. The bridge itself consisted only of a narrow platform
leading nearly to either side of the ship and surrounded by railings made of iron pipe. Protection from wind was afforded by
canvas siding laced on by many turns of light rope (a heavy cord
known as "white line"). This canvas had received so many
coats of paint that it had the consistency and stiffness of sheet
metal. The two outermost ends of the bridge were slightly
widened to accommodate extra working room around the gyro-
compass repeaters mounted there. Immediately below the "upper
bridge," or "navigating bridge" as it was sometimes called, was
the "lower bridge," of almost identical construction except that
it was entirely roofed over by the floor of the higher one, whereas
the upper bridge had only a canvas awning over the central
portion. At the center of the lower bridge, integral with it and
the base of the foremast, stood a heavy, squat, vertical steel
cylinder with narrow eye slits through its thick material. This
was the command conning station in battle, the conning tower,
equipped with all necessary ship-control facilities, impervious to
damage from everything but a direct hit by a large-caliber projectile. Directly above it, held forward and clear by heavy brack-

ets built into the base of the navigating bridge, hung the ship's bell, fully two feet in diameter and two and a half feet high.

In the engineering spaces, roughly extending from the boilers under number one stack to the stern, the complex of compartments contained sixteen boilers, two engines and all their associated machinery—entirely below the water line and encased in an armored citadel consisting of armored deck above, side armor, and armored ends. The engineering spaces were interconnected by a series of passageways and watertight doors, so arranged that access to the firerooms was through an airlock (a telephone-booth-sized cubicle with airtight doors on opposite sides). Outboard of the firerooms, occupying the intervening space between them and the side of the ship, in effect combining convenience with added armor protection, were the ship's coal bunkers, equipped with one door to each fireroom. Thus, once coal was in the bunkers, getting it to the firerooms was a relatively easy matter, involving only opening the bunker door and shoveling it out on the fireroom floor plates. As the bunkers were depleted, however, the coal passers had to go deeper into them and haul the coal out in buckets. Filling the bunkers, or coaling ship, a task everyone hated, was something the U. S. Navy had not yet learned to do without. Oil burning boilers for U. S. ships of war were still in the design stage.

To the vocal regret of many old Navy men, the U. S. Navy did away with the white, buff and black color scheme of its ships in favor of gray "war-color" immediately after the cruise of the Great White Fleet. The purpose was to make the ships a little less visible on the horizon, a little harder to aim at; "war-color" they have been ever since. At the same time, the scroll and crest were removed from the bows of all ships—a change probably very little lamented by the sailors whose job it had been to keep the golden scrolls shiny.

In June, 1915, Dad was skipper of the armored cruiser *Washington,* flagship of the Cruiser Force, on detached duty in the Caribbean. There came grave trouble in Haiti. A murderous President—its seventh in seven years—was himself murdered. The despairing people, many of them relatives of the President's victims, were rioting. American lives were in danger; so *Washington* was sent to Port-au-Prince. There, for several months, Father spent most of his time ashore in charge of special forces of U.S. Marines and sailors he had landed to restore order. Primary among his assumed responsibilities was that of ensuring a fair and impartial presidential election, a rarity in that country. So well did he succeed in this duty that he is still remembered with warm nostalgia in Port-au-Prince as the bald, medium-height, gray-mustached naval officer who, with his ship, brought tranquility and a stable government when desolation and revolution seemed to be their only prospect.

A week before the *Washington* had arrived, the new President had incarcerated 168 members of his political opposition. He, at least, was determined to stay in office longer than the pattern established. The morning before the *Washington* arrived, a squad of prison guards moved methodically from cell to cell, shooting through the bars at the prisoners and then rushing in with knives and bayonets to make sure. Thus were killed 164 of the educators and political leaders he had rounded up. The firing at the jail was heard in town and caused an honest riot (as opposed to the jaded bought-and-paid-for "revolutions" to which Haitian politics had degenerated). A small band of angry men led by a one-time chief of police assaulted the palace, and the villainous President, an ex-convict, jumped over the back fence of the palace grounds and sought refuge in the French Legation, which abutted against them. But this was little protection. The infuriated mob, by this time much augmented, burst into the legation, found their President hiding in a toilet, dragged him out and hacked him to pieces in the city streets. When the *Washington* arrived on the scene, no one felt safe in the city of Port-au-Prince, least of all members of foreign embassies and the few non-Negroes in the country for business or other reasons.

Captain Beach's orders, classic in their simplicity, were to protect the lives of Americans. The most direct way this officer could carry out these instructions was to protect the lives of all white people in Port-au-Prince, whether they were French, German, Danish, English, or American, since assuredly the mobs then roaming the streets could make little distinction among them themselves. In fairness it must be admitted that later events proved to Father that there was little real danger to foreigners from the mob, who were searching only for their own Negro persecutors. At any rate, he set up headquarters ashore and in a short time, with the help of the marines and sailors whom the *Washington* landed, he was able to establish order and stabilize the situation.

It is not recorded that under the circumstances any of the foreign legations objected to being summarily protected by Father's American marines; and in all candidness it must be stated this book could not now be written had this occurred. One of the French families who came under unofficial American protection had a daughter who later became the second Mrs. Beach, and, in due course, my mother.

The United States has reason to believe that one of the few bright spots in Haiti's tragic history has been the period beginning when American sailors and marines, under the over-all command of the commander, U.S. Cruiser Force, Rear Admiral William B. Caperton, and under the direct supervision ashore of his flagship skipper, Captain Beach, restored order and tranquility to a country ripped by internal strife, overcome with hatred and despair and ground into the most degrading individual—as well as national—poverty. It was United States forces which restored to the people of that pathetic land, the wretched, bewildered victims of the world's most fantastic misgovernment, some modicum of peace and tranquility. Our marines were the best friends the people of Haiti ever had.

The history of Haiti before and after the period when U. S. Marines were there has not been such as to inspire confidence in the ability of Haitians to govern themselves. Many, many Haitians have suffered under their own rule, have been imprisoned and murdered. All have been impoverished, except the cynical rulers or their cohorts, who have spirited the natural wealth of Haiti away to foreign banks. None of this happened while our marines policed the country. After all, the "good of the people" is closer to American ideals than the theoretical "independence" so loudly shouted by despots and supported, in all honesty, by our own good-hearted and well-meaning citizens. "Freedom," as we understand it, should mean freedom of the individual from oppression, not freedom for the oppressors to pillage their people.

Late in September, with newly elected President Dartiguenave in office, Father received distressing news: His wife of many years lay seriously ill in Boston; her life was despaired of. He dashed home, was with her when she died. The Navy, trying to do its kindest for him in its inarticulate, official way, detached him from command of the *Washington,* gave him leave followed by only nominal duty, promised a tour at the Naval War College in Newport for his next assignment. Blackness lay heavily on his spirit. But a few weeks later a telegram ordered him to report to the office of Josephus Daniels, Secretary of the Navy. Expecting to spend only a few hours in Washington, he took an early morning train and brought no baggage. In the capital, Daniels sent him to the Secretary of State, with whom he spent an hour. "Captain," said Mr. Lansing, "the treaty you handed President Dartiguenave for the State Department is in danger of not being passed. I am told that you have the good will of the legislators and that they will listen to you. Can you go back there immediately?"

Upon his return to the Navy Secretary's office, orders restoring him to command of the *Washington* were handed to him and he was shown a telegram to Admiral Caperton, directing him to employ his returned flagship skipper on special duty as desired by the Secretary of State.

Dad had to run to catch the train for Key West. When he arrived, there was no steamer for Havana; so he commandeered the best launch at the Naval Station there, steered all night for the coast of Cuba, arrived in Havana at dawn, raced to the railroad station. He handed a new toothbrush to an expostulating customs official with the explanation that it was his only baggage, caught the departing morning train for Santiago de Cuba, and next day was back aboard the *Washington* in Guantanamo Bay. The ship left immediately for Port-au-Prince.

Dad now became a full-fledged naval officer-diplomat. He got the treaty desired by Lansing through the Haitian Senate where it had been stalled; participated in the framing of a *modus vivendi,* pending ratification by the U. S. Senate; accepted appointment as "Acting Financial Advisor to the Republic of Haiti." All this was with the full approval of the Commander, Cruiser Force, who remained on board the *Washington* and to whom regular reports were made.

In January, 1916, the *Tennessee* came to Port-au-Prince to relieve her sister ship in order that the latter might return to the

United States for a navy-yard overhaul. But Admiral Caperton did not wish to lose the services of his experienced flag captain; the skipper of *Tennessee* had no great desire to remain in the Caribbean. The result was telegraphed orders from the Navy Department for the two commanding officers to exchange ships, and on the twenty-ninth of January, 1916, unusual twin formal ceremonies—a double change of command—took place. A few days later, with Admiral Caperton now flying his flag in *Tennessee,* the *Washington* departed.

Early in March, *Tennessee* circled South America with the International High Commission of the Pan-American Congress embarked. The senior person aboard was William G. McAdoo, Secretary of the Treasury of the United States, whose vivacious young wife was also along. Father always remembered this interlude as one of the most pleasant cruises he had ever made. He came to know and appreciate his new ship, for he had to drive her hard to keep up with the rather demanding schedule of the Commission, but he visited a variety of interesting ports and had interesting company while at sea. During the cruise there was recorded one of the few instances when a lady Pollywog crossed the Equator aboard a man-of-war and, after having a fair trial and doing penance, was duly and properly welcomed as a shellback by Neptunus the King, the Queen, Davy Jones, the Royal Baby, and all the rest of the trusty band of hardened shellbacks. The lady involved was, of course, Mrs. McAdoo, daughter of President Woodrow Wilson, and she insisted upon being initiated like everyone else. This caused some careful thought, since even shellbacks—perhaps more than anyone else— are very aware of the limitations of authority; but after what must have been a fairly difficult trial before Davy Jones' court, she was found guilty of only a few high crimes and misdemeanors, for which she was sentenced to sing "Home Sweet Home" to the crew assembled that evening.

During this trip the *Tennessee* traversed the Panama Canal, passed through the storied Strait of Magellan in a single day at 23 knots, and returned to Hampton Roads, Virginia, in May, 1916.

Shortly after her arrival, *Tennessee* was renamed *Memphis,* in order to release the name *Tennessee* for a battleship then under construction (the same which was later damaged at Pearl Harbor).

Seafaring men are traditionally superstitious. If they are not born so, they become so from the heritage of the many fears and worries that sailors of olden days carried forward as traditions. For example, it has always been unlucky for a ship to be launched or to go to sea on a Friday, to see St. Elmo's Fire in its rigging, or to sight an unidentified ship in the vicinity of Cape Horn. For fairly obvious reasons, it was always considered unlucky to make an unexpected landfall, and particularly so at Cape of Good Hope or Cape Horn. Even the most sophisticated of seamen cannot but be affected by the accumulated weight of the legends of centuries.

One of the traditions of bad fortune concerns the changing of the name of a ship. Dire were the predictions when the crew of the *Tennessee* were informed that their ship was henceforth to carry the name *Memphis,* and especially so when workmen arrived during the short layover in Hampton Roads to remove the raised letters spelling out *Tennessee* on the stern of the ship and replace them with new ones spelling *Memphis.*

"Mark my words," said one sailor, assuming a dark air of omniscience and foreboding, "no good will come of this." His hearers nodded sagely. Thereafter many of the normal vicissitudes of ship life—such as the occasional minor injuries which are inevitable in a crew of nearly one thousand, or the happenstance cycle of damage to ship's boats which the *Memphis* began to experience just at this time—were ascribed to the action of displeased gods of the sea. Not that anyone went so far as actually to believe in the existence of these gods, but many knowingly wagged their heads at the inscrutable fate which seemed to dog the movements of their ship with all the force of dark malevolence.

There were those, of course, who refused to accept the general belief in bad luck. The cited "proofs" were to them only chance circumstance. Most of the officers and not a few of the crew were of this persuasion and were more concerned over the cumulative effects of lowered morale than over any other result of the belief in good or bad fortune. Some, in their own ways, made considerable efforts to propitiate Lady Luck and their own messmates.

One man, W. E. Gerhart by name, a boatswain's mate first class, wrote a poem entitled, "Welcome to You, *Memphis,* and Good-bye, Old *Tennessee."*

The little rechristening folder in which this poem was printed gave testimony to latent pride in the ship and attempted to evoke it by listing statistics of her length, displacement, the horsepower of her engines, how many boilers she had, the number and size of her guns, and the fact that she was still one of the most powerful and speediest big ships possessed by our Navy. It also stated that during her entire career to date, from July 17, 1906, to May 23, 1916, *Memphis* had steamed a total of 175,181 nautical miles. In June, she got underway for the Caribbean Sea carrying a detachment of Marines to reinforce our forces in Santo Domingo.

The situation there in 1916 was somewhat similar to that in Port-au-Prince the year before, in that U. S. Marines had been ashore for some time maintaining the public peace and establishing an honest financial administration. The situation having become somewhat stabilized, and Rear Admiral Caperton having established an outstanding reputation for his handling of Caribbean problems during the preceding year and a half, the Navy Department promoted him to full Admiral and ordered him to command the entire U. S. Pacific Fleet. His relief was Rear Admiral Charles F. Pond.

The City of Santo Domingo, on the south coast of the Island of Santo Domingo, these days occupying both sides of the Ozama River, was one of the first cities founded in the New World. Indeed, the remains of Christopher Columbus are reputed to lie buried here in a mausoleum in the cathedral of Santo Domingo, and the remains of the house built by his son, Diego, still exist. For centuries the Island of Santo Domingo, or Hispanola as it was then called, was known as the "Pearl of the Antilles," and the city of Santo Domingo was one of the most prosperous in the entire New World. The Ozama River, which bordered the old city on the east, gave it excellent port facilities for ships of commerce of those days, but the larger vessels of the modern era were forced to anchor in the open roadstead off shore. Deep water reached close to the curve of the bluff-lined shore, shoaling suddenly from more than 100 fathoms to 10 fathoms and thence shoaling more gradually to a series of rocky reefs at the base of forty-foot-high bluffs. On the west mouth of the river stood the ancient Spanish walls of old Fort Ozama, where were quartered the marines we had ashore in that unhappy country. Built upon the battlements was a wooden signal tower where signalmen maintained a constant watch and through which messages could be sent to and from naval vessels at anchor, a mile or so away.

In view of the exposed nature of the Santo Domingo anchorage and the fact that any southerly or easterly storm would strike freely upon ships at anchor there, Admiral Pond and Captain Beach took counsel as to proper precautions necessary to insure the safety of the ship. One factor was that the West Indian hurricane season was about to begin and it was known that West Indian storms could arise very suddenly. Another was the probability that *Memphis* might be held in this area for several months because of the unsettled conditions in Santo Domingo, Haiti, and the other neighboring islands. A third was the war in Europe, which was becoming increasingly serious and which demanded readiness for quick reaction to unexpected requirements.

A fourth factor was the necessity to conserve fuel. A coal burner is always hard pressed to replenish her fuel supply and, of course, the general scarcity of coal of a proper quality was a worry. In addition, the constantly recurrent need to coal ship, with the attendant necessity of completely scrubbing both ship and all hands attached immediately thereafter, was heartily disliked by everyone.

A fifth point of consideration was that all ships of the Navy were constantly in competition with each other in all categories of performance, including fuel economy. While captains were expected to be ready for any eventuality, there was no allowance in the competition for prudent seamanship.

Father, nevertheless, earnestly proposed keeping fires lighted under four boilers, as he had always done under Caperton, in order to be ready to get under way in minimum time if a hurricane arose. Admiral Pond did not approve. Two were ample for auxiliary power, and there would be plenty of time to light fires under additional boilers when bad weather was noted, he said.

The matter, of course, was one of professional judgment. Seamen are customarily very alert to the signs of approaching bad weather. In those days, before the airborne and electronic sensing devices which we now have, they were adept at translating local signs into accurate weather predictions and, of course, into necessary preparation to meet it. It was with some misgivings, therefore, that the Skipper acquiesced to the Admiral's wishes. The matter was compromised by setting up special emergency steaming watches and the arrangement that four extra boilers would be maintained fully ready to be lighted off at a moment's notice. This meant that the men responsible for operating the engines would actually be in the engine rooms ready to warm them up and prepare to get under way at all times, and that the men designated to operate the extra boilers would likewise be in the engineering spaces and immediately available.

Specific arrangements were the responsibility of Lieutenant Claud A. Jones, Senior Engineer Officer of the ship, assisted by Lieutenant (junior grade) Horatio J. Peirce, Assistant Engineer Officer, and three warrant machinists: Newton R. George, in charge of engine rooms; George R. Thompson, in charge of auxiliary machinery; and Charles H. Willey, in charge of the firerooms. A detailed watch bill, listing the duties of all personnel concerned, was devised, approved by Jones and the Captain, and placed into effect.

Second to the Skipper in responsibility for the ship was the Executive Officer, Lieutenant Commander Yancey Williams, of diminutive stature but possessed of high qualities of energy and leadership, plus a sense of humor which endeared him to officers and crew. The navigator, next senior to Williams and responsible for maintaining a close check on the weather as well as for the ship's position at anchor and at all times under way, was Lieutenant Tommy Withers, an intelligent, precise individual of medium height, who was slender enough to go by the name of "Skinny" among his friends, and who, unfortunately, suffered from periodic attacks of rheumatic arthritis.

On the evening of the twenty-second of August these special arrangements were put to the test. Signs of bad weather suddenly were noticed; the barometer began to drop, and the special underway procedure was put into effect. It so happened that the United States Minister to the Dominican Republic, Mr. W. W. Russell, and his wife had just come aboard for dinner, which was to be followed by the showing of a movie. The entertainment they received was of quite a different kind, for suddenly they found themselves in the midst of a bedlam of boats being hoisted, hatches being closed, chittering boatswain's pipes and hoarse shouts through voice tubes—all the ordered rush and confusion attendant upon getting a big ship under way with a well-trained crew.

In exactly forty minutes from the first warning, the *Memphis* had steam up and was ready to start heaving in the anchor. But the signs of bad weather abated. The hurricane never came. In a few hours the barometer rose again and all was serene—except that no one aboard saw a movie that night. The false alarm was a nuisance, but it was nevertheless gratifying to the Captain and officers. It showed that they had, indeed, the capability of getting steam on their big ship and having her under way in less than an hour. For a ship of this size (14,500 tons nominal, 18,000 tons actual full load), it was no small feat; but *Memphis* was accustomed to performing specially. The proof of this ability, as Captain Beach remarked, enabled him to rest more easily.

The effect upon Admiral Pond was not noted, but it may be surmised that his own seaman's instincts were also reassured. The ability of the ship to get under way in such a short time probably reinforced his judgment that, provided due vigilance was maintained, it was perfectly safe to lie at anchor with fires for auxiliary purposes in only two of her sixteen boilers, even during the West Indian hurricane season.

Chapter 2

TUESDAY, AUG. 29, 1916, AT SANTO DOMINGO
--UNTIL MIDAFTERNOON

August 29 dawned entirely unremarkably. The day was dull and somewhat cool for this latitude, although there was promise that, as the sun climbed higher in the sky, some of the dullness would burn off. Memphis rode easily to her anchor in approximately fifty-five feet of water in a completely smooth sea. The starboard anchor was down with 70 fathoms of chain run out, the link marking the seventieth fathom just touching the water as it lapped quietly along the ship's side. Responding to gentle prevailing northeasterly winds, the 18,000-ton Memphis lay all day on an easterly to northeasterly heading, with the anchor stretched out approximately 70 fathoms, or 420 feet, to the east. Adding the ship's own 500-foot length, she was thus free to describe a circle 900 feet in radius about her anchor; or, in naval terms, her anchoring circle was 600 yards in diameter. USS Castine, a pre-Spanish-American War gunboat barely more than 200 feet long and displacing 1,200 tons, was anchored in the next berth inshore, approximately six hundred yards from the Mem-

31

phis. Like the cruiser, she rode to her anchor on an easterly heading, but, with less chain out, would describe a smaller circle about her anchor as she swung to the wind and tide. These two ships were the only vessels at anchor in the roadstead this day. The log of the *Memphis* records that at ten twenty-eight in the morning the U. S. tug *Potomac* stood out from the Ozama River and headed to sea.

The log also records that boilers one and three in fireroom number one were in use in *Memphis* for auxiliary purposes, that is, to provide steam for general-purpose power and heating throughout the ship, such as to the dynamos for electricity and to the galley for cooking.

The sixteen boilers with which the cruiser was fitted were arranged in eight firerooms, numbered from one to eight, forward to aft. In accordance with maritime convention, boilers and firerooms on the starboard side of the ship all had odd numbers while those on the port side bore even numbers. Thus boilers one and three were located in number one fireroom, the farthest forward on the starboard side, and vented their gasses of combustion into number one stack. Boilers two and four were in number two fireroom, the farthest forward on the port side, and also tied into number one stack. Boilers were built facing each other from opposite sides of their common fireroom and each pair was the responsibility of a single fireroom crew.

According to the ship's emergency under-way bill, the four boilers in firerooms seven and eight, the aftermost firerooms in the ship and nearest to the engine room, were to be kept ready to be fired immediately. Their fireboxes were already filled with coal distributed properly over the fire gratings, and the water drums and boiler tubes were filled with water. The fires needed only to be started, and this was customarily done by bringing live coals from the boilers already in use.

One other maneuver was also necessary, however, before the boilers could be used. To protect the interior surfaces of the water areas from corrosion, they had been filled all the way up with boiler water. Addition of heat would first cause expansion of the water, and the resulting pressure rise would damage the boiler long before any steam could be formed. It was therefore necessary, at the same time as fires were lighted, to "run down" the water in the boilers to the designed steaming level, where it could be visually observed by a sight glass installed on the outside of the boiler casing. The water level in the sight glass must never be allowed to get too low—or too high—for proper and safe operation of the boiler. For this reason the most important man in a fireroom is always the water tender, for it is he who personally regulates the level of the water and is in charge of the safe generation of steam. The firemen, in contrast, merely maintain the fires underneath the boilers and are not directly responsible for the water level.

Each fireroom had access to the one directly across from it through a watertight door, and to the two forward and aft by other doors. The two forward firerooms could be reached by a pair of iron ladders descending through air locks and an armored hatch from the berth deck. The two after ones, firerooms seven and eight, not only had corresponding ladders leading to the firemen's washroom (itself constituting an air lock), above number eight, but also each had a standard air lock leading to the corresponding engine room. For convenience only the starboard engine room air lock was utilized for passage, since the starboard engine was considered senior to the port and it was here that the Engineer Officer of the Watch had his log desk and station. Persons desiring to pass from either engine room to number eight fireroom would first pass through the starboard engine room and number seven fireroom.

The walls and floor plating of each fireroom were black, relieved only by the red reflection when one of the six furnace doors in the front of each boiler was opened, and there was a gritty impression everywhere, as though the ten years since the ship had been commissioned had so ingrained particles of fine coal dust into the very pores of the metal that they could never be removed. A few sparse light bulbs encased in "steam-tight" glass shields failed to relieve the blackness, succeeded only in casting into relief the various equipment and tools with which the walls of each fireroom were adorned. Ceiling or "overhead" there was none, save the grating of a narrow water tender's walkway for closer inspection of water-level-gauge glasses and boilertop appurtenances. Light glittered from the underside of the grating and partially gave the impression of an overhead, but above this there was a suggestion of great, formless, convoluted masses of huge pipes and air ducts, some of them many feet in diameter, some dull black and some a dirty off-white in color, twisting and writhing in the shadows above the lighted area, finally disappearing beyond the shadows where, indubitably, there must exist a closure to contain the air. All this, of course, was static and each of the convolutions had its designed purpose, but the constantly moving shadows and the reflections which dimly caught one's eye gave an impression of movement as though they were the intestines of some great, prehistoric, iron-sided beast.

Evenly spaced along the face of each boiler were six furnace doors leading to its firebox, and here was the heart of the ship's power. As the coal passers wearily performed their endless chore of climbing into a coal bunker, filling a bucket of coal and bringing it out to the floor plates of the fireroom to maintain the heap of coal in its approximate center, each fireman constantly made the rounds of the three furnace doors assigned to him, endlessly shoveling, checking the level of the fire, feeding the thin spots, loosening clinkers with his clinker bar and devil's claw as they formed on the firebox gratings, insuring to the satisfaction of the water tender in charge that his fires had the proper degree of "whiteness." In addition to a series of glassed, ruby-colored peepholes into his fireboxes, the water tender had another measure of the power being generated by the two boilers under his immediate supervision—by comparison of the amount of water he was pumping into each. So long as the water level in the sight glasses was approximately right, obviously the boiler taking more water was making more steam.

The crew of each fireroom consisted generally of a water tender in charge and an assistant, plus two firemen for each boiler, and three or four coal passers.

If the water tenders were the elite of the fireroom crew and the coal passers at the bottom of the scale, the firemen were conscious that it was their sweat, their muscles, and their willingness to face the shriveling heat of a wide-open furnace door while they worked on their fires that made the ship go. While they would have sneered at the word "romance" as being entirely inappropriate to their feeling for their job, and in fact would have insisted that they had no such feeling, in the soul of each lurked the secret knowledge that the job the firemen were called upon to perform was a little more demanding, a little tougher than most. They were the source of power, and they knew it. Ashore, the self-conscious way in which they rippled their fire-hardened muscles and stood wide-stanced in disdain of lesser men, betrayed their knowledge. At sea, with the ship rolling in a seaway and calling upon them to drive her, some of them would strip to the waist, and would knot a sweat-rag around their foreheads or necks. With a rag held in the palms of their hands to help protect against the fire-induced heat of their tools, they would angrily pit their bare, sweat-streaming, reddened torsos against the pitiless heat of the furnaces. The older men wore heavy shirts, buttoned down to the wrists, and work-stained gloves with large gauntlets. Once the shirt and gloves were permeated with sweat—which happened almost immediately—they provided almost perfect, if temporary, protection for the body against the radiant heat of the open furnaces.

The air-lock doors at the rear of the two aftermost firerooms led to the engine rooms, the starboard of which, by standard custom, was the control or "lead" engine room. To permit independent operation of either engine in spite of possible damage to the other, communication between them was permitted by only a single low watertight door in the bulkhead separating the two engine rooms. This connecting door, so low that it was commonly referred to as the "half-door," was in the approximate center of the bulkhead, near the main throttles. On either side the overhead of the engine rooms was trunked upward, through the armored berth deck, the gun deck, and the main deck, to the engine-room hatches on the boat deck. To permit ventilation through these hatches, maintain the integrity of the armored berth deck, and yet allow the lifting of some of the large component parts of the engines, heavy, removable "battle bars" of case-hardened steel, spaced a few inches apart, spanned the overhead at the berth-deck level. The engineer officer of the watch had his log desk in the starboard engine room, adjacent to the half-door connecting with the port engine room, and thus had easy access to both main-engine throttlemen, either through the door, which normally would be kept open, or by voice tube when it was shut.

The engines, of course, dominated the two engine rooms; but despite their huge cylinders and their heavy crankshafts, connecting rods and bedplates, they were more impressive for the lack of that great solid structure which, because of familiarity with railroad steam locomotives, is customarily associated with steam engines in general. The fact is, of course, that most of what one sees of a steam locomotive is the boiler and firebox section. The steam engine proper consists only of the pistons and drive shafts near the forward driving wheels. In a ship, boilers and fireboxes are located in other compartments and supply their steam through great insulated pipes. Thus, all one sees in the engine room of a ship are the steam cylinders; the great, perfectly balanced connecting rods moving up and down at tremendous speeds; and the fantastically heavy and powerful crankshaft, also perfectly balanced, spinning the great propeller drive shaft which extends aft and downward, through the huge thrust bearing, the smaller line support bearings in the shaft alley, through the bottom of the ship to the propellers. It is because of the propeller shafting that the main engine of a ship is never exactly upright. It is always at an angle, since it must be aligned with the propeller shaft instead of with the keel of the ship.

Memphis' engines were listed as four-cylinder, triple-expansion, which meant that the four cylinders were made in three different carefully figured sizes, so that the amount of work done by each piston would be the same. Thus the high-pressure cylinder, one of the two center cylinders, was the smallest in diameter. After the steam had expanded so as to release exactly one-third of its energy in operating this cylinder, it was led to the intermediate-stage cylinder, approximately one-and-a-half times the diameter of the high-pressure cylinder and immediately abaft it. Here the expanding steam would deliver another third of its energy. The exhaust therefrom was divided equally between the two equal-sized low-pressure cylinders (a single low-pressure cylinder would have been impossibly large) located at each end of the engine. The exhaust from these, now fully expanded and therefore depleted of its energy, passed through extraordinarily large pipes across the engine room to the main condenser, where it was condensed and returned to the boilers as feed water to repeat the cycle.

With two hundred and fifty pounds steam pressure and wide-open throttles, *Memphis'* reciprocating engines could spin their tremendous steel crankshafts and propeller shafts, with a three-bladed, 26-feet-in-diameter propeller at the end of each, at a speed of 120 revolutions per minute. This was normal full speed, equivalent to 22 knots. In emergency they were limited only by the amount of steam the boilers could produce, and in one recent case had gone 128 revolutions per minute and driven *Memphis* at a shade better than 23 knots.

The log of the *Memphis* for the morning of the twenty-ninth of August shows nothing of particular interest. At 8:15 A.M. various men under confinement were released, having completed their terms in the brig. At 9:15 A.M. quarters were held for muster and drill—no absentees. Magazine temperatures were taken and the flooding system tested. Sentences imposed at Captain's Mast for various infractions of the regulations were read out, ranging from a fine of four dollars for being two hours' over leave to ten days on bread and water for striking another person in the naval service.

At 10:28 the *Potomac* stood out and at 12:50 the commanding officer of the USS *Castine,* Commander Kenneth Bennett, came on board for dental treatment. At 1:00 the recreation party was called away.

The status of our Marines and naval landing forces in Santo Domingo at this time was that of a peaceful presence, which is to say that they had been put ashore at the request of local authorities to assist in the preservation of law and order. Understandably, nevertheless, they were not popular with the Dominican people, and there had been considerable rioting and upheaval. By consequence normal "shore leave," or liberty, was not allowed. The Marines were billeted in old Fort Ozama, on the west mouth of the Ozama River. In order to obtain a little more room for exercise and recreation, a plot of land about half a mile upstream from the fort and on the opposite side of the river had been assigned, and it was for this area that *Memphis'* liberty party was headed. The men going ashore were largely members of the ship's baseball team, which only a week before had defeated the Marines by a score of 7 to 5. Some of the others, perhaps, might have come along because of the probability of being able to obtain beer at the recreation area. The U. S. Navy had long since learned that morale of a crew cooped up aboard ship, with no possibility of normal liberty, could be almost measurably enhanced by occasional opportunities for a portion of them to get ashore for a few hours in this way.

Lieutenant (j.g.) Horatio J. Peirce, *Memphis'* assistant engineering officer, was sent ashore in charge of the party, assisted by Chief Boatswain's Mate Kaskurg and a patrol of ten men. The total number of men in the recreation group, including the patrol, was fifty, well below the full-load capacity of the motor launch which brought them from the ship.

The American Consulate at Santo Domingo was under charge of a slightly built, studiously inclined young man by the name of Carl M. J. Von Zeilinski. Noting that both Admiral Pond and Captain Beach had professed interest in history and associated subjects, on this day he had, with some special trouble, arranged, in the ancient cathedral of Santo Domingo—the same where the body of Christopher Columbus was reputed to be entombed—a lecture by an American Archaeologist, De Booy by name, on the subject of "Dominican Antiquities." An invitation had been extended to both Admiral and Skipper; the former, a gregarious person, endeavored in a good-natured but insistent manner to entice his comrade to go ashore with him. There was, however, considerable ship's work to be done. Among other things, *Memphis* was scheduled for target practice in the near future and there were drills to be held and reports to be prepared. Furthermore, the Captain had forbidden officers to go ashore during drill hours, except on duty. Under these circumstances he felt he himself could not go ashore; so at 2:05 in the afternoon only Admiral Pond, accompanied by two aides, left the ship. The trip ashore occupied about fifteen minutes and they were met at the landing by Minister and Mrs. Russell, Acting Consul Von Zeilinski, and Mr. De Booy. A few minutes before three o'clock in the afternoon the party was seated comfortably in the cathedral.

Early in the afternoon a group of five ship's cooks and bakers, with time on their hands before preparing the evening meal, requested permission to use one of the two recreational dinghies to row about the ship. Permission granted, they happily paddled about, causing a certain amount of merriment from more experienced sailors watching as they splashed uncertainly, caught crabs with their unaccustomed oars, and wobbled un-nautically in avoiding other boats about the ship. At about three o'clock they apparently had had enough and brought the boat back alongside the ship. Ensign Myron J. Walker, officer of the deck, directed them to bring the boat forward to the boat falls so that it could be hoisted aboard. The ship was rolling very gently, as it had been every day, to the long, easy swell which came in during the afternoon from seaward, and the amateurish dinghy crew had the misfortune of catching the gunwale of their boat under the projecting rim of an ash chute as she rolled toward them. The dinghy's gunwale was immediately pushed under water, the boat filled, and all five men suddenly found themselves swimming. Fortunately there were many men watching on deck and many boats nearby; and of course, Ensign Walker had his eye on them at the time the accident occurred. All were quickly fished out of the water, and one of the motor launches was assigned the task of picking up loose equipment floating about from the dinghy and helping to salvage the boat itself.

In the meantime Commander Bennett of the *Castine,* having been released from *Memphis'* dental chair, had gone to Captain Beach's cabin to pay his respects and chat for a moment. The two men discussed events ashore, *Memphis'* forthcoming target practice, and other professional and personal matters. Subconsciously it is probable that they noticed that the ship had commenced to roll gently, but this was nothing unusual for ships at anchor off Santo Domingo on a summer afternoon. In the absence of any untoward reports from the officer of the deck, a leisurely cigarette was smoked and a satisfying cup of coffee drunk, both served by the Skipper's devoted steward of many years, Taliaferro Watson. Also present, before the open communications and code safe, which regulations prescribed should be kept in the captain's cabin, was Ensign Robert T. Darrow, Radio Officer, who was decoding a message.

Lieutenant Commander Yancey S. Williams, executive officer of the *Memphis,* looked like a little bulldog and was beloved of the crew. He was short in height, about five feet six, stocky and muscular of build, had a square, bullet-shaped head and square facial features. The executive officer is the discipline officer of the ship, who automatically charges all infractions of discipline and decides whether or not to bring offenders to the Captain at Mast. He is the leader of the ship's officers, presides over the wardroom mess, and with the single exception of the navigator, who for obvious reasons must always have direct access, is their intermediary in all things with the captain. Being energetic and gregarious, Williams managed to retain the good feeling of both officers and men, and was, as he should have been, the Skipper's right-hand man.

A true story about Yancey Williams began one of those legends apocryphally attributed to a large number of persons through later years. In the Navy the rule is that if a man is on leave from his ship and desires an extension, he may telegraph his request to the "exec," with the understanding that, if granted, a telegram to that effect will be sent collect. Failure to receive a reply is understood to be the same as a negative reply. R. J. Ganley relates that having once wangled a ten-day leave and gone to upper New York several hundred miles from the ship, he ran short of funds and wired as follows:

TO LIEUTENANT COMMANDER Y. S. WILLIAMS, EXECUTIVE OFFICER, USS TENNESSEE. NEED TWENTY DOLLARS TRANSPORTATION MONEY TO RETURN TO SHIP. ADVISE.

He received an immediate reply, likewise by telegram, collect:

REQUEST FOR FUNDS DENIED. FIVE-DAY EXTENSION GRANTED. WALK BACK.

A few minutes before 1:00 P. M. on August 29, Ensign Walker had sent word to the Executive Officer that he was ready to send the recreation party ashore. Williams came on deck, noted that the sea was smooth with a light breeze from shore, that the barometer stood at 30.01 corrected, and that the temperature was 79 degrees. He granted permission for the boat to proceed to the recreation area and went below to the officers' wardroom, where he had scheduled a conference with the Heads of Departments at 1:30. Terminating the conference at 2:30, Williams strode through the lower decks making a quick inspection, as was his custom at odd times, and returned to the warrant officers' mess room at 0315. A summary court-martial was taking place on a coxswain named Potter, and Commander Williams had been routinely called as one of the witnesses in order properly to introduce the man's record into evidence.

It was here that the messenger from Ensign Walker found Williams with the report that the dinghy had been swamped by being caught under the lip of the ash chute. The Exec went on deck immediately. "What's the barometer reading?" he asked Walker.

The somewhat flustered Ensign, embarrassed to be presiding over damage to the boat, the loss of equipment and, most important, the resulting danger to five crew members, answered, "29.58 uncorrected—30.09 corrected."

Bracing himself against the moderate roll of the ship, Yancey Williams nodded. This was not the first time boats had been caught under the lip of the ash chute or some other projection, and good seamen should know enough to keep clear. Likewise, officers of the deck should not let amateurs get into trouble. He said nothing, however, but bounded up to the superstructure deck where a group of men were preparing to hoist the recovered boat aboard. It was imperative that it be emptied of water before being hoisted. Otherwise, the hoisting pads might pull out of their sockets in the light frame of the dinghy, or the boat break its back from the weight of the water inside. Idly he looked about and, as he later expressed it, he "did not like the looks of the sea."

It was still smooth with hardly a ripple on its oily surface, but there were undulating swells to be seen off shore, deeper than usual. On several previous occasions the sea had become too rough for safe boating, and it had become routine to send for the liberty and recreation parties early whenever it showed signs of acting up. Williams ran down the ladder to the quarter-deck again. "Walker," he said, "send in two motor launches for the recreation party immediately!"

"Aye, aye, sir," replied Walker, "but won't one boat be enough, sir? We sent them all in a single boat. There aren't that many——"

"I know. This is just a precaution. It looks to me as if we have some rollers coming in from sea and I want to be sure the boats aren't overloaded."

"Aye, aye, sir," said Walker again, making as if to move away to set the events in motion.

"Just a minute, Walker. I want to send someone in charge of the first boat to make sure everything is straight and no confusion ashore. Send for your Boatswain's Mate of the Watch."

The officer of the deck normally keeps his boat's crews standing by if they are not actually engaged in operating their boats, and in addition he has a deck watch crew of a dozen men or so of varying rates and capabilities. In a moment Ashton C. Lindsay, Boatswain's Mate Second Class, was standing before the Exec.

"Lindsay," said Williams, "I am sending two boats for the recreation party, and you will go in charge of the first one. I want you to tell Lieutenant Peirce, when you get there, that there will be another boat following you and he is not to put more than half of the men in each boat. Is that clear?"

Lindsay saluted as he began to speak, with just a hint of a Virginian drawl. "Yes, sir," he said. "I'm to tell Mr. Peirce that there's another motor launch coming after me and he's not to put more than half of the people in each boat. Aye, aye, sir."

Returning Lindsay's salute, Williams waited until he had finished, then turned to the young O.O.D. "Get the boat off right away, Walker, and send the other one after her as soon as you can."

"Yes, sir," replied Walker. "Right now it's picking up the stuff from the swamped dinghy, but that won't take much longer, and we'll have her on her way over in about five minutes."

The Exec nodded and strode to the quarter-deck companionway hatch which led to the deck below, where the Captain's cabin and the Admiral's quarters were situated. He paused with one hand on the neat rope-braided companionway hatch cover, "Good," he said, "keep your eye on the swells to seaward and keep me advised. I'm going down to report to the Captain."

Deep in the recesses of the Caribbean Sea, hundreds of miles to the south of Santo Domingo, there is a fault in the ocean floor where the rocky layer underlying the mud and ooze of millions of years hides a deep crack many miles in length, a crack created by stresses when the earth cooled into its present shape and the continents were formed. The fault reaches deep below earth's crust to the heavy elements forming its core, into the heat and pressure of the fluid interior. When a tremor or shift occurs along such a fault, it may not be noticeable on the surface of the sea placidly covering it, though it may be recorded on seismographic instruments. The effect, however, is to send out shock waves in all directions from the source of the disturbance. Even the shock waves are themselves unnoticeable, but since water is incompressible they will give witness somewhere. They might be remarked by a storm-tossed vessel as a confused cross-buck in the sea, an exceptionally large wave, or an unusual shift in the rhythm of rolling and pitching. In an otherwise calm sea the only evidence might an extremely broad, benign elevation in its surface.

The effect on a nearby shore, however, would be something else again, and would depend on the configuration of the land, the speed with which the huge wave moved, and its direction.

About noon on August 29, 1916, the earth shifted in the vicinity of the submerged fault. There was a slippage of basal matter, a great amount of water moved suddenly, and shock waves radiated from the disturbed area.

The day previous there had been the beginnings of a storm several hundred miles to the east. The near-hurricane blew strongly for a few hours, then died, leaving no damage in its wake. The wind was nowhere felt on the land; it did, however, make a disturbance in the water at its center, and large swells radiated outward on the placid sea surface. These swells moved at a considerably slower speed than the shock waves from the seismic movement. The locus of the intersection of the two sets of oceanic disturbances ran through Santo Domingo on a northwest-southeast line.

There have been only a few recorded, reliable reports on the chance formation of huge waves. USS *Ramapo,* a Navy tanker on passage from Manila to San Diego in 1933, measured and reported a tremendous wave, calculated at 112 feet in height, which overtook her from astern, lifted her, and harmlessly passed under. This wave was far larger, in all dimensions, than its companions and could only have been the result of some as-yet-little-understood concatenation of circumstances, some accidentally perfect resonance of all the factors, known and unknown. It was entirely unprecedented that it should have developed to such a noticeable extent at sea, and even more so that a ship was there to see it. The fact that a storm was in progress, with standard-sized waves formed by the wind, must have contributed.

The effect of the moon on the tides, while predictable from experience at any given locality, cannot with certainty be predicted in one place by observation of the effects in other areas. Other factors—the configuration of the land, for instance, its resonance with the tidal cycle—though not well understood, have a great effect. An example of this is the radical difference in rise and fall of tide at the two ends of the Panama Canal, only fifty miles apart. Another occurs in the Bay of Fundy area, renowned as a place where local conditions cause a twice-daily maelstrom, and where the height of the water changes as much as fifty feet in an insane rush to keep its diurnal appointments with the moon. A third takes place in the Gulf of San José, in Argentina. At sea, on the other hand, the slight rise in water level due to the moon's transit, though representing more potential energy than the mind of man can grasp, cannot even be noticed. Obviously, while the moon may be the prime mover of tides, there are many other things which figure in the movement of the tremendous volume of water involved.

It is everywhere recognized that the diurnal rise and fall of the normal tide involves a fantastic combination of forces, world wide. But even though all the waters of the earth are affected, it is only in relation to the immovable land, the *Ramapo*'s experience notwithstanding, that the change in water level ordinarily is noticeable. At sea, even a most unusually high tide, or tidal level, occurs far too gradually and is spread out over far too wide an area to have any affect on ships or marine life; and on land, even though many cubic miles and billions of tons of sea water may be displaced, the regular rise and fall of the tide is everywhere accommodated.

Naturally it must be, for it has been going on in each place in the same way for eons. Occasionally, however, an unusually high tide will take place because of a hurricane in the vicinity, and the excessive water level in such cases can be destructive along the affected seacoasts. These tides cannot be predicted until the atmospheric disturbance causing them is detected and its progress charted, and the highest water level comes, as one might expect, at the time of the regular high tide. Such extraordinarily high tides are properly referred to as "hurricane tides."

One of the effects of a storm is the creation of waves in a pattern generally emanating from the storm center, and the resulting displacement of water, the "hurricane surge," is the proximate cause of the hurricane tide as it reaches the seacoast. Should the high winds themselves also strike the coast, the storm waves will add to the resulting destructiveness of the situation. These storm waves are sometimes erroneously referred to as "tidal waves," and they may reach far inland in shallow areas and create great havoc and loss of life.

The true tidal wave is most usually seismic or volcanic in origin. (Some insist it should be known by its Hawaiian name, *Tsunami*, to eliminate any inference of a tidal nature.) It may be far higher than any tide, gives no warning of any kind save its own sudden appearance, and may be upon its victims with the force and surprise of the bursting of a dam. In the Pacific, in the Hawaiian Islands, native legends of early days frequently mentioned such waves and their effect upon the early history of the Hawaiian people. During the past 142 years it is said that forty-one tidal waves, or *Tsunami*, have struck the islands. One of the worst occurred in 1946, bringing a death toll of 159 persons. With regard to Santo Domingo, there is a local story that many years ago a pirate fleet anchored off the city with plunder its objective. But before the pirates could set foot ashore, a series of great waves raced in from seaward, smote the threatening ships, and destroyed them all.

One would surmise that both Hawaiian and Caribbean areas may be so situated in the earth's geological structures as to be, perhaps, particularly susceptible to tidal waves. Perhaps both areas have some deep-seated flaw which permits more earthquakes—and therefore more tidal waves—in these two locations than elsewhere. Perhaps it is only that islands are particularly susceptible to onslaughts from the sea, and that their inhabitants, whose lives must largely revolve around the sea, can never forget them.

Someday, when the relationship between seismographic indications and water movement is more perfectly understood, it may be possible to warn areas about to be affected. A concerted effort is going forward in this direction, led by the Coast Guard and centered, as one might surmise, in Hawaii. A warning system has been established, and the power of the human mind will ultimately have its triumph. But there is much to learn in this area. For storms and gales, we have achieved a warning capability, though we have yet to penetrate deeply into the root causes. For a tidal wave, originating in the foundation of the earth, we have as yet no explanation, and no way of predicting its movement.

The situation in the harbor of Santo Domingo is particularly hazardous because it is open to seas from the south, and because the coral shelf which forms the relatively shallow anchorage drops off precipitantly, almost like the edge of an underwater cliff, from 10 fathoms to over 100 fathoms. A tidal wave from the south, carrying its millions of tons of water, would sweep up the steep slope, find itself standing on the unyielding shelf, and thus —as though from nowhere—startlingly crest in huge elevated masses of muddy sea water and then hurl itself insanely into the shallow basin of the anchorage.

When Yancey Williams went down the companionway toward the Captain's cabin, the steep stairway momentarily disturbed the habitual stance with which all seamen normally and subconciously react to the motion of their ship so that it is neither noticed nor felt. As a consequence, he was aware of *Memphis'* rolling motion when he reached the bottom of the ladder, and for this reason his first words upon entering the Captain's cabin, instead of the report on the mishap to the dinghy which he had intended, were something of an ejaculation of surprise. "That was a heavy roll we just had," he said.

Startled, because they, too, had subconsciously felt it, Captain Beach and Commander Bennett looked inquiringly at Williams.

"I just noticed it as I came down the companionway ladder, Captain," said Williams. "I came to report to you about the dinghy and also that I've recalled the recreation party." Briefly the executive reported the situation.

Both captains reached for their caps. "Well I'd guess we better go and have a look," said Beach.

A moment later the three officers stood on the quarter-deck.

After a swift survey to seaward through his binoculars, Beach turned deliberately and gazed shoreward. Bennett was looking at his own ship, the *Castine,* six hundred yards inshore. She was rolling a little, too, he noticed.

"Captain," ventured Williams, "I've only been below a few minutes, but the rollers already look a little bigger than before."

Captain Beach put down his binoculars with a decisive movement, leaving them hanging by their straps around his neck. "Bennett, I think you'd better go back to your ship. We may not be able to use the boats much longer."

"This doesn't look like hurricane weather to me," said Bennett, "but it might be a good idea at that. May I ask the Officer of the Deck to send to the *Castine* for my boat, sir?"

"Don't bother, I'll send you in a *Memphis* boat. We have one right here and it will save time." He turned to Ensign Walker, who had hurried over when his Commanding Officer appeared on the quarter-deck, and said "Walker, call away the steamer. When it is alongside, have it take Captain Bennett back to the *Castine.*"

The O.O.D. moved away to attend to the necessary arrangements. Williams excused himself to return to the boat deck to superintend completion of salvage of the dinghy. The two captains continued to observe the sea. As they braced themselves against the slow, even motion of the *Memphis,* Bennett spoke. "You know, Captain, it's true that our motion has picked up some in the last hour or so. I guess our afternoon rolling period is upon us."

"You're right," returned the other, "but there's one thing a little unusual. Look at the surf along the shore." He handed his binoculars to Bennett, lifting the strap from about his neck as he did so. Adjusting the eyepieces, Bennett stood looking for a long minute, handed the glasses back without comment. Both officers glanced up at the mainmast peak, where Admiral Pond's blue, two-star flag was flapping idly, and at the starboard yardarm, some twenty feet below, where the blue and red international pennant for the letter "E," indicating the Admiral's absence, was likewise moving lazily in the light breeze. The in-port colors, hoisted on the flagstaff at the stern of the ship, not many feet away from the quarter-deck where the two officers were standing, were streaming gently to an offshore north breeze of about 2 knots.

Several minutes passed. *Memphis'* Skipper had started to wonder what was delaying the boat, had half-turned to investigate, when Ensign Walker approached, aimed his salute to include both commanders. "Captain," he said, addressing Captain Beach, "the first steamer is alongside the starboard gangway, ready to take Captain Bennett back to the *Castine*."

"Very well," responded the *Memphis* skipper, returning the salute. Turning to Bennett, he thrust out his hand, "It was good of you to drop in, Bennett, and I'm sorry to seem to be sending you away, but I don't quite like the looks of the sea and surf. I'm going to get steam up and be ready to get out of here. You had better do the same."

"It does look like a good idea." Bennett grinned. "I have only two boilers—the old Scotch type—and one's down for repair. But the other one's cooking away for auxiliary power. We'll be able to get under way just as soon as I call the boys together and heave in the anchor. Thanks for the boat, sir."

The two officers had by this time reached the starboard gangway and accommodation ladder, at the foot of which waited a boat with a tall slender smokestack projecting through a full-length canvas canopy. Bennett saluted Beach, turned and saluted Walker, mumbled the long-tried formula, "Sir, I have permission to leave the ship." At the top of the gangway he turned aft and saluted the colors, and then swiftly trotted down the steps of the ladder and into the steam launch.

"Shove off, Coxswain," cried Ensign Walker. 'Take your orders from Captain Bennett!"

The Coxswain saluted, and with a sibilant hiss and a puff of smoke from its toylike stack the little steamer surged off toward the *Castine*.

The decision to send Commander Bennett in a *Memphis* boat had pre-empted Walker's attention. The steamer had already nearly come alongside to port when he recalled his protocol—that all officers, especially captains of ships, should be received and dispatched at the starboard side. He had waved the boat away from the port side and sent it around to the starboard gangway, where the remaining business involving *Castine's* skip-

per was carried out. In the meantime he had directed the gasoline motor launch, with Lindsay in charge, to clear the port
gangway, lie off, and await orders. Lindsay, of course, might just
as well have been sent directly on his mission. But such is not the
proper, military way to handle boats, especially when the operation
concerns another skipper and is going on under the eyes of your
own. Not till the steamer had been properly dispatched to the
Castine, therefore, did the young O.O.D. cross to the port gangway, hail the motor launch, and send it on its way. Lindsay and
boat crew departed at 3:25, having waited perhaps seven minutes
in a heaving boat aimlessly drifting about near the port gangway. Meanwhile, Captain Beach continued to pace the quarter-
deck of the *Memphis,* gazing to seaward, where long rollers were
now visible, and looking at the shore, where it was evident that
the surf was considerably heavier than it had been a few minutes
earlier.

A couple of turns of the deck, and *Memphis'* Skipper reached a
decision. He beckoned to Walker. "Send word to the chief engineer to get steam up immediately. Start fires in the standby boilers. Call your deck crew and take in the boats."

He had as yet no clear idea of impending danger. The ship was
rolling about 10 degrees and the mastheads were describing
sweeping arcs across the sky. The air was so light that the Admiral's flag at the main truck was being whipped in opposite
directions as the motion of the ship dragged it through the still
atmosphere. But there was no denying that prickly worry forming at the back of his mind. It was better to be forehanded than
not, he reasoned, and anyway, as in the case a week before when
he had nearly taken the Russells to sea with him, it would keep
his engineering department on their toes and be a good drill for
all hands.

Walker beckoned to young Seaman Thomas, his Messenger of
the Watch, and sent him with the message for the Chief Engineer. Lieutenant Jones, he told him, would be found in the
warrant mess room, where he was counsel for the defense before
a summary court-martial then taking place. The time was 3:28
P.M. as the messenger swung himself down the ladder and disappeared.

At about 3:30 salvage of the dinghy had finally been completed and Yancey Williams rejoined Beach on the quarter-deck. The second motor launch, which had been retrieving articles lost from the dinghy and was now free from this duty, came alongside the gangway as previously instructed. Ensign Walker reported that the boat was ready to go in to the dock to pick up the other half of the recreation party. *Memphis* had by this time, however, commenced to dip the ends of her boat booms into the water as she rolled, alternately submerging the accommodation ladder platforms on either side of the quarter-deck, or raising them impossibly high out of water. The motion was still an easy, comfortable one, not unpleasant, but it was distinctly more than normal. The sea was still completely smooth, unruffled on its surface, yet beneath there was the impression of tightly bound muscles, flexing together in a secretive, oily, altogether malevolent way.

"My God, Yancey," the Captain suddenly burst forth, "look at those breakers inshore of our boat!" Beach handed the binoculars to his executive.

A low whistle broke from the latter's lips. "Why, I've never seen any breakers that big before," said Williams. "Those are really big rollers! They'll be dangerous for the boat. Maybe we'd better get it back before it reaches them!"

"Walker!" shouted the Skipper. "Hoist the recall for the motor launch! Blow the whistle to attract attention!"

Another messenger was immediately dispatched to the bridge with the necessary instructions. In the meantime the two now-anxious officers continued watching the motor launch as it approached the breakers. The whistle blew at about the time the boat was seen to enter the breakers and pass safely through them, but the recall signal was not yet flying. "Belay the recall, Yancey," said the Skipper, but Williams was already running for the bridge. After a moment, the Captain proceeded there also, selected a piece of paper from the hooded chart table, and began to write a message. Having canceled the signal, Williams approached him.

"Captain, I don't think we'd better hoist these boats before leaving the anchorage. The swells are too big, and we might damage them. The sea is getting heavier by the minute, and I think we'd better have them follow us out to sea where it will be safer."

"You're right, Yancey. I've already decided the same. Go ahead and cancel the order. Here is a message I'm going to send to the Admiral." Father handed the paper to his executive.

TO COMMANDING OFFICER FORT X SEND WORD TO AMERI-
CAN CONSUL TO TELL ADMIRAL HE CANNOT RETURN X SEAS
BREAKING ACROSS BAR X SEND ACROSS RIVER FOR MEMPHIS
RECREATION PARTY X KEEP THEM IN FORT DURING NIGHT

"Captain, how about adding 'Do not let *Memphis* motor sailer return?' " said the Exec. "I hate to think of it trying to come back through this surf with all those people."

Beach said nothing, put the pad of paper down on the desktop, wrote an additional sentence. When drafted, the complete message read:

TO COMMANDING OFFICER FORT X SEND WORD TO AMERICAN
CONSUL TO TELL ADMIRAL HE CANNOT RETURN X SEAS BREAK-
ING ACROSS BAR X SEND ACROSS RIVER FOR MEMPHIS RECREA-
TION PARTY X KEEP THEM IN FORT DURING NIGHT X DO NOT
LET MEMPHIS SAILER RETURN X SIGNED BEACH

Handing the message to Quartermaster Blattner, who had been watching attentively, Beach said, "Send this immediately to the fort!"

As Blattner reached out his hand for the paper, Williams spoke. "Chief, use every means to expedite that signal. It's very important!"

The Executive Officer had picked up a pair of binoculars from a nearby rack and now the two officers stood side by side looking shoreward.

"Yancey," said the Captain, "the breakers are receding from the shore. They are coming closer to the ship!"

"That's right, Captain. They are already halfway between the river mouth and the *Castine*. If this keeps up, she may have a rough time!"

Beach swung his glass to seaward. "Good Lord, Yancey! Look at this!"

The two officers on the bridge of their gently rolling ship in a quiet harbor stared horror-struck to seaward, where only a few moments before there had been a placid horizon, marred only by the rollers which had first been noticed about twenty minutes before.

Now there was no horizon to be seen. Instead, an ugly mountain of ugly, yellow frothy water completely obscured the horizon over the entire sweep of view from east around through south to the westward. The great wave was possibly seventy-five feet high. In length—impossible to guess. In breadth, likewise impossible to tell, for it was so high that one could not see over the top to make an estimate. But the fact that it had arisen where, but a few moments before, had been nothing, boded ill for the ships and boats in harbor.

"Yancey," Beach said urgently," that thing will be on us in a few minutes! Rig the ship for heavy weather! Put in all gun shutters! Get everybody at their stations! Find the bugler and have him sound Officers' Call!" The surge of adrenalin in his bloodstream left him with face contorted above the heavy gray-tinged mustache, complexion reddened by the suddenly called-on imperative of command. More reflectively, in the next breath he said, "I've never seen or heard of a thing like this in all my years at sea!"

Williams jerked off his binoculars, quickly replaced them in the rack from which he had taken them. "Aye, aye, sir," he said swiftly, as he turned to dash down the bridge companionway ladder. Then, with a foot on the top tread, hand gripping the rail, he turned back to his skipper for one final word. "Captain," he shouted, his face mirroring his consternation, "this isn't natural! This is volcanic!" Then he turned and dashed down the ladder.

The time was 3:45 P.M. on the afternoon of August 29.

Chapter 3

Chief Machinist Newton R. George, a precise, competent engineer, a shade under average height and spare of build, had been Engineer Officer of the Day since 0800. The duties of his watch were to maintain readiness to implement the ship's emergency station bill for getting under way, and to supervise regularly prescribed ship's work. On watch with Machinist George was a complete engine room steaming watch, consisting of Chief Machinist's Mate George W. Rudd and six other men. The emergency procedures prescribed that four boilers should be kept continuously ready to be lighted and that adequate personnel should always be available in the engine rooms to carry out initial warm-up procedures. All officers attached to the Engineering Department were directed to proceed immediately to their respective stations whenever the emergency watch was called, but until their arrival the Engineering O.O.D. had over-all charge of the entire engineering plant.

Since George's regular assignment was Chief Machinist in Charge of Main Engines, his regular responsibility was for the condition of the engines, repair of machinery, and accountability of all spare parts and equipment—all separate from and in addition to the supervisory duties over the entire Engineering Department which, by virtue of being on the duty list, he held on this day. With the ship at anchor and no intended movement in prospect, Lieutenant Jones had given permission to carry out certain routine repairs. The circulating water pump, which supplied cooling water to the port main condenser, had been showing excessive leakage of steam through some of its turbine gaskets; so like the careful engineer that he was, George had scheduled it for overhaul. In order to avoid putting the entire port condenser and therefore the port main engine out of commission at the same time, the starboard circulating pump had been cross-connected so that it could serve both main condensers. This was standard procedure, planned for in the design of the plant and accomplished by opening a cross-connection valve so that the starboard pump took its suction through the port condenser instead of from sea directly, and discharged it, as usual, through its own condenser and overboard.

With similar rationale, Machinist Charles H. Willey, in charge of the fireroom, had obtained permission from Lieutenant Jones for some of the deck plates of fireroom number eight to be unbolted from the angle-iron foundations to which they were normally secured in order to permit the otherwise idle "standby watch" crews to clean and repaint the ship's bilges beneath them. Operations of the boilers would, of course, require that the deck plates be restored to their proper positions, only a few minutes' work. The heavy plates had been lifted from their foundations and temporarily stowed in out-of-the-way corners while the men squatted below the foundation brackets, chipping and scraping at the old paint beneath.

Machinist Willey, unlike George, was not on watch, but since his regular assignment was Machinist in Charge of the Firerooms, he was nevertheless fully cognizant of and responsible for everything about them. Like George, he was a precise, methodical man. In physical stature as well as repute the two were quite similar, though Willey's almost somber usual expression and reserved, fastidious personality caused him generally to be considered the less gregarious of the two. Conscientious, deeply aware of their responsibilities, these two officers epitomized the finest type of career enlisted man in the Navy. Both had enlisted at a very young age. The records of both were unblemished by irresponsibility of any kind, and now, in their mid-thirties, they had attained the rank of Warrant Officer and enjoyed the respect and confidence of everyone aboard.

At 3:30 in the afternoon, having during the course of the day made numerous trips below to check on the work in his firerooms, Willey shifted into the "uniform of the day"—uniform jacket buttoned up to the neck over a clean white shirt (the Navy had not yet adopted the double-breasted style with necktie) —and donned his best cap. Then he climbed up two decks to the boat deck to take a turn about topside. Neither he nor anyone else gave any attention to the slightly increased roll of the ship as she lazed at her anchor in the soft Caribbean breeze. This was, after all, quite normal for the time of day.

Down below in the starboard engine room, Machinist George was at the same moment engaged in checking over the inventory in the starboard engine room spare parts storeroom.

Ensign Walker's messenger found the Chief Engineer, Lieutenant Jones, where he had been told he would, ranged opposite three other officers, all in full and impeccable white uniform, at a green baize-covered table in the warrant officer's mess room. Seated nervously bolt upright in a chair alongside Jones was Coxswain Potter, accused of attempting to bring liquor on board and, when apprehended, striking another person in the Naval Service. At one end of the table, equally attentive and also somewhat ill at ease because of the requirement for meticulous accuracy in preparation of the record, sat Ensign Meyer, the Recorder of the Court. The accused had pleaded "Not Guilty" to the charge, thus by the nature of the summary court-martial procedure greatly augmenting the natural gravity and complexity of the proceedings. Navy Regulations, the Ship's Orders, and unwritten tradition specified that no members of a court could be interrupted while carrying out court-martial duties except by matters of the greatest consequence, of sufficient import to justify possible reversal of the entire proceedings of the Court. These rules were rightly intended to guarantee an accused man the undivided attention of all members of the Court. They were then, and still are, rigorously observed. Young Thomas, only a few months in the Navy, first had to spend several moments convincing the Marine orderly on guard at the entrance to the wardroom that his message was of sufficient importance to interrupt the proceedings. This hurdle passed, he found himself inside the room, under the severe and annoyed gaze of the three members of the Court, the recorder, and the defense counsel.

"What is it, son?" testily snapped Lieutenant Withers, by virtue of seniority president of the Court. While his arthritis was not preventing him from carrying out court-martial duties, it was not conducive to a mild temper.

Young and inexperienced though he was, the messenger had been on deck and had observed the reactions of his august superiors. He knew little about the sea, but he had noticed the ship beginning to roll and was inwardly pleased at participating in something which tended to break the monotony of his life in a large ship filled with superior beings. He delivered his message effectively, if slightly garbled.

"Mr. Jones, sir, the Officer of the Deck requests that you get the ship under way immediately!"

"What's that?" asked Jones, caught by surprise. "We're to get under way immediately?"

"Yessir. The Captain was there, sir, and he told Mr. Walker. He said he don't like the looks of the sea, sir, and he said for you to light off the forward boilers."

"That's the wrong message!" snapped Jones as he and the other members of the Court exchanged glances. What the Captain had directed was clearly "four more boilers," but in the mind of each was the thought that perhaps he was acting a little skittish over the possibility of hurricane weather in this unprotected anchorage. The same thing had happened only a week earlier, and all their trouble had been for nothing. The bonds of discipline held firm, however, and nothing was said.

"Very well," said Jones. "Messenger, you go find Mr. Willey. Tell him we are putting the emergency station bill in effect and that I want him to go below and get started. Tell him to put number one fireroom under forced draft right away, and number seven and eight as soon as they're started. Then you go down and tell Mr. George in the engine room the same thing. Tell them both I'll be down myself as soon as I can. Hurry, now!"

"Aye, aye, sir," the lad responded and dashed away. Jones stood up. "I'm afraid I shall have to ask to be excused, sir," he stated formally. Withers nodded to indicate reluctant assent, and Jones likewise left the room.

At this moment Captain Beach was on the bridge of the ship at the chart table writing the message to the fort signal tower. The time was approximately 3:40 P.M.

Seated at the end of the green baize table opposite Ensign Meyers was Yeoman First Class "Pop" Ezzell, who had been assigned as the Reporter of the Court. He had before him a pad of paper filled with shorthand notes of the proceedings thus far. Lieutenant Withers thought a moment. The defense counsel had abruptly left the room, but possibly the proceedings might yet be salvaged if he could avoid making some fatal judicial error. He cleared his throat, announced in a juridicial tone, "The Court will be closed." This meant that everyone else must leave the room to permit the members of the Court to consult in private. The Reporter made a note on his pad. Everyone rose. The three members of the Court remained standing while the others trooped out of the room.

Inside the wardroom, Withers spoke decisively. "There is not much we can do, fellows. I intend to reopen the Court and then recess it subject to reconvening upon future call, probably tomorrow. Any objections?" The other two members of the Court, Lieutenant (j.g.) W. J. (Josh) Carver and Passed Assistant Surgeon George Robertson, the ship's medical officer, shook their heads.

"All right. I'll tell the Recorder of the Court to take a good look at the Manual of Courts and Boards to be sure that this is properly reported in the record of proceedings. I'll also tell him to be ready to advise me when we reconvene."

The other two nodded.

At a further signal from Withers, the door to the passageway was opened and those outside were allowed to re-enter and resume their places. Lieutenant Withers rose again to his feet. "The Court is reopened," he said. "The Court will be recessed until further call. You are all warned that the oaths you took are still binding and that you may not discuss this case with anyone."

While standing, he had to brace himself against the table as the ship rolled. He rapped on the table once with his knuckles as though with a gavel, and suppressing a grimace of pain, strode swiftly to the compartment door. As he reached it, Lieutenant Jones opened the door from the other side. He had discarded his immaculate white service jacket, now wore a stained dungaree jacket and a dirty cap. The hairs of his chest peeped above the curved neck band of his white undershirt, and, incongruous below the jacket, he still wore the creased white trousers and white shoes with which he had outfitted himself for the court-martial.

"Ah, I see you've adjourned," said Jones.

"Not quite, Jones," said Withers. "We've recessed. We'll reconvene tomorrow morning after this exercise is over. I'm just as glad. My legs are killing me, and since I'm officially on the sick list, I think I'll lie down for a little while. I suppose we've got at least an hour or so before you'll be able to get under way, don't we?"

"More like forty-five minutes, Withers," said the engineer. "Maybe we'll be able to beat our time last week. I've already talked to the engine room by voice tube from my stateroom, and they're already starting. Do you think this is just a drill?"

"More than likely, I expect. But we are rolling a little more than usual. Maybe the Old Man just wants to play it safe."

"That's probably right." Jones grinned. "Well, I've got to get down below!" The Chief Engineer departed on the run.

As Seaman Thomas ran out of the messroom, he knew that the most likely place to find Machinist Willey at this time of the day was in his stateroom, or possibly just returning from the firerooms to "warrant officers' country," as that area of the ship was known. In his few months of service he had become accustomed to searching for certain officers intimately connected with the ship's capability to operate. It was but a few feet to Willey's stateroom from the warrant officers' messroom. Hanging on a hook on the front of a locker door, swinging through a small arc as the ship rolled to and fro, was the old dungaree jacket which

Willey always wore in the engineering spaces. Above it swung the battered "steaming cap," which was also part of his working uniform. Obviously Willey was not below, but somewhere else in the ship, possibly topside or perhaps conferring with one of his chiefs in the CPO quarters. Thomas ran back to the messroom.

"Where's Mr. Willey?" he asked Charles Howard, the husky Negro Warrant Officer's Steward on watch in the tiny pantry.

"Not here," the latter pronounced gravely, as though this bit of negative information possessed great potential usefulness, apparently oblivious to the fact that the virtual emptiness of the compartment must already have communicated itself to the young messenger.

A bit nettled, Thomas turned to the solitary individual in the messroom, a heavy-set officer who, having apparently entered on the heels of the recessed court-martial, was holding in his two cupped hands a very blond cup of coffee in a large, white, handleless mug and looking at him over its rim with what Thomas hoped was a helpful stare. "Mr. Thompson, the Chief Engineer wants me to find Mr. Willey right away, sir," he said. "We have to get ready to get under way as soon as we can!"

Thompson lowered his cup. "He's probably up topside getting some air. Why don't you look on the boat deck?" Apparently unimpressed with Thomas' feeling of urgency, Thompson raised his cup again to his lips.

A sense of panic was growing in Thomas, though he would have been hard put to it to explain just why. He had been on deck when the Captain of the *Castine* had been sent back to his ship. He had seen and partly overheard his own Captain's conversations with both the Officer of the Deck and the Executive Officer and had observed their interest in the surf and the rollers to seaward. Also, he was not yet enough of a seaman to have become completely inured to the motion of the ship and was therefore very much aware that it had increased during the past several minutes. He dashed out of the warrant officers' messroom, raced forward and, two steps at a time, up the ladder leading to the next deck and up a second ladder. Panting, he arrived in a burst of sunlight as he scrambled through the hatch opening on the boat deck approximately abreast the aftermost of the ship's four tall stacks.

The deck was encumbered with various paraphernalia, not least of which were eight big ventilator intakes, one on either side of each of the stacks, which led down to the forced-draft blower mechanisms and thence into the firerooms. The ship's boats and various components of boat-handling gear were located on this deck, most prominent of the latter being two great boat cranes which towered more than half as high as the smoke pipes. Abaft number four stack and covering most of the space between it and the mainmast was the skylightlike cluster of large square engine-room hatches, wide open to permit escape of the engine-room heat. Three decks below the hatches, at the level of the armored deck—or berth deck—and supported by heavy members of the ship's structure, were the battle bars, or battle gratings—heavy steel bars placed close together so as to permit ventilation and at the same time stop or deflect any projectile which might happen to penetrate to their level. On the theory that their deflective ability would be improved if they were not rigidly mounted, and also because of the frequent need for access for repair of the machinery, the battle bars were set in sockets, but not otherwise firmly attached. Upon being struck by a shell from an enemy gun, they would undoubtedly be dislocated and damaged, but the looseness of the bars would contribute to their ability to absorb shock. At least, so was the theory.

Deep below the battle gratings were the engine rooms. At night, when the ship was under way and lights were low topside, one could peer into these hatches and squint between the shadowed battle bars to see the people on watch far below, moving amid the orderly confusion of the machinery.

Despite all its paraphernalia, the boat deck had considerable clear deck space and was a favorite area for members of the ship's company, not otherwise occupied, who wanted to get an hour or two of sun, or watch the sea go by. Here Thomas judged he would find Willey, and here, by good fortune, he did so.

Breathlessly he reported Lieutenant Jones's instructions. Willey, never one to be unduly loquacious, listened impassively. "Thanks, I'll go right away," he said, turning and descending by the companionway through which the messenger had just come up.

His mission as yet incomplete, Thomas clattered down the

ladder after Willey and down two more ladders. At exactly 3:45 he was repeating his message to Machinist George. "The chief said to start fires in the ready boilers and put number one fireroom under forced draft. Also put firerooms number seven and eight under forced draft as soon as you get the fires started. Mr. Jones is on a court-martial and will be here as soon as he can!"

George was already wiping his hands on a piece of waste as Thomas entered the spare-parts storeroom. He nodded with a trace of impatience, for he had just received the same message from another messenger, who had answered Lieutenant Jones's call on the voice tube. He stepped out of the storeroom into the starboard engine room. Chief Machinist's Mate Rudd, he knew, would be in the port engine room, supervising the work on the small steam turbine which ran the port main circulating water pump. He stepped to the low watertight door connecting the two engine rooms. Stooping, he brought his head below the top coaming. "Rudd!" he called. A group of men had just dismantled the circulating water-pump turbine and were examining it. One of them, grease and grime to his elbows, wearing a battered and greasy chief petty officer's cap perched on the back of his head, detached himself from the group and, likewise wiping his hands and forearms on a piece of waste, approached George.

"Here, Chief," he said pleasantly, balancing himself against the roll of the ship.

"Rudd, we've got to get under way right away! Orders from the Chief Engineer. Secure what you're doing, cross-connect your condensers and get steam on the main-engine jackets as soon as you can."

The ship heaved. Both Rudd and George braced themselves against the nearest handrailing, gripping it with the waste in their hands so as not to leave dirty fingerprints. "Aye, aye, Chief," said Rudd. "It is kicking up a bit, isn't it?"

"Feels that way, agreed George. "Mr. Jones said he'd be down here right away, as soon as he gets clear of this Summary Court he's sitting on. You start things moving in here. I'm going up forward to check on the firerooms."

"Right," replied Rudd. "This won't be any problem back here to get warmed up. Are they going to send us any help?"

"Yes. The emergency under-way bill is in effect and you'll be getting your regular crews down here right away. Stillman should be here in a minute or so and will take over the starboard engine room. You're supposed to get things started for him before he gets here, though."

"Aye, aye, Chief," said Rudd again, smiling confidently.

Just as George had complete and total responsibility for all the main propulsion machinery, his two main subordinates, Rudd and Stillman, each held complete responsibility to him for one of the two engine rooms. Both men were chief petty officers, or CPOs, had had years of naval service and were on their way up the same ladder which George himself had already climbed.

Settling his cap more firmly on his head, instinctively using the bit of waste to protect its greasy, cracked visor, George retraced his steps to the forward end of the starboard engine room. Since the firerooms were not at the moment under forced draft, both doors of the air lock connecting with the after starboard fire-room, number seven, were open. George paused, one foot already over the coaming of the first door, to hear Rudd start events in motion with the shout, "All right, you guys, let's stow all this here gear and warm up them engines!" These were exactly the words George would have used—had used many times. The faintest touch of a grin crossed his face as he ducked his head through the watertight door and into number seven fireroom.

Willey preceded Thomas down from the boat deck, but in-stead of going immediately to the firerooms, he went to his own stateroom. There he swiftly hung his uniform jacket on a hanger in his locker and neatly placed his good cap in its accustomed place on the shelf. In one often-repeated motion, he crammed his steaming cap on his head, swept his arms through the frayed and discolored dungaree jacket hanging beneath it, and stepped back out the door, patting the pockets of the jacket to assure himself that his gauntleted leather gloves were in their accustomed place. As he strode toward the hatchway which led to the ladder into the fireroom spaces, he swiftly buttoned the dungaree jacket and then drew on the gloves. The iron ladder upon which he was about to descend was always hot, and the gloves had by this time become quite second nature to him. There was some thought also in Willey's mind that just possibly, if this were only a drill or perhaps only a temporary emergency, as had been the case a week ago, he might, as he had then, salvage the clean shirt he was wearing. Willey's experience in the firerooms with the heat, coal dust, and perspiration did not, however, give him much cause to hope in this regard. Just as he swung himself through the hatch and onto the fireroom ladder he heard the first twittering of boatswain's pipes and the hoarse shouts, scarcely clear enough to be directly understood, but by long habit and association recognized by all: "Now, man your stations for getting under way! All hands, man your stations for getting under way!" Halfway down the ladder, he faintly heard the notes of a bugle sounding the well-known notes of Officers' Call.

Willey arrived in number seven fireroom at about the same time as George re-entered it from forward, whence he had gone to see the conditions in number one fireroom. The time was now about 3:46 P.M.

Newton George was the first one to speak, "Willey, what's going on topside?" he asked.

"Dunno, Chief," replied Willey, who, being a rank below George, occasionally used the title in friendly deference. "I had just finished down here about half an hour ago and was taking a turn around the boat deck when a messenger from Mr. Jones told me to come right down here and light off these boilers. What word do you have?"

"Not much more. A messenger found me a couple of minutes ago and said the same thing. He told me the Chief was on a Summary Court up in the wardroom and would be down as soon as possible."

"Well," said Willey, "that doesn't sound too serious. I didn't see anything special topside, except some cooks and bakers took the dinghy out for a row and, like the lubbers they are, they capsized it under the port ash chute when the ship rolled. . . . Come to think of it we are rolling fairly much right now."

Both men were shifting their weight and swaying in cadence with the ship's motion. "Well, anyway, Willey, I got orders from the Chief to get ready to get under way, same as you, and Rudd is warming up the engines. I've already been to number one fireroom and told them to build up their fires and get the fireroom under forced draft. The four-to-six dogwatch has just come on, and they have already started to clean fires. That's too bad, because they won't be in the best of shape for a while. Anyway, Water Tender Grant knows that we'll be needing to take fires from his boilers to start fires in the after-boilers."

"Okay, Chief," said Willey. "Is the emergency watch bill in effect?"

"Yes, it is. That's the word I had from the messenger anyway. He said Jones will be down right away. Now that you're here, I'll turn over to you. You take charge of all preparations in the firerooms for getting under way, and I'll go back to the engine rooms—okay?" Willey nodded his agreement.

Men comprising the fireroom-watch sections as listed on the emergency under-way bill were already arriving as Willey inspected the two boilers in fireroom number seven. As George watched, his first move was to check the water level to confirm that they were full of water as they should have been. By this time, Water Tenders Porter and Quinn had arrived on the scene. Under Willey's instructions, each took one of the two ready firerooms and immediately opened drains in the bottoms of the boilers to bring the water down to the steaming level. Boiler feed water is precious in any ship, and although the quickest way of lowering the water level is to dump it right into the fireroom bilges, as Porter and Quinn were doing, this is far from the preferred procedure, which involves running it back into the feed tanks. In the interests of saving time, however, and in spite of the loss of boiler feed, dumping it had been specified in the emergency procedures.

George remained a few more minutes in fireroom number seven. Then, as a fireman appeared holding a coal shovel behind him, half full of red-hot coal carried aft from the steaming fireroom, the Chief Machinist unobtrusively made his way back to the engine rooms. The time was now about 3:50 and *Memphis* had commenced to roll noticeably. Carrying a shovelful of live coal through two empty firerooms to reach number seven, stepping over coamings, along narrow passageways beside the boilers and through three sets of watertight doors, by consequence had become a fairly difficult operation. The shovel was always held behind, to keep the heat and smoke out of one's eyes, and it required two hands, leaving only an elbow, placed strategically akimbo against the bulkheads, to help maintain equilibrium during the journey. Many of the red-hot coals fell off the shovel as the firemen jostled them through, and the deck plates of the walkways alongside the boilers quickly became luminous with hundreds of tiny glowing dots lining their surfaces.

In the meantime, the coal passers as they arrived had opened the bunker doors and begun to drag out coal, which they piled on the floor plates in the center of the fireroom, ready for use.

Fireroom number eight had a special problem, having had its floor plates removed to permit work on the bilges beneath. One of Willey's first orders had been to direct that these plates be immediately replaced. With the ship rolling back and forth the heavy plates showed a tendency to shift suddenly with sudden motions of the ship, and the workers' difficulties were compounded by their lack of adequate footing, since it was this very footing which had been taken up. To secure the plates in place, they normally had first to be fitted back precisely into their old locations and carefully lined up so that bolts could be inserted into their holes at each corner and tightened. As a concession to haste, however, this step was for the most part skipped; but not until the floor plates had been at least set in their proper places, with or without bolts in the corners, could regular firing procedures begin on the two boilers located there.

With events moving as well as possible in firerooms seven and eight, Willey went forward to evaluate the situation in fireroom number one, noting by the fireroom clock there that he arrived in that compartment at 3:50 P.M. First checking by the glass peepholes and then opening the furnace doors and peering inside, Willey was not pleased by what he saw. While some of the fires looked clean enough, and fresh, others had been allowed to deteriorate with the evident expectation that the unpopular job of cleaning them would be done by the on-coming watch. Despite George's information upon Willey's arrival, it was not strictly true that the crew of the afternoon watch had been completely relieved by the men designated for the "first dog watch" (4:00-6:00). The watch was actually still in the process of being relieved. Men of both sections were present, and additional men were arriving upon their heels in response to the provisions of the emergency bill for getting under way. The presence of so many extra men, about three times as many as needed, naturally interfered with the process of getting the fires in the best shape.

Chief Water Tender Kenney now appeared and took charge of fireroom number one, his duty station on the emergency bill. To him Willey transmitted instructions to get rid of unnecessary personnel, do his utmost to force his boilers, and make as much steam as possible just as soon as this could be done. Willey then returned to firerooms number seven and eight, where his battle to get up steam would be fought. It was about 3:55 and he, too, noticed that the ship was now rolling heavily.

When George returned to the engine room, he found the situation under good control. The starboard main circulating pump was running and both condensers were receiving cooling water through the cross-connect system. The forced-lubricating system had been tested and was operating. Steam had been placed on the jackets of the main engines, warming up the cylinders in preparation for the admission of operating steam, and little wisps of vapor were escaping from the labyrinth glands around the piston shafts, reversing gear mechanism and throttle.

Chief Machinist's Mate H. P. Stillman had arrived and had taken over the starboard engine room. Chief Machinist's Mate Rudd, in the port engine room, reported everything in readiness on his side also.

At about this time, Lieutenant Jones arrived in the engine rooms. "Main engines are just about ready, Mr. Jones," reported George. "We're still checking them and watching them, but preparations for getting under way have been completed and reported to me."

"Very well," said Lieutenant Jones, returning his chief machinist's salute. His dress, the first real indication George had had that this was not a drill situation, was enough to cause George to make special note of it. Had it been only a drill, and not a real or believed emergency, Jones would have been aware of it in advance and would certainly not have risked his nice uniform trousers and shoes in the engineering spaces.

"Mr. Jones, is the emergency watch bill in effect?" asked George of his chief. It was important for George to know this, just as it had been for the others, since the duties and responsibilities of the individuals were affected. It was also a tactful way for George to insure that Lieutenant Jones and he held the same appreciation of the division of responsibility.

"Yes, it's in effect, Chief. I'll take charge of the engineering department as of now. You take over the engine rooms."

"Aye, aye, sir," said George. "The engine rooms are ready in all respects to get under way. I'll keep you advised, sir."

"Very well, Chief," responded the chief engineer. "You've done well. I can see that we're all ready back here. What we need now is steam." He emphasized the last word as he spoke; then, bracing himself against the now quite heavy rolling of the ship, he turned and went forward into the fireroom compartments.

The firemen in the meantime had been having their problems. As Willey walked back from number one fireroom aft, he met Lieutenant Jones who had just stepped forward from the starboard engine room.

"Willey, why haven't you got the forced draft blowers on yet?" asked Jones, who had instantly noted that the blowers were not yet running.

"Number one fireroom has orders to get the blowers going right away, Mr. Jones, and we're not ready yet in seven and eight."

"Well, start all the blowers right away," ordered Jones.

This disturbed Willey. Because of the delay resulting from the floor-plate difficulty, not all the furnace doors in number eight fireroom had yet received fire. Running the forced-draft blower over a cold fire bed would delay rather than speed the formation of steam. In addition, the blowers were yet another drag on the still critically short supply of steam. But something in Jones's demeanor stopped the protest that Willey was about to voice. There were plenty of idle men about, since the emergency station bill manned all eight firerooms even though there were immediate plans to use only two additional ones, and Willey at once drafted a number of men to check the uptake and air-lock doors secured, notify the dynamo rooms, and start the blowers.

When Willey entered the firerooms, steam pressure on the two boilers in use had been one hundred and seventy-five pounds. This was standard for auxiliary purposes. The engine rooms had, however, absorbed a considerable amount of steam in order to warm up the main and auxiliary machinery and to start the

main feed pump. When one runs steam into cold machinery, the
first and most immediate effect is for the steam to condense on
the cold metal and dissipate much of its heat—that is to say,
power—in bringing the metal itself up to operating temperature.
This condensed steam does not go into the condensers, but instead drips out through strategically placed drains and along the
abnormally large clearances between operating parts, which can
only be steam-tight when the machinery is at operating temperature and all expansion of metal due to heat has taken place. The
more rapidly machinery is warmed up, the more steam is needed
at the early stages; thus more is lost in the form of condensate
drained from stategic low points in the machinery. As a consequence of the extra loss of water, requirements for fresh feed
water were increased. The extra feed water, of course, had to be
taken from the main feed tank, requiring more pumping, thus
still more steam; and this water, being cold, was also harder to
convert into steam than condensate water from the condensers
would have been.

The resultant effect of these factors was that steam pressure
began to drop.

The time was now 4:05 P.M., or 1605, in the twenty-four-hour
time system since adopted, and the motion of the *Memphis*
could be described as "lively." That is to say, she was rolling
heavily from side to side, pitching gently at the same time, tugging at her anchor chain intermittently. The action of the anchor could be felt as the anchor chain snubbed her motion. The
behavior of the ship could be likened to that of a spirited horse—
not yet in open rebellion against its tether, but uneasy under the
restraint, tossing its head, backing away from the halter, nervously shifting its weight and pawing the ground.

Down below it is usually difficult to tell how far a ship is
rolling since the entire environment goes with it. There is additionally a certain amount of centrifugal force which minimizes
the noticeable effects upon persons below the center of gyration.
By contrast, rolls are more noticeable to people above the center
of gyration and, of course, to someone high on a mast even moderate rolls feel pretty violent. Most engineering spaces consequently harbor an inclinometer, or pendulum, frequently the
obvious product of some sailor's spare time, mounted in an un-

used space somewhere near the center line of the ship. Its purpose is simply to satisfy the curiosity of the engineering personnel as to the degree of roll. There was, however, no instrument to measure periods between successive rolls. This could only be known by timing with a watch, or by sensing intuitively. The intuitive sense was not long lacking in *Memphis'* engineering spaces. To George, Willey, and Lieutenant Jones, the motion of the ship, her heavy, rapid rolling, made it gradually but abundantly evident that something serious was taking place and that there was every reason to make a maximum effort to get the engines ready.

At 4:05 P.M., Chief Machinist George stepped through the doorway between the starboard engine room and number seven fireroom and approached Lieutenant Jones. "Chief," said he, "the bridge just called. The Captain wants to know how soon we will be ready to get underway."

"What's your status back aft, Chief?" responded the engineer officer.

"We're fully ready to go, sir, just as soon as we get steam."

Willey broke in. "Mr. Jones, steam pressure is dropping. We can't keep up with it with two boilers, and the other four boilers aren't producing any steam yet. It would help some to secure all unnecessary machinery."

"Make it so," replied Jones. "Secure the evaporators and the ice machine and all machinery not actually needed. George, shut off your main air pumps until steam pressure gets back up. You don't need 'em now anyway."

"Aye, aye, sir," replied George. "When shall I tell the bridge we can get under way, Chief?"

Sweat stood out on the Chief Engineer's face. It was hot in the fireroom, but not all the sweat was due to heat. He had been observing the difficulty in number eight fireroom and had been too long in engineering duty to have any illusions about the problems his men faced. Already he bitterly regretted the few minutes, now irretrievably gone, it had taken to start things moving.

"Tell the bridge we'll be ready to get under way in about half an hour"—and then, speaking directly to George and Willey in a lowered tone, he added, "That will give us until about four thirty-five."

George left immediately, bracing himself with arms outstretched to either side against the motion of the ship. When he arrived at his engine-room log desk, secured to the amidships bulkhead opposite the starboard engine throttle, he first relayed Claud Jones's response to the bridge through the voice tube and then set about cutting out the unneeded machinery Jones had specified. As he did so he noted the steam-pressure gauge attached to the bulkhead overhead. The needle stood at one hundred and twenty-five pounds. Except for reducing his demands for steam, there was nothing more George could do.

Willey's problems were far different. The uneven and rapid metal expansion resulting from the quick heating of the boilers had caused leaks in various handhole and inspection plates on the boiler surfaces, necessitating that he assign two men to crawl over the boilers with wrenches and tighten all plates. The ship was now rolling and pitching rapidly and heavily. In number seven fireroom there was suddenly a heavy spray of water, punctuated by the rapid beat of the forced-draft blower blades. It stopped quickly and the blower, which had cleaerly been heard to slow down momentarily, resumed its normal running. The fireroom crew stared at each other wonderingly. This water could only have come in through one of the ventilators on the boat deck, which reached almost half as high as the stacks—a height approximately fifty feet above the normal water level! The water spread around on the floor of the fireroom, soaking into the pile of coal in the center of the deck space. The rolling of the ship continued to increase, both in amount and rapidity, and coal passers coming out of the coal bunkers with their heavy buckets of coal frequently found themselves unable to control the heavy weights. Sometimes they lost them and a cascade of coal and bucket would fling itself across the floor plates, scattering itself in the puddles of water, adding its degree of difficulty to the problems of the firemen. To this was added the sometimes labored charge of a young coal passer, bucket and all, desperately fighting for balance the entire length of the fireroom, from coal bunker outboard to the inboard bulkhead on the ship's centerline.

Overhead, attached to the underside of the walkway gratings

around the water-level sight glasses, were various firebox tools such as slice bars, clinker bars, and devil's claw rigs, all located there for quick use when needed to work on the fires. These now commenced to slide back and forth in their racks. During one particularly heavy roll to port, one of the slice bars, six feet in length, shot completely out of its rack and, like a spear, struck the far bulkhead with enough force to blunt the tip. Luckily, no one happened to be in the way, or he would have been trans-fixed by the heavy, sharp-ended instrument. As a result of this incident, however, all tools in the overhead racks were removed and placed on the floor plates out of the way.

In hurrying to get the fires going under the boilers in fireroom number eight, many of its loose floor plates had not been prop-erly secured. As the rolling of the ship increased, some of them shifted position, opened up holes in the floor or, tilting between the brackets, dropped the coal piled on them into the bilges. Extra men were detailed to secure the floor plates, a dangerous operation because of their weight and tendency to move unex-pectedly. The matter was urgent; tools were improvised from slice bars, clinker bars, and other ordinary fireroom equipment. And after a few minutes of concentrated effort—a few more im-portant minutes lost—enough bolts had been put in place to hold them firmly and provide some kind of assured walking sur-face for the firemen working on the fires.

In the meantime *Memphis'* motion had increased to the vio-lent stage, even as felt from below. More and more water con-tinued to come in through the blower ducts. The bilges began to fill up. If allowed to be too full, water would ultimately spill over from the bilges into the furnace fireboxes. It was imperative to get this water out and, despite the fact that it took more precious steam, Willey started a bilge pump for the purpose.

It was during this period—time not exactly specified but prob-ably in the neighborhood of 4:25—that a shout from one of the firemen attracted Willey's attention. The man had his furnace door open and was looking at his fire. Willey stooped swiftly and looked with him. The fire was dull, dirty red in color, not evenly spread. As they watched, it slowly returned to a more normal condition. "What happened?" said Willey.

"Dunno. I was looking at it and all of the sudden it got dim. . . .

There it goes again, sir!" As they watched, the fire again dimmed, and after a moment sprang back cheerfully. And now Willey could hear a new noise—a hissing, slithering, spattering noise, akin to that resulting when fires are put out with a hose. In this case there was no hose. There could be only one explanation. There was only one place this water could come from—down the smokestacks directly into the fires!

Willey became conscious of a tingling sensation in his nerve ends. The tops of the smokestacks were seventy feet above the water line. Granted that the ship was rolling pretty wildly and that the water might be entering the stacks when she was well heeled over, nevertheless waves able to throw spume or spray that high must be unbelievably high! Then another thought entered his mind and drove the first one out completely. If a really heavy slug of water came down the smokepipes, enough cold water really to deluge the hot steam drum at the top of the boiler, the resultant reaction would probably be enough to rupture something. If so, everyone in the fireroom would be killed and, depending on the steam pressure at the time, the ship herself, perhaps, seriously damaged.

Willey resolved to say nothing about these fears to his men, but to communicate the intelligence of what he had seen to Lieutenant Jones as soon as possible.

The engine room had a somewhat better appreciation of what was going on topside than did the firerooms, partly because of the glass ports built into the engine-room hatches on the boat deck abaft the funnels, partly because it was in voice communication with the bridge, and lastly because of the arrival of occasional messengers. At 4:15 P.M. a messenger came from topside with the news that the motor launch returning the recreation party from the baseball field had overturned in the surf. A few minutes later by bridge voice tube it was learned that the *Castine* had got under way, was also in the surf and making very heavy weather of it, and that her survival was despaired of. Interspersed with these communications were several demands from the bridge to know the condition of the engineering plant and when they would be ready to get under way. To each of these, George responded with the same information he had given the previous time. Lieutenant Jones and Willey were doing their utmost in the firerooms, and George knew enough of the conditions there to realize that there was nothing to be gained by querying them. He answered all inquiries with the standard answer that the ship would be ready to get under way at 4:35.

In the after part of each engine room was a great ventilator grill, the lower terminus of an air duct from the quarter-deck. The upper end of each air duct was part of the after section of the superstructure, just forward and on either side of the after turret. Being protected from ahead by the bulk of the ship, these airshafts were seldom troubled by heavy weather. For the last few minutes, however, a little Niagara of water had been pouring intermittently out of each, and the intervals between Niagaras were becoming less and less. Now there was nothing but continuous solid water coming in, and it was impossible to maintain one's station in the vicinity. The ventilator intakes had covers held open by steel cable and they had not been closed for years. Recognizing that something really extraordinary was happening topside and that extraordinary measures were necessary, George detailed two volunteers, J. G. Sontheimer, Machinist's Mate First Class, and E. W. Tator, Machinist's Mate Second Class, to go to the boat deck with chisels and sledge hammers and cut the wire ropes holding the covers open. This would permit them to shut of their own weight and, while not as perfectly as a regular hatch, would inhibit the flow of water. The men were instructed to pass upward through the interior of the ship, not going on an open deck until they reached the boat deck, and only then if it was safe to do so. On their way back they were also, if possible, to try to make the main engine-room hatches tighter.

At about 4:25, in the middle of a deep lurch to starboard, the heaviest roll the ship had yet experienced and, thought George, also the heaviest he himself had ever experienced in his life, the natural light in the engine rooms suddenly grew dim. Instinctively, everyone looked up, and it was as though a tarpaulin had precipitantly been drawn across the eye-ports in the hatches above. Within seconds a sheet of water landed in the engine room, splashing high over all machinery and splattering everyone in the two compartments. The word had previously been passed to batten down all hatches for heavy weather, but these were so high that, though closed for rain and spray, their watertightness against solid seas coming aboard the boat deck had never been a serious problem. Through the years, their light construction had accumulated some small damage so that a completely tight closure was difficult, and in fact had never before been a concern. Their location high on the boat deck had been for the precise purpose of being a source of ventilation for machinery spaces when otherwise completely closed up. In the extraordinarily short time available from the first warning of danger, all hands had been employed in securing portholes, deck hatches, and gun ports for heavy weather, or, in the case of the engineers, working to get the ship under way. Nevertheless, these hatches, which were the responsibility of the engineering department, should have been tightly shut, a responsibility freely admitted by George. The problem at this stage was only who was to do it. He could not spare anyone else from the engine rooms and he had no immediate communication with any other engineering personnel except those in the firerooms, who had sufficient problems of their own. So George called the bridge by voice tube. "Bridge, this is the engine room. Can you have someone batten down our engine room hatches on the boat deck? We're taking water down below through them!"

"Bridge, aye, aye," said the voice. "We'll try. We're taking solid seas over the main deck fore and aft and some are coming up on the boat deck too. . . . How soon will we be able to have the engines?"

It was the same old question. There was nothing George could do but answer it as before—"4:35"—and wait for steam. The steam gauge had dropped to a low of seventy-five pounds per square inch and was now slowly climbing again. At this time, 4:25, it read eighty pounds per square inch. In the engine rooms, men were unable to keep their footing and were forced to cling to hand rails and solid objects. No one worried any longer about fingerprints on the shiny rails.

In addition to the problem of merely hanging on under the now-violent motion of the ship and avoiding being drowned with the great gouts of water coming in, the engine rooms now began to experience a missile hazard similar to the one in the firerooms. Unsecured loose gear hurtled about from side to side, smashed itself against bulkheads or some portion of the main engines or condensers. There was worse in store, however, for the battle bars at the berth-deck level were not designed to withstand the amount of displacement from the horizontal which the ship was already experiencing. Inevitably, if this increased, at some point the bars must come loose.

At 4:35 steam pressure read ninety pounds per square inch, and at precisely 4:35 the bridge voice call tinkled again. "Engine room this is Bridge. How soon can we operate the main engines?"

As George was answering the call, he saw Jones approaching. "One moment, Bridge," he replied.

"Ask them if we can have five minutes more," said Jones.

George turned to the voice tube. "Bridge, this is the starboard engine room. The Chief Engineer requests five minutes more time before using the engines." Placing his ear to the voice tube, George turned about to catch his chief's eye and to his surprise found him gone, his retreating back visible in the forward part of the engine room, hurrying back toward the firerooms.

There had been a growing note of urgency in the calls from the bridge during the past many minutes, but now there was a note that could not be overlooked. *"Engine room, this is Bridge. We must have the engines now! The ship is in danger. Stand by to answer all bells. Answer bells as received from the bridge. Do you understand, engine room?"*

"Engine room, aye, aye," shouted George into the voice tube.

The ship was now thrashing about at a frantic rate, rolling in great shuddering heaves from side to side, with each of her heaves bringing up sharp on her anchor chain, which was stretched taut to its maximum length, the entire fabric of the heavy steel hull quaking and shivering, resounding like a tuning fork under the stresses. There was something extraordinary about the motion, too. Most of the time it was much faster than usual; *Memphis* shook as though alive, whipping back and forth like a great terrorized fish at the end of a line, or a wild animal panicked at its steel tether. And then, every once in a while, there would be a sudden delay, as though *Memphis* were laboring under a great weight which she was endeavoring to shake off. The noise of the sea against the plates of the hull, which had become noticeably louder, would suddenly cease during these periods of quietness. It was noticeable that the quiet periods were also those when the greatest amount of water came from the two ventilators aft, and when truly tremendous quantities poured in through the as-yet only partially closed engine-room hatches on the boat deck.

Shortly after one of these quiet periods most of the water coming in through the ventilators stopped, first in one engine room and then, after several minutes, in the other. Sontheimer and Tator evidently had reached their objective. Similarly, someone —or more than one—on the boat deck was putting a canvas cover over the engine-room hatches. Great quantities of water had, however, been taken into the engine room and it had already become necessary to start a pump to keep the level down below the main engine oil-sump tanks. It would be serious to permit water to get into the oil, for this would ruin the engine bearings.

George recognized what the quiet periods were: they were when the ship was submerged. During the active periods she was surfaced again, and jerking back and forth under the continuous pull of her anchor, rolling, shaking, bouncing, and jumping, strained and stressed in every fiber of her tough steel being. It must be hell up on topside, thought George, and at the same time hell in the firerooms, too. . . . And here we are in the engine rooms, all ready to go, but we can't do a thing!"

These thoughts passed through George's mind in a flash, along with an intuitive realization that worse might lie ahead, but outwardly he remained composed. To the anxious throttlemen of the starboard engine, watching him and awaiting instructions, he said quietly, "Stand by to answer bells!" The steam pressure at this time was ninety pounds per square inch.

Almost immediately the starboard engine-room telegraph rang up full speed astern and, a moment later, the port engine telegraph rang up full speed ahead.

Chapter 4

The *Castine* had been launched in 1892, one of a number of tiny gunboats built for general patrol duties when our Navy finally obtained authority to construct modern ships to replace the wooden Civil War relics to which it had until then been restricted. Alongside her modern consort, she was a tiny thing, only two-fifths her length and one-fifteenth her displacement. The lowest point of *Castine*'s hull projected only 12 feet below the surface, as compared to the 27-foot draft of the *Memphis,* and each of her tiny engines developed only five hundred horsepower. Nevertheless she had twin screws, and an assigned complement of eleven officers and one hundred forty enlisted men.

Castine had only two boilers, of a long-outmoded type. On 29 August, 1916, she was already twenty-four years old, but she had two great advantages over the much newer and bigger *Memphis*. She was of much smaller draft, and, with but two boilers, half her steam plant—wastefully—was in operation to supply auxiliary power. Though the other boiler had been opened, drained of water, and was under repair, she was thus immediately capable of a speed of about 9 knots.

The *Memphis* steam launch returning Commander Bennett to the *Castine* arrived at her gangway at approximately 3:40 having covered the quarter of a mile from the *Memphis* in two or three minutes. *Castine* was rolling gently as the boat's coxswain held the steamer alongside.

One hand gripping a stanchion strategically located in the steam launch for the purpose, Commander Bennett waited until *Castine*'s motion came into cadence with the boat and her gangway platform came level with the gunwales of the steam launch. He then easily stepped across and immediately ran halfway up the ladder. Once sure that submergence of the lower gangway platform would not catch him in lubberly delay, he paused, turned to the launch. "Thank you, Coxswain!" he called. "Shove off and return to your ship!"

Three more steps up and Bennett passed through the opening in the high bulwarks which led to the main-deck area set aside as the quarter-deck.

Lieutenant (j.g.) R. E. Schuirmann, Officer of the Deck, and Lieutenant Thomas Moran, Engineer Officer, met their skipper with a salute.

"Schuirmann," said Bennett, "where is our boat?"

"It's about five minutes away, Captain," responded Schuirmann. "The bridge lookout reported it in sight a few minutes ago. I was going to send it over to the *Memphis* for you as soon as it came back."

"Good! As soon as the boat arrives, hoist it aboard and make all preparations for getting under way. I want to leave here just as soon as we can!"

"Aye, aye, sir," said Schuirmann with a note of surprise. "The Exec is still ashore, sir—he's not due back for a couple of hours. Besides you know that we have only one boiler in commission. It will take us several hours to get number two back together——"

"I know it," interrupted Bennett, his enunciation taking on a staccato quality. "We'll just have to do without it, and Rogers will have to wait till we get back. There's something funny happening out at sea. We may not have to get under way, but I want to be ready!"

As in the *Memphis,* ordered bedlam promptly broke out on *Castine*'s deck. Boatswains' mates ran to the hatches, blowing their pipes so that they could be heard below, shouting, "Station the special sea detail! Make all preparations for getting under way! All hands on deck to furl awnings! Take in all boats!"

Men came running up from below deck. A group went immediately to the forecastle to test and make ready the anchor windlass and cast loose the chain stoppers. The windlass was powered by a small steam engine, and getting it ready required cutting in steam lines and warming up the engine before throwing in the clutch which connected it to the anchor-hoisting mechanism. The same engine operated the capstan, which would be needed to hoist the heavy boats.

Superintended by their petty officers, another group of men began to hoist in by hand the starboard gangway, over which Bennett had just returned to his ship. *Castine* was far too small to carry the towering boat cranes of *Memphis*. She used davits for all her boats, and her designers had for some unfortunate reason located the gangways directly beneath the most frequently used boat davits. Thus a boat could neither be hoisted nor lowered while the gangway was in place. The design had a degree of economy in that, if necessary, one of the boat davits could be used to help with the gangway, but this, of course, further eliminated its use for boats. The lower platform of the gangway was supported by its own davit, stepped into a socket on the side of the ship and itself projecting into the boat-handling area. This, too, had to be removed prior to swinging a boat in or out.

As the accommodation ladder was dismantled and taken in, the boat davits were swung out. Heavy "hoisting blocks" at the base of the hoisting falls were lowered to the vicinity of the water, where they could be picked up by the boat's crew when it came alongside. The running ends of the boat falls were carefully laid clear on deck, passed through two large, strategically located and specially built pulleys (technically, "rove through two fair-lead snatch blocks") and their ends led up to the forecastle, ready to be wrapped around the capstan for heaving in.

Hoisting a big boat is always a tricky business, particularly when there is a little sea and current alongside the mother ship. First it is necessary to center the boat directly under the falls and hold it there with the help of rudder, engine, and a sea-painter tended by a man detailed for the purpose so that it may be

instantly released. On signal, one man in the bow of the boat
and another at the stern simultaneously clutch the heavy hoisting
blocks on the ends of the boat falls and attempt to pass the hooks
attached to each through the hoisting shackles in the bow and
stern of the boat. Since the boat falls cannot quickly be raised or
lowered, the hoisting blocks are always moving up and down
with the role of the ship. The boat alongside, in the meantime, is
rising and dropping bodily with its own cadence, always entirely
different from that of the ship. At one moment the hoisting
blocks are too high to be fitted into the boat's hoisting shackles,
and the next moment they may come crashing down on the boat
and be much too low. Since the blocks themselves may weigh fifty
to one hundred pounds each, the existence of even a small seaway will produce enough relative motion to cause grave danger
of injury to the men in the boat. Not least among the additional
concerns is the importance of getting both blocks attached nearly
simultaneously and—especially important—not permitting the
after block to be attached before the forward one is hooked on. It
would be bad enough to lift only a single end of the boat, but far
worse, in any kind of current, if that end be the stern.

To hoist a boat in a seaway, therefore, requires a maximum of
seamanship, co-ordination, and cool nerve; and many have been the
devices invented by seamen to make things a little easier.

The preparations went forward rapidly on *Castine*'s decks, with
all hands participating who were not involved with making the
engines ready, down below. Nevertheless, the necessary arrangements took time to complete; and, in the meantime, the rollers
in the vicinity of the gunboat were increasing perceptibly.

Castine's motor launch arrived only minutes after the *Memphis* boat which had brought Commander Bennett, at about
3:45, and was motioned to the port side of the ship where a door
in the bulwark had been opened and a Jacob's ladder thrown
over the side through the opening. Johnnie Priest, coxswain of
the boat, brought it alongside as directed, and Ross Garrison,
using a boatbook, held the boat momentarily alongside the
Jacob's ladder. *Castine*'s mail orderly with his leather sack slung
over his shoulder clambered up the ladder and arrived, wet to
the knees, on the quarter-deck through the bulwark doors. Lieutenant Schuirmann shouted to the coxswain, "Priest, we're get-

ting ready to hoist the boat. We're taking in the gangway now, and we'll be ready in a minute. We'll pass you a line from the stern and you can ride to that until we're ready to take you aboard!"

Priest, standing in the stern sheets of the boat with the tiller in his left hand, acknowledged with a salute. Seymour, the boat engineer, threw the propeller in reverse, Garrison pushed clear with his boathook, and the boat drifted aft. This was a completely routine situation. In obedience to a nod from Priest, Seymour put the propeller ahead again as the boat passed *Castine*'s port quarter, nudged it near the rising and falling stern of the gunboat and held position with light and judicious use of the throttle. In a few moments someone threw them a line, which they made fast right over the stem of the boat, through the bow-chock (as opposed to the sea-painter chock just off the bow on either side, which is used only when riding alongside in a current). To a man-of-war's boat crew, boating is frequently a matter of waiting; so the three men settled themselves to await completion of preparations for getting them aboard.

But not for long. "Geez, Cox," said Garrison, "I never saw it get this rough this quick before."

"Me neither, Gary," responded Priest. "I was just thinking the same thing. Looks like it's already too rough to take us aboard. Bet they'll have to send us back to the dock at the fort, and we'll get to spend the night on the beach."

The seas had risen perceptibly in the few minutes which had passed and the boat, at the end of a fifty-foot line from the stern of the *Castine,* was already rocking and pitching heavily. *Castine* herself had begun to roll deeply to either side, the seas completely submerging the pad-eyes on her side where the lower gangway platform had been. Some of the larger rollers splashed up almost to the upper platform, at the bottom of the side bulwark doors, where someone, kneeling, was attempting to pull out the steel pin attaching the accommodation ladder to it. The boat falls, which had already been swung out with their davits to hooking-on position, were alternately splashing deeply into the water and jerking high into the air, swinging back and forth with the motion of the ship and with every roll banging against her side with a loud crash.

What had been clear for some minutes to the boat crew was now also clear to Commander Bennett. At his instruction, Lieutenant Schuirmann appeared at the stern of the *Castine* with a speaking trumpet. "Coxswain," he shouted, "we're not going to try to take you aboard! It's too rough, and we're getting under way!" He paused, lowered the megaphone, raised it again to his lips. "Do you understand me?" he finished, for with the boiling and turbulence of the successive rollers against the side of the ship, the noise of the hoisting blocks and the many groans of *Castine*'s ancient hull, he realized that he had strong competition so far as noise was concerned.

Still holding to the boat's surging tiller, but seated this time, Priest waved his free hand to signify that he understood. "Very well, Coxswain! Cast off and proceed to sea. Join the *Memphis* boats at sea. Do you understand?"

Priest again waved his hand. "*Memphis* boats have already gone out to sea," Schuirmann concluded, "and *Memphis* will be getting under way in a few minutes also. After you get out in smooth water, stay with the *Memphis* boats. We will come by later and pick you up. Just take it easy and we'll have you aboard in time for dinner!"

Priest waved his hand a third time, then cupped his hands around his mouth and bellowed back, "Shove off and join the *Memphis* boats. Aye, aye, sir!" The engine fired immediately. Cautiously, for the boat was now bouncing and rolling actively, Garrison crawled up to the bow and detached the bow painter. As the boat drifted away from *Castine,* Seymour gunned the engine to about half-speed, Priest put the rudder over, and it described a wide circle to a generally southerly course, crawled past the stern of the *Memphis* and headed out to deeper water.

There were long, deep swells, but the boat was so small in comparison with the distance between their tops that the only noticeable effect, so far as the men in the boats were concerned, was that they rather quickly lost sight of both ships when they were down in the hollow. All three boats got out past the deep-water line before the wave from the sea arrived on the edge of the shelf and, so far as is known, none of them saw anything other than the heavy swells which they had no trouble in riding over.

Relieved of the problem of the boat, *Castine*'s crew quickly "two-blocked" the falls, that is hoisted them until the hoisting block was snug against the upper block, swung the davits in, and secured all gear. The work of getting in the gangway was quickly finished, and the bulwark doors on both sides of the quarter-deck were tightly dogged shut.

Commander Bennett on the bridge of his diminuitive ship, called down to the engine room by voice tube. "Engine room, this is the bridge. Are you ready to get under way?"

"We're ready, Bridge," came the reply in Moran's steady voice, "but we only have one boiler. We can only give you about eight knots."

Bennett was well aware of the status of his boilers. Eight knots would have to be adequate. "Very well," he yelled into the voice tube. "Stand by." Then, picking up a speaking trumpet, he shouted to the forecastle: "Focs'l!—Heave up the anchor!"

"Focs'l, aye, aye!" someone shouted from the group clustered about the anchor windlass. The Skipper waited a moment. There was no rewarding rumble and clank of the anchor chain being heaved in.

He raised the speaking trumpet again. "Any trouble up there, Focs'l?" Though distance to the bow was only twenty-five yards, he put the trumpet to his ear to hear the reply.

The voice sounded disembodied, but clear enough above the rapidly rising noise level: "Trouble with the clutch, Captain! We'll have it in a minute!"

The ship, now rolling heavily, had begun to tug strongly at her anchor. Hoisting preparations included rousing additional chain out of the chain locker and passing it around the chain grab at the base of the windlass so that rotating it would pull the chain in. The windlass—that part of the anchor machinery which could be seen above deck—was connected to the "anchor engine" under the forecastle deck by a heavy shaft and a clutch with two large jaws which could be separated to allow the windlass to turn freely. To mesh the separated jaws it was necessary to align the shafting by rotating the windlass-head by hand. In their hurry, the forecastle crew had placed the chain on the windlass grab prematurely and could no longer turn it far enough to line up the jaws of the clutch. The remedy was to pull a little more chain out of the chain locker and readjust it, with more slack, around the chain grab.

All this, having to be done by hand in the most exposed part of the tiny ship, already pitching her bows under the extremely heavy rollers, took several more minutes. Soon, however, there was a welcome call to Commander Bennett on the bridge. "Bridge, we're ready to heave in now!"

"Very well, Focs'l, heave right on up!" shouted Bennett.

There was a single clank of chain as the windlass took the strain of the anchor from the chain stopper, a slight pause while the stopper was disconnected and removed from the chain, and then the steady rumble of the chain clanking around the windlass and feeding into the pipe leading down into the chain locker. All these were familiar and welcome sounds to Commander Bennett. Bending to the voice tube again he shouted, "Engine room. This is the bridge. Stand by to answer bells!" And again he was rewarded by the immediate reply, "Engine room standing by to answer bells, sir!"

Castine was now heaving extensively and rolling heavily. The surface of the sea was still completely smooth and still retained its deceptive oily quality, but the rollers were becoming large. Alternately, the sea would rise up, lifting the gunboat as much as ten or fifteen feet, and then it would subside and drop her down an equal distance. There was a strong sensation of rising and falling as this was taking place; and as the crest of the rollers approached and passed beyond the little ship, she would first lean into them, then roll away, then lean back into the following hollow, in the process bringing up hard on her anchor chain. The wind, though light, had nevertheless blown the high-sided *Castine* around so that she lay in a northeasterly heading, almost broadside to the approaching rollers. Since she had been riding to her port anchor, the chain now lay across the bow, and with the normal clatter as it came aboard could be heard the unmistakable "clink, clink, clink" of the links being dragged across her pre-Spanish-American War, ram-shaped stem. This additional resistance slowed the heaving-in process. Bennett subconsciously noted that it would be necessary to put a boat over the side at the first opportunity and repaint the bow.

The ship's head was pulled around to east as she approached

her mudhook. At 4:05 P.M. a shout from the forecastle, "Anchor's at short stay!" indicated that the anchor chain was nearly up and down, and that the anchor, though still on the bottom, was about to pull free.

"Heave right on in," shouted Bennett through his speaking trumpet and then, more quietly to Lieutenant Schuirmann, "Put your rudder right full, and tell the engine room to answer bells." He moved to the vicinity of the engine order telegraph, deliberately waited until Schuirmann lifted his face from the voice tube as though satisfied, and put both engine telegraphs to Full Speed Ahead. *Castine* was at this time headed almost due east, and it was necessary to change course almost 90 degrees, to south, in order both to clear Torrecilla Point, an out-jutting point of land forming an extension of the east bank of the Ozama River, and to get head on to the sea.

The time was now approximately 4:06 P.M. and at this moment the port bridge lookout reported that a *Memphis* launch was coming out of the Ozama River. By this time the rollers in the location of the *Castine* were very heavy. Although her engines were going as fast as her single available boiler could drive them, and the ship had actually changed course about 15 degrees to the right—to about 105 degrees true—every succeeding wave drove her bodily to the north, toward land. She labored heavily under the drive of her engines and, at the moment quartering into the sea, she rolled mightily from side to side, shipping great gulches of water through her scuppers onto the main deck, through the bulwark doors at the gangway locations, and through her ancient gunshields, none of which could be made completely watertight around her antique three-pounder guns.

There was, however, a feeling of security in Commander Bennett's heart. With the exception of the three men in the motor launch, and Lieutenant Rogers, his executive officer, who had asked for a few hours off for a tennis match ashore, he had his crew on board, his ship under way, and he was starting to head out of the anchorage which had so suddenly become uncomfortable. At this point he still had no thought but that he would quickly be able to get to sea, would shortly rendezvous with his boat in the smoother water off shore, and that in a few hours the situation would be restored to normal.

Chapter 5

In addition to the furious activity in the engineering spaces, there was also much for the rest of the crew of the *Memphis* to accomplish, for with the menace of the oncoming wave in the offing she had to be made as watertight as possible; to compound the difficulty, she was allotted a shorter time in which to do this than had ever been the case before, or indeed than any of her designers had ever contemplated. At 3:35 she was wide open for ventilation, totally unprepared for bad weather, or for seas of any kind. Although accustomed to a certain amount of rolling most afternoons in this exposed anchorage, the always open gun ports had never been threatened. On this afternoon she lay at anchor in the sultry heat of a Caribbean August with every "eye-port" open, every gun-port shutter dismantled from around the broadside guns and stowed in the racks nearby. Eye-ports, the customary round glass ports with which every ship everywhere is fitted, were easily closed. But the gun-port shutters, for a single gun consisting of a set of four sections of curved steel each approximately three feet square and about 150 pounds in weight, were extraordinarily difficult to handle even with the ship completely at rest. With the rapidly increasing motion to which *Memphis* was subject, getting the shutters installed became an individual, personal battle with the sea.

Yancey Williams' orders were clear and vehement: "secure ship immediately for heavy weather!" Some men understandably were slow to appreciate the urgency which so peremptorily drove the Captain and Exec, but this soon gave way to real concern as individuals able to see and evaluate the oncoming sea wave communicated their reactions to others not so advantageously situated. It is noteworthy that many of the officers and men began to secure ship of their own accord, even before being ordered, or hearing the formal call to stations. The gunnery officer, Lieutenant (j.g.) Henry G. Shonerd, gave an illustrative account:

> There was a heavy sea running, and I went down to close the gun ports. The Chief Gunner's Mate and I joined with the gunner's gang, and Lieutenant Carver was there also. We got all the six-inch gun-port shutters in place. Some of the gunner's mates were working on the three-inch gun ports. Most all the deck force were deck closing hatches, etc., getting ready for sea, so the assistance that we had was the engineer's force that was on the gun deck at the time. We all worked trying to get the gun port shutters tightly secured, but I do not think that single six-inch port shutter on the starboard side of the gun deck was entirely secured. The cause was that these shutters secured from the inside, and the pressure of the water would cause the dogs to carry away before enough of them could be gotten into place. There is one long bolt for each shutter which is supposed to be bolted first, and we would get that one fixed, but before we could set up enough on that bolt to get the other dogs in place, a sea would come and carry the long dog from the catch.

Lieutenant (j.g.) William J. Carver, first lieutenant of the *Memphis,* had been a member of the Summary Court-Martial. Following its termination, his story is much like that of Lieutenant Shonerd:

> I proceeded to the gun deck where I helped in charge of several

members of the engineers force to put in one of the forward six-inch
shutters. I do not know how long we worked at this individual shutter,
but soon someone reported to me that we were shipping water through
the starboard gun shutters. Soon water started flowing across the deck
from the starboard side. More water continued to enter the ship with
nearly every roll; everything loose about the decks, and mess tables
and mess benches which had fallen down, were washing back and
forth on the gun deck through the athwartships passages. I made futile
efforts to secure some of this floating wreckage, also endeavoring to
keep the men clear of the athwartships passages as much as possible.

By 3:50 *Memphis* was rolling 15 degrees to each side and jerking at her anchor chain. Like *Castine,* she had also swung in
obedience to the off-shore breeze, though not as far as the lighter
vessel, and was lying on a northeast by east heading with the
starboard chain stretched taut on the starboard beam. An extremely heavy surf had now commenced breaking inshore, and
the mountain of yellow water had moved perceptibly nearer and
appeared considerably larger.

With concern, Captain Beach reflected upon the position of his
ship. He had dropped his anchor in the spot recommended by
Sailing Directions as the preferred anchorage. His anchor had
been placed in an area described as "good holding ground" and
the depth of water was ideal—about 55 feet, exactly double the
draft of the ship. In accordance with the accepted best-seaman-
ship practice, she was riding to a scope of chain eight times the
depth of water. Perforce, however, *Memphis* was moored in a
basin of relatively shallow water just inshore of a steep underwater slope leading to extremely deep water. The size of the
wave he was looking at, even though monumental in terms of the
amount of water it contained, would not pose his big cruiser
much of a problem could she but meet it at sea. The effect of this
great mass of water when it debouched upon the shallow anchorage was entirely beyond his experience, or indeed, that of anyone
of the maritime profession, but his knowledge of the sea gained
from more than thirty years of naval service warned him that
when the oncoming sea-wave hit the shoaling bottom, there was
bound to be a violent effect upon the basin in which he lay
anchored.

The action of the sea during the passage of a wave has been

noted and remarked upon by all seamen, but description has sometimes not been adequate. As is well known, there is no actual movement of the water. That is to say, as a wave passes, a floating marker would simply move up and down. Unless the action of gravity caused it to slide down a steep wave front, it would suffer no significant lateral displacement. This has led to the often-repeated statement that the sea actually does not move, and that waves are merely compressions and rarefactions on a heroic scale. All this is, of course, true, in a sense, but as is well known, water is not compressible; and furthermore everyone who has been to sea can testify that the water, indeed, does move. The fact is that a great deal of water is in violent motion, mostly up and down, relatively little of it from side to side, and none of it permanent. That there is fantastic power involved in this simple motion can be appreciated by calculating the horsepower required to lift a million tons of water an average of forty feet straight up in one second!

If a stone is thrown into a quiet pond, a series of ripples will spread from the point of impact in ever-widening concentric circles. These ripples are, in effect, shock waves; and as the water reacts from the shock of the entry of the stone, a compression wave, or series of compression waves—expressed as the rise and fall of the water constituting each ripple—is set up. The ripples are created from a combination of the inertia of the water molecules and the attempted compression and rarefactions which follow the shock wave. To illustrate the action, one might place one's hands side by side about six inches apart in a basin of water and then rapidly move them toward and away from each other in very short movements of a quarter of an inch or so, timing the motion with the natural period of the waves created. The result will be that for very small motions of the hands, repeated over a period of time, relatively large vertical reaction will be observed in the water. There will actually be very little displacement of the water from side to side, but it is evident that the accumulation of pressures as the hands move together will cause a rise of the center, and likewise there will be a lowering when the hands move apart. It will also be noted that the greatest motion of water will actually occur at the sides of the basin, where the water climbs a steep slope.

To return to the stone tossed into the pond, it is as though a million tiny hands were all operating in strict sequential co-ordination, one with the other, so that the ripple seems to move across the surface of the water. Again, the ripple moves, but not the water. So far as any single unit or molecule of water is concerned, its motion is almost entirely in the vertical plane. Horizontal motion is confined to very small movement back and forth of a relatively small amount of water, just enough to account for the volumetric changes involved.

If two stones are thrown into the pond, each will send forth its own set of ripples, and the different sets of ripples will be seen to intersect and cross each other with no apparent impediment to their passage. When a ripple from one source happens to be exactly in phase with that from another, the two effects reinforce each other, and a considerably higher than normal ripple will result at the intersection. The reverse is also true, and there is a cancellation effect when the wave crests of one set of ripples get into phase with the hollows of another. Thus, larger-than-normal ripples may be followed by miniature ones, or none at all if the forces are exactly equal and exactly opposed. There is apparently an affinity in the water, too, at least partly resulting from the phenomenon known as "surface tension," which causes some ripples or waves to tend to continue to travel together once they have joined forces, even though the actual direction of both wave fronts is thereby altered in favor of a resultant which is the sum of the two original directions.

Thus are great waves formed at sea. But if such a great "super-wave" passes suddenly from deep water to shallow, there is a tremendous discontinuity created in its foundations. In the first place there is an interference with the motion and rhythm of the successive contractions and rarefactions. Secondly, the tre-mendous volume of water in motion, drawing its substance from the entire depth of the sea and displacing itself back whence it came in the time and rhythm ordained, is suddenly brutally cast upon the shallows. Billions of tons of sea-water, no longer able to be accommodated in the accustomed slight movements in the infinite fluidity of the deep sea, must instead swiftly mount the ledge and, towering higher than ever before, as swiftly collapse into a violent, destructive maelstrom.

Breakers are, of course, the normal resultant of normal-sized waves when they hit the shore; and everyone recognizes that their size is directly related to the size of the off-shore rollers from which they were formed. It is also a common observation that bigger rollers and bigger breakers result when there is deep water close inshore.

Consider, then, the size of the breakers resulting from the appearance of a wave millions of times larger than any ordinary wave! They would contain millions of times as much water, possess a thousand times the battering force, and in height and breadth measure anywhere from twenty to fifty times the dimensions of the "ordinary" wave.

The background of a lifetime of observation of the sea was with Captain Beach as he evaluated the situation at 3:50. Intuitively, he knew that he and his ship had been caught in the seaman's most feared trap: a lee shore, an untenable anchorage—and with no power to move. That great wave itself posed no danger if he could get *Memphis* to sea, for despite its height, she would steam over its gradual slope with little or no difficulty. It would, in fact, simply lift the ship and pass harmlessly under.

All hinged on whether or not there was enough time left to get up steam. With steam, safety was easy. Without it, disaster was sure. The possible need to get under way on short notice had been well considered, his plans well laid, his preparations adequate for any forseeable contingency. Indeed, only last week they had been put to the test. But, for a big ship in harbor, just how quick is quick enough? Had he kept steam up on all his boilers, or on half of them—eight instead of two—the need to warm up engines would have been the only delay. But this would have burned valuable coal, day after day, kept extra men on watch, gained perhaps only half an hour in preparation time. In emergency conditions, of course, all boilers could have been kept steaming, the engines warmed up as well, and getting under way would then have depended only on disconnecting the anchor chain and slipping the anchor if there were no time to hoist it—five to fifteen minutes delay at most. But there would have been great cost in fuel and to his crew. The ships wrecked in the famous hurricane at Samoa had had more than twenty-four hours of warning, and no blame was ever attached to their inability to get underway. *Memphis,* by contrast, had maintained readiness to move within one hour. This had been demonstrated. She need proceed only a short distance to sea, less than a mile or so, to cross the ledge into deep water and safety. One mile. At a speed of 10 knots this would take six minutes.

The whole question revolved around the matter of time. How much time was there left before the sea avalanche was upon his ship? There was nothing further that Beach, as Commanding Officer, could do at the moment. His years as a junior officer in the engine rooms and firerooms of older ships convinced him that excessive interference with the urgent business of his engineers was the worst possible course for him to embark on at this critical moment. Steam in quantity, and as fast as it could be produced, was the key to the problem—and the only one. The Skipper's business was to be on the bridge, to mastermind the situation and direct such steps as appeared best to meet the developing situation. Lieutenant Jones and the rest of the engineers knew their own business thoroughly, down below, and would produce steam just as fast as it could be done. There was nothing he could do to hasten this, except to minimize directives and requests for information. Once he had sufficient steam to operate his engines, then would his long-learned skill as a seaman and skipper of a first-line ship of the United States Navy be put to the test. Then would he be called upon to maneuver his ship, to extricate her with her crew of nearly one thousand men from the suddenly fierce Juggernaut which the sea had become. Until then he must wait, as patiently as he could, and put his faith and trust in his men, as they were putting theirs in him.

At about 3:50 P.M. Yancey Williams reappeared on the bridge. "Captain, we've sounded Officers' Call and we're shutting all topside openings. There is nothing more the Officer of the Deck can do down on the quarter-deck, so I recommend we shift the watch to the bridge." Beach nodded concurrence. "In addition, Captain, I've taken a good look at the situation from the boat deck and the boat-crane head, and I don't think we ought to keep our boats with us until we get under way. If things get much worse than they are already in this open roadstead, the boats will have a hard time living in the seas. Besides, they'll have a devil of a time keeping up once we start moving."

"I think you're right," said the Captain. "The situation is going to get worse here in the harbor, but it doesn't look too bad out at sea. Send the boats out there clear of the anchorage and tell them to wait for us. We'll pick them up after we get clear."

"Aye, aye, sir. I'll do it right away!" Williams dashed off the bridge again.

In addition to setting in motion the necessary action to get up steam, warm up the engines, and batten down for heavy weather, on the bridge Captain Beach urgently directed his attention to two other matters: the rudder and anchor. The steam engine which operated the rudder was located in a large, dark, and isolated compartment—known, appropriately, as the "steering engine room"—at the very stern of the ship, three decks below the quarter-deck. In the sultry Caribbean the steering engine room was hot even when the ship was anchored and the engine secured. When *Memphis* was under way the steering engine operated several times a minute and had steam to it all the time. The intermittent but constant demands of the helm caused it to leak steam at every joint and gasket, and consequently the bulk- heads and deck of the steering engine room remained covered with heavy condensation until the steam valves were shut again, sometimes days or weeks later. Because of its importance, the compartment was always manned while under way, but its re- moteness, its oil-laden, humid atmosphere, and the puddles of steam condensate which oozed from side to side under their sur- face of oil drippings caused this station to be one of the most unpopular in the ship.

As Chief Quartermaster Frederick L. Rose, on the bridge, ran through his check-off list of necessary preparations to get under way he was a little dismayed to find that, after the rudder had been reported ready, it still failed to respond to the helmsman's testing rotation of his wheel. Normal procedure for getting under way allowed enough time for a thorough check of the system, but today, of all days, there was not that kind of time.

It so happened that Rose, a career Navy man every bit as well- versed in his portion of the naval profession as Newton George or Charles Willey were in theirs, had actually witnessed the rise of the sea. He had, more nearly than anyone else, seen it race in from the horizon on the placid bosom of the Caribbean, heaving the unruffled surface into a gently rising slope which must lead to some as-yet-unseen watery plateau in the far distance, encompassing in total a volume of water so incalculable that the entire sea surface appeared slanted, as though the force of gravity acting on it had in some way become disoriented from the vertical.

When *Memphis* was at anchor, the ship's standing orders required that bearings upon all navigational landmarks be taken and logged once an hour. Rose, who for years had performed this routine duty himself, had by consequence come subconsciously to survey the land and the sea several times an hour, almost as the reflex action of a primordial memory tracing back to man's earliest ventures on the sea. All was calm and peaceful at 3:30 in the afternoon—1530 by the sailor's twenty-four-hour clock—about the time that Rose lifted his eyes from the chart he was in the process of correcting and swept the seaward horizon. Something about its shape caused him to observe it a little more closely than usual, and then, puzzled, reach for a pair of binoculars. He never was able to define what troubled him, later thought that perhaps it might have been the binoculars themselves; these particular glasses, he had observed, tended to make curved lines appear more curved than normal. A few minutes later, however, the Captain's appearance on the bridge and his preliminary orders to batten down hatches and prepare to get under way confirmed Rose's vague feelings of uneasiness, and at the first free moment he again swept the horizon with his binoculars.

This time, to his consternation, he could see a rising of the waters, a matter of the horizon becoming more convex than it had any right to be, an impression of concaveness in the unbroken sea between himself and that distant line. Without taking his binoculars down from his eyes, he half-opened his mouth to shout a cry of fear and warning, thought better of it, turned to see where the Skipper and Exec were and found them completing a message to the signal tower at Fort Ozama. Immediately thereafter the interchange between them made it obvious that any report from him at this time was unnecessary except insofar as it pertained to the ship's readiness to get under way.

Several minutes later, Rose had run a second and third time through his check-off sheet. The steering engine had been reported tested and ready. The steering cables were unquestionably whole. There was no possibility of their slipping. No work of any kind had been done upon them; this he would have instantly been aware of and, indeed, would probably have initiated. But whenever this remotely located machinery was secured, as he had more than once remarked to Lieutenant Withers, it was amazing how many valves would turn up wrongly set, controls go out of adjustment, perfectly reliable mechanisms go mysteriously awry, in the interim before the steering engine was started again.

Precipitantly, Rose left the navigation bridge, ran below to the conning tower—the Skipper's armored station in battle—where he hastily eliminated the possibility that some critical change affecting the navigating bridge above had been made at this steering station. He ran back up the ladder. "Peltier!" he called. Vincent Peltier, a third-class quartermaster who had been testing annunciators and engine-room telegraphs a few feet away, came instantly, his face mirroring the same anxiety that his chief felt in his own mind.

Rose spoke rapidly and precisely, his voice carrying the barest trace of the impatience he felt. "Run down to the steering engine room, on the double! Tell that first-class quartermaster down there to open all the petcocks on all the cylinders and drain out the water that is in them. When that is done, close them again. Make sure they're closed tight. Then have him disconnect the wheel ropes and operate the steering engine with the trick wheel from full right rudder to full left rudder and back again until it is operating right. You know how to do it—stay there while he does it. If he doesn't do it, you do it. Got that?" Peltier nodded. "Then connect up the wheel ropes again and ring me on the bridge buzzer until both of you see me operating the engine with the bridge steering wheel. . . . Got that straight? . . . On the double, man!"

Peltier set off on a dead run. The time, he noted as he left the bridge, was just after 4:00 P.M. He did not hear Rose's half-mumbled comments immediately afterward: "Damn that Schaivoni anyway! He's already reported ready! He's supposed to check those drains and work out the engine on his own without somebody going there to tell him! That's what his report means, he knows that! What does he think we've got a first-class quartermaster down there and a check-off list on the bulkhead of that hell hole for, anyway!"

Shortly after Peltier's departure, no one on the bridge could fail to be fully impressed with the urgency of their situation. The anomaly in the sea level noted by Rose had almost immediately afterward grown into the huge ocher-colored roller observed by their skipper, was now perceptibly nearer, and still growing in size. Various excited estimates were made of its height, ranging from conservative guesses in the neighborhood of a hundred feet, to far higher figures, and within minutes the great wave's fore-runners had reached the *Memphis* and were throwing her about. There was little doubt among the entire ship's company that something most remarkable was happening; the unusual motion of the ship gave sign that the situation might even be fairly serious, but the full appreciation of the ship's predicament could be had only by the navigating and ship-control group clustered on the bridge, impotently fingering their useless equipment and staring at the oncoming wave, an utterly incomprehensible, never-before-witnessed, seismic sea-wave racing toward them, a billion-ton battering ram destined to strike within minutes!

The other critically important item was the anchor. The ship should either hoist the anchor and get out, if steam could be had for the main engines, or drop another anchor—two more, if possible—and attempt to ride out the sea right at her anchorage. Of the possible courses of action, getting to sea was clearly the thing to do if it could be done. Based on the forty-minute time required to get the ship under way a week ago, it did not seem illogical to hope that the same success could be achieved now.

Through his speaking trumpet the Captain shouted orders to the ship's Boatswain, Plagemann, who was on the forecastle. "Make ready the port anchor for letting go!" he called, and a moment later, the apparently contradictory order, "Connect up the anchor windlass to the starboard chain and prepare to heave short!"

Both of these preparations were immediately accomplished. The port anchor could be dropped, of course, without using the windlass, but this would not be done until it was apparent the ship could not get under way. On the other hand, there was no point in heaving in on the starboard anchor until there was enough steam to operate the engines. It was logical, however, that the extra delay in leaving the anchorage which would be required to hoist two anchors with a single anchor engine should be avoided if at all possible. For better holding with the single anchor in use, it might be desirable to increase the scope of chain to it, as soon as it was clear that the resulting increased radius of swing could cause no embarrassment to the *Castine;* but the amount of chain already out supposedly had already ensured the best possible holding, and any increase would also increase the time necessary to haul it all back in.

In any case, either veering chain or dropping a second anchor were simple evolutions which, it appeared, could safely be delayed until it could be determined whether or not the ship could move in time.

A third solution was also possible: Instead of hoisting the anchor, the chain could be broken at one of the shackles and allowed to run out, leaving anchor and chain on the bottom until there was an opportunity to return and drag for them. This was a comforting thought to the beleaguered skipper, for it permitted him to await availability of the main engines until the last possible moment.

At this point, though Father was certainly far from easy in his mind in the face of the onrushing cataclysm, it has been my impression that the ship's performance exactly a week earlier in getting under way in forty minutes had given him full confidence that it could be done again. Forty minutes measured from a roughly equivalent time-frame, 3:40 P.M., would give 4:20 as the time at which he might therefore logically expect to be able to move the ship. No bad weather in his experience, nor in that of anyone he knew, had ever arisen fast enough to trap a ship able to get under way in less than one hour. His crew had already demonstrated their ability to move this great cruiser in the unprecedented time of forty minutes. Surely, he felt, all maritime experience was in his favor!

But there was no blinking the fact of that huge roller of yellow-green sea-water and sucked-up bottom sediment sweeping toward Santo Domingo. The separated effects which had given it birth were far distant, virtually unnoticed, and already past; but their juxtaposition had produced a sudden cumulative shock wave, which had raced across the ocean, growing ever larger, until now it was about to burst upon the *Memphis!* All this Father sensed, rather than deductively reasoned. He had no way of estimating how fast the wave was traveling. Therein, as he needed no reasoning to appreciate, lay the difference between safety and disaster.

In addition, one other factor was operating which had not existed on the twenty-second of August: the heavy rolling of the ship. It was obvious to everyone that this was greatly hindering preparations topside. No reports of difficulties below were received, however, and in the absence of any indication of trouble, a direct question to that effect might have suggested that the Captain lacked trust and confidence in his Chief Engineer. Father was personally in direct communication with the engine rooms, speaking by voice tube with Newton George, but the Chief Engineer did not himself at any time come on the voice tube. Thus the only information available to the bridge on conditions below was relayed second-hand. The Captain never had the benefit of talking directly with the officer upon whom he was forced most to depend. While there was nothing which he or anyone could have done to help the engineers at this point, it is logical to suppose that fuller awareness of the difficulties they were actually experiencing might have caused an earlier decision to get out additional anchors and give up the effort to get under way. It is questionable, however, whether merely talking with Lieutenant Jones would have made all this clear at this time, inasmuch as Jones himself was still confident of success.

As it was, Beach ordered that no chain be veered, that the port anchor be held in readiness but not dropped, and that the starboard chain be broken in the chain locker so that it could be slipped with minimum difficulty as soon as the engines were able to turn.

It was by this time nearly half an hour since he had made the original decision to light fires under the extra boilers. Now, at 4:05, he directed that the engine room be asked how long it would be before they would be ready to get under way. The answer Father hoped and expected to receive was in the neighborhood of fifteen minutes. Instead, the reply was that the engineering department would be ready to get under way in half an hour.

Even though a little disappointing, the estimate of half an hour more did not seem too long. The weather was still completely calm, flags were still hanging loosely on their halyards or responding to the fitful breeze from shore. The surface of the sea itself was still smooth, but there was the undeniable heavy rolling of the ship, those great rollers undulating underneath the smooth, oily surface of the sea, and that great yellow mountain of water, now perceptibly nearer than when it had first been seen.

Inshore, tremendous seas had begun to break near the bar at the entrance to the Ozama River. Breakers twenty to thirty feet in height—so high as momentarily to obliterate the bluffs above the shoreline—threw spray as high again above the bluff. Soon it was apparent that several lines of breakers had formed, and it was remarked that they were continually being formed farther from shore. All of the participants of this day were unanimous in their description of what they termed the "receding lines of breakers." This meant, of course, that they receded from shore as they increased in size, and that if the process continued the *Castine,* at her anchorage, would soon be engulfed in them. If they continued to move seaward, they would in a short time be swollen to even larger size and be reaching the vicinity of the *Memphis.*

At 4:05 P.M., to the dismay of Beach and Williams, the motor launch sent to fetch the recreation party was seen coming out of the mouth of the Ozama River. There was a strange feeling in the pit of Beach's stomach as he realized that somehow, though there had been more than adequate time, his message directing it to stay ashore had not been received. On it came, oblivious to the size of the breakers it would soon be facing. All eyes on the bridge of the mother ship were fixed on the developing tragedy, recording the sight in their memories forever.

Apparently the boat had no difficulty with the first few breakers where they broke across the partially sheltered river mouth, and was not dissuaded by sight of the larger ones farther off shore. Perhaps Lindsay and its crew were so preoccupied with the sea over the bar that they failed to evaluate properly the conditions farther out, where breakers normally did not exist. Possibly those in the boat were so low to the water that they simply could not see over the tops of the near waves and consequently were not aware of the much larger ones farther out. In any event, they continued to head straight for the *Memphis*. Like a tiny water bug, the boat climbed comber after comber, her bow first thrusting up through the frothy spray at the top of the breaker, then the entire boat following, spanking down upon its back and coasting out of sight into the hollow between it and the next wave. The watchers on *Memphis'* bridge and boat deck stared in fascination and dread. Their own ship was rolling heavily, but the surface of the water between them and the boat was perfectly smooth, marred only by uneasy, hurried strength beneath. And yet their motor launch, less than half a mile away, was sliding down the back of one huge breaker after another, while before it was ever the white-and-dark line of the gathering of still another breaker, poising itself, ready to hurl itself upon it. And then that wave, too, would sweep down upon the boat, curl over it, bury it out of sight—and then the bow of the boat would appear again up through the wave, followed by the rest, and slide down its back in momentary surcease to await the next onslaught.

No doubt Lindsay and the boat's coxswain, Smith, would have liked to turn and run for the shelter of the Ozama River, but the boat sometime previously had passed the point of no return. Now it dared not turn. It must keep its bow headed into the sea. Now that they were in the breakers, Smith and Lindsay were doing the only thing they could do, which was to meet the seas head on, at reduced speed, in the hope of getting through them before the boat filled. By this time, no doubt, it was impossible to see beyond the next wave ahead of them, except while actually passing the crest. Only the upper works of the *Memphis* would have been visible, and for this Smith steered. Probably after each breaker had swept by, Smith and Lindsay thought they were through the last big one and that from there they would have to contend only with large smooth rollers, rather than with the furious white water curling over and breaking. Such, indeed, would be the normal experience; but in this case new breakers were being formed successively farther out from shore. Every time the boat got through one breaker, there was another bigger one being formed farther to sea.

Finally, the inevitable occurred. All hands in the boat were bailing desperately, using hats or their bare hands, but then one of the breakers broke at precisely the right point and filled the launch half full. Flooded, the engine stopped. Seaman Snell, one of the boat's crew, could be recognized as he half-stood, braced himself in water to his knees over the floor boards, raised the boat's signal flag as though to signal. But there was no time to do anything. Deep in the water, the dark gray hull of the disabled boat lay helpless. No one moved. The tableau of disaster was fixed; the moment, separated from time. The boat was within six hundred yards of both *Castine* and *Memphis,* and everyone realized the significance of what was happening. Another great breaker raised its broad, hunched, rolling shoulders between the viewers and the motor launch, and when it rolled by there was no launch to be seen. A group of round black heads clustered in the water in the vicinity of a larger object, the bow of the boat, now standing straight up and down in the water.

"Man the lifeboat!" shouted Beach. "Man the port lifeboat! All hands tend the port lifeboat!" He turned to Chief Quartermaster Rose. "Hoist the recall!" he ordered. This last was in reference to the two motor launches, still only a few hundred yards away, which had been sent to sea for safety just a few minutes before. Possibly they could turn back and be on the scene faster than the lifeboat.

Several hundred men on *Memphis'* boat deck had seen the catastrophe to the motor launch and there was no dearth of volunteers to man the lifeboat. Carl Wass, First Class Master-at-Arms, was the first one in it. Chief Master-at-Arms J. Denig was second; W. P. Arrowsmith, Boatswain's Mate First Class, third; and Tom Wallace, Seaman, fourth. Alvin P. Mosier, the pugnacious ship's barber, unsuccessfully pleaded his much greater experience at the oars in an attempt to get a berth in the boat. "Some young fellow," as he later related the story, "had got there before me, and he wouldn't give up his place."

Yancey Williams, as usual, was on the scene. He directed all unnecessary material in the whaleboat to be thrown on deck and had all hands in the volunteer crew take off their shoes and clothes, with the exception of underclothing, and put on life belts. Opening a life-belt locker nearby, he had a dozen additional life belts thrown into the boat. Within two minutes of the capsizing of the motor launch, or at about 4:10, the lifeboat was ready to be lowered. But in those two minutes the breakers had swept on farther to sea and had completely engulfed the *Castine,* which, with black smoke pouring from her tall funnel, had just managed to get under way.

"Do *not* lower the lifeboat!" bellowed Captain Beach from the bridge.

His stentorian voice, developed through years of service and amplified by the speaking trumpet through which he shouted, had no difficulty in reaching the Executive Officer and the men assisting him, some fifty yards away. "Do *not* lower the lifeboat!"

Though the surface of the sea was oil-smooth, there were now great, swelling waves, following one after the other with tremendous rapidity, coming from the southeast in quick succession. The inertia inherent in the cruiser's ponderous displacement would not allow her to rise to each passing roller as could, for instance, the lighter *Castine.*

It was noticeable that the water did not dash itself upon the ship, or splash on deck, as seamen are accustomed to seeing it do. It merely rose quickly—too quickly and with too short a distance to the next wave for *Memphis* to rise with it—and flowed on deck. The first wave covered the quarter-deck and forecastle to a depth of only a few inches, but immediately afterward came another which buried the quarter-deck a foot or more. By 4:15 the successive rollers were sweeping over *Memphis'* main deck, normally more than twenty feet above the water. All hatches on the main deck had been closed, and all on the boat deck except for one, near the center, kept open for access below. Considerable water came on board, nevertheless, through the hastily shuttered gun ports on the gun deck and, as the seas continued to rise, through the superstructure casemate gunports as well; but internal hatches also having been shut throughout the ship, all of this water remained above the armored citadel which contained the vital operational components of the vessel.

As a result of nearly frantic efforts on the parts of the officers and men attached to deck divisions, it had been possible to get all gun shutters in place, but they could not be made completely watertight. They had been designed only to be proof against spray and driving seas, and the two-inch clearances which existed in certain spots admitted hydrantlike streams of water under the complete submergence to which they were now being subjected. The shutters had not, moreover, been designed with an eye to quick installation. Twenty minutes per gun port had been considered a reasonable time to get them in place under normal conditions. No one in the U. S. Navy had ever contemplated that they would have to be installed under conditions worsening as rapidly as these, with the ship rolling through ever-increasing arcs approaching 45 degrees to each side during the period of maximum effort by the men at the gun shutters.

While none of the water on main and gun decks penetrated below the armored deck, nevertheless an appreciable quantity quickly accumulated in the ship's berthing areas and in the casemate between the turrets under the boat deck, where it sloshed back and forth every time the ship rolled, piling up and reaching to the overhead on the down side. All equipment normally stowed in these spaces burst from its confines, rolled or slid back and forth with each wracking heave the *Memphis* made in response to the ever-mounting size and frequency of the attacking waves.

The signals directing the return of the motor launches that had been sent to sea were hauled down at the same time as the order to belay sending the lifeboat was given. It was apparent that no boat could have lived in the mad seas now raging farther inshore. To have lowered the lifeboat, or to have sent other boats into the vicinity of the men in the water, would have simply meant dooming their crews also.

One element which made this decision easier to take was the *Castine*. Now herself in the breakers, great seas sweeping completely over her and tearing at her decks and upper works as though they would rip them off, *Castine* had reversed her engines and was backing toward the men in the water. At the time not appreciating that this action was caused as much by her own need as for any other purpose (though it must also be pointed out that in later years Father saw no need to revise his initial opinion), in his official report he gave his reaction in these words:

Realizing that to have lowered the lifeboat would have caused the death of every man in her, and that there was no possibility of getting anywhere near the men who had been in the capsized launch, and also realizing that if there was anything possible to be done for these men, it would be done by Commander Bennett of the *Castine,* I ordered the lifeboat not to be lowered and hauled down the recall of the other motor sailer and the steam launch. I desire to state that I have never seen or heard of anything more magnificent and courageous than the attempt of Commander Bennett to save the men from the *Memphis;* nor have I known of a more magnificent exhibition of seamanship than the way he handled his ship and saved her, in spite of a broken steering engine and but little steam power. It did not at this time seem conceivable that the *Castine* could possibly be saved.

As the men on the bridge of her consort watched in admiration, *Castine* backed slowly toward the men in the water, herself alternately buried entirely out of their sight. At one point, when she struggled out of the smother, men on her deck could be seen heaving objects overboard toward the tragic cluster of black dots in the boiling water.

During these few minutes since the launch had been swamped, the size of the breakers had increased astonishingly, and it was now obvious to everyone that not only could *Castine* do nothing for the men in the water other than throw life jackets and other floating stuff to them; but were she to approach closer she might actually crash down upon some of them. This was even more obvious to Commander Bennett, and just as the *Memphis* skipper was saying mentally, "No closer!" it became evident that *Castine* had put her engines ahead and was clawing her way clear.

A few minutes later, now riding much easier, the little white-hulled ship passed astern of the *Memphis,* quite close aboard and with the scars of her recent brush with disaster plainly visible. Water was still cascading out of her scuppers, she carried a heavy list to port, and her topsides looked as though a freight train had driven through them. Her anchor hung loosely from a short length of chain in her port hawsepipe, its flukes dragging in the water, and every time she rolled, it struck her side with a crash clearly audible on board the *Memphis.* The hull around it was heavily pitted and scratched, with gray iron showing through where great chunks of the white paint were newly gone. Her bridge area had suffered severely, the bridge seemingly having been bent askew, and on it could clearly be seen the figures of the quartermaster at the wheel and her skipper standing alongside him.

At the nearest point of approach, actually very close since Commander Bennett was no doubt taking advantage of the lee afforded by the much larger hull of his consort, a spontaneous cheer broke out from the *Memphis*, led by her skipper on her bridge and joined by all those watching on deck. It was a well-deserved tribute.

Memphis by this time was also rolling violently, the tips of her masts describing gigantic arcs against the blue sky. She was tugging and leaping at her anchor chain, pulling the heavy forged steel links—each of them as much as a man could lift—until they were straight taut and the entire tremendous chain vibrated in tune with the ship's own stress. The main decks were continuously flooded, and water now began to come over the boat deck, too, some thirty-five feet or more above the water line. This sea-water was noticeably warm, yellowish-red in color instead of the customary gray-green of the sea, and as described by one young seaman in a letter home, oily or mucky in feel.

The breakers had, however, as yet not reached the *Memphis*. The water was still only flowing over the ship. Since *Memphis* lay broadside to the direction from which the swells came, she dropped into the trough of the first swell, and then simply was unable to rise fast enough before the next one was upon her. Each trough robbed her of buoyancy, and each huge roller added to the weight of water upon her main decks. She struggled to free herself with great, heaving rolls from side to side, cascading the warm brine from her topsides, and indeed occasionally struggled to the surface. But except for these intervals, the only parts of the ship that were consistently out of water were the boat deck, the masts, and the bridge.

At 4:20, concerned over the prospect of holding his anchorage in the face of worsening conditions and the imminent arrival of the great sea-wave approaching from seaward, Father ordered the port anchor dropped. This could not immediately be done, since it was first necessary to warn the people in the chain lockers to stand clear. One minute later Captain Beach directed that the port anchor not be let go, since he had received word that steam would be available very soon. One minute after this, according to Commander Williams, all hands on the forecastle were driven off by the continuously mounting seas and forced to take refuge in the forward section of the superstructure, under the bridge and just abaft the forward turret.

Inside the superstructure there were portholes with a view of the foredeck, and the men inside looked out through the heavy glass upon what some of them have always recalled as the most unforgettable sight of their lives. More than half the time the portholes were completely under water, causing the sun's rays suddenly to appear as though filtered through a yellow-green filter. At other times the water level would be down lower and some of the forecastle structure—the cat davits, the tops of the anchor windlass, and capstan heads, the turret with its two ten-inch guns—stood out individually above the bright surface of the troubled sea. All those who took their turn at peering out the ports were impressed alike with the bright normality of the sun and sky, and the fact that the sea was neither angry nor splashing except where its even flow was interfered with by some underlying projection of the ship.

Their initial feeling of urgency long since replaced by full recognition of a state of emergency, Captain Beach and Commander Williams were in the midst of an all-out battle to save their ship. The Captain, of course, had to remain on the bridge, so Williams became the inspector and executor, constantly roving about the decks, topside as well as below, to insure that all watertight closures were closed, all men in a place of safety, all loose gear properly secured for heavy weather.

The main deck under the boat deck was the area where the lashing down of loose equipment became of greatest importance. This casemated space, sometimes called the "air castle" was, except for such necessary items as stacks, ventilator shafts, and boat-crane foundations, entirely unobstructed from side to side—about seventy-three feet. Practice shells for its four six-inch guns and ten three-inch guns were stowed in racks along the bulkheads, as well as dummy ammunition for drill, the crew's mess benches, cleaning-gear lockers, and the ship's piano. Some of the men on their own had already made attempts to pass extra lashings around some of these items, but Williams, recognizing the special danger inherent in the piano, directed that special lashings be placed around it. With the turmoil of the ship's violent motion, this unfortunately, was not accomplished soon enough, or well enough; and the piano, breaking loose, began a self-destroying and lethally dangerous traverse back and forth across the seventy-three foot width of deck. Gracefully, and sometimes by sheer brute force, it avoided the efforts of the sailors who were attempting to lassoo it. Yeoman First Class Roy Ezzell, known as "Pop," less than an hour before court reporter for the Summary Court-Martial of Coxswain Potter, thought he saw an opening during a momentary lull in the ship's motion when the swift lunges of the piano were also temporarily stilled. With the piano cornered, he advanced upon it with a length of line with which to lash it to a nearby stanchion. Just as he did so, the ship took a sudden lurch and Ezzell suddenly found himself converted from pursuer to pursued. Agilely, he jumped for the overhead, gripping one of the steel beams supporting the deck above, and swung his legs clear. But "Pop" Ezzell was no longer young and agile. He could not retain his hold on the overhead and his plump form fell on top of the piano which he gripped frantically for a downhill dash of some fifty feet to the far side of the ship where it paused, as *Memphis* righted herself, long enough for the shaking Ezzell to drop off and scuttle clear. Paymaster McIntosh then organized a party to tackle the smoothly rolling instrument, pressing into service two of his pay clerks, as well as barber Mosier, his assistant, Tom Wallace, and Fireman First Class T. J. Leary. The piano soon managed pretty well to batter itself to pieces and lose some of its mobility, and finally it was thoroughly corralled, but not before Leary had the misfortune to come between it and one of the supporting stanchions of the deck above, sustaining a broken leg and severe internal injuries in the process.

Commander Williams sometime during this period also became a casualty, when a sudden heave of the ship flung him into a group of lockers in a corner of the casemate with such violence that he was knocked unconscious. It was a badly bruised face that Dad saw the next time he confronted his executive officer.

By 4:25 the situation on the bridge was desperate, not to say frightening, and it was the more frustrating because the one thing necessary to save the ship—steam—was still denied. The great wave of yellow water was now close at hand on the starboard side, completely blocking out the horizon as far as the eye could see, reaching to a height higher than the bridge of the ship. To port, although no breakers had yet reached the *Memphis,* it was obvious that very shortly they would. The swells rolling into the anchorage as advance agents of the great wave were now reaching the boat deck with regularity and splashing high as the water encountered obstructions in its sweep across the deck. Again the Captain directed that an urgent message be sent to the engine room. "How soon can we have the engines?"

But the monotonously regular answer continued to come back: "Four thirty-five, Bridge!" There was now no hope of dropping the port anchor nor, indeed, of slipping the starboard one, unless the ship could somehow, by some maneuver or good fortune, get her forecastle clear of water long enough for Plagemann and his men to rush out on deck for the one or two critical operations required.

Lieutenant Withers, the navigator, despite the painful arthritis which had put him on the "binnacle," or sick list, had reported to the bridge when Officers' Call was sounded. He quickly forgot all about his own troubles as he stationed himself alongside his skipper, continuously taking bearings of navigational points ashore. At about 4:30, after a particularly heavy roller had gone past, he remarked, "Captain, I think we hit bottom that time! I distinctly felt a jolt as though we had struck while the ship was submerged!"

The Captain nodded. He, too, had felt the shock and knew what it portended. He forced calmness in voice and demeanor. "Are we dragging?" he asked quietly.

"No, sir," replied Withers. "There is no sign of that yet. I've been keeping a continuous navigational cut of our position, and we haven't moved. It's just that these seas are so big that we're hitting the bottom of the bay in the trough!"

Sailors are accustomed to the motion of ships. There is always something a little indefinite about it; the ship has momentum in whatever direction it is going—forward or back, up or down, or rolling from side to side. Whatever motion is on the ship, it changes smoothly, transitions into the next motion. A heavy roll comes gradually to a stop, even though, under certain severe conditions, it may appear to stop more abruptly than at other times. Another roll in the opposite direction begins gradually, reaches its maximum of angular velocity and then, under the accumulation of opposing forces, gradually reduces velocity until again it comes to a stop at the limit of angular displacement. A graphic plot of velocity would show a series of curves resembling sine waves in that there would be maximum velocity at midpoint of the roll, when the ship is upright, and a smooth transition of direction at the points of zero angular velocity, at the limit of rolling.

It is true that a ship driving through heavy weather will feel the shocks of striking the successive seas, especially if they are taken head on; but the major exception to the idea of the smooth transition of motion is the anchor. A ship tugging at her anchor in heavy weather, or dragging anchor, will experience a series of violent shocks as she brings up taut against the unyielding chain or as the anchor flukes break loose and it drags on the bottom. These will be communicated throughout the entire corpus of her hull in the form of sharply felt changes in the direction of movement, accompanied by singing vibrations along her keel and structured members, and shrieks and groans of protest from the unwontedly stressed steel plates of her fabric.

The normal motion of a ship, in other words, is a combination of reaction to the yielding forces of the sea and the momentum inherent in her own heavy weight. But when a ship strikes the bottom, there is a very different sort of motion, something so strange, so out of the ordinary, that it is immediately felt by everyone aboard. In the first place, and most obvious, there is virtually an immediate change in the direction of motion, a sharp break in the otherwise smooth curve of the plotted sine waves. Second, the lifting effect of the fluid medium, the sea, may be considered as though it were concentrated at a mathematically calculable point, the "center of buoyancy"; but the effect of striking the ocean floor is concentrated, naturally enough, at the point of impact, generally somewhere near the keel. A ship aground no longer has the same stability she had while at sea. Staunch vessels have rolled over in this unfortunate condition.

Thus the sailor reacts instantly and with alarm to "touching," before even considering the probability of damage. Instantly, the ship *feels* different, and subconsciously he knows she *is* different from the vessel whose idiosyncracies and capabilities he had come to understand. Small wonder that to the seaman these are the harbingers of danger, the precursers of the mighty catastrophe which can be wrought upon a ship caught between the sea and the shore!

Memphis was stoutly built and could stand hitting the mud beneath her keel a few times—provided only that there were no rocks at the spot, and that she did not strike too hard. If she could be got to sea immediately there might, by good fortune, not yet be any significant damage. And she had to go at once, for the great wave was nearly upon her, rearing in majesty and malevolence only a couple of miles away!

How Dad must have wished that he had happened on deck a little sooner, that he had evaluated the situation just a bit faster, that the decision-taking, at the very beginning, had been swifter; or that etiquette for a departing Captain had not caused a crucially important loss of time in sending Lindsay after the recreation party. If only he might have given some extra time, only a few minutes, to the Chief Engineer and his men in the engineering department! Most of all, in his discussion with Admiral Pond he should have insisted with even greater passion on keeping two extra boilers steaming, as had been his custom.

For Dad knew well the operations that had to be accomplished before a big ship can get under way. Possessing himself with such patience as he could muster, he had waited for the engineering department to be ready, and except for such natural expressions of urgency as increasingly frequent requests for a status report ("When *can* we use the engines?")—all of which were answered unequivocally that the engines would be ready at 4:35—he had accepted the Chief Engineer's time scale. By this example of forbearance, he had rendered full support and approval to his engineering department in this critically important time of extreme need.

There were psychological implications of the situation, too, stemming from the history of steam engineering in our Navy. When warships began to depend upon steam for their prime motive power, it was, of course, necessary to have personnel who could operate the original crude engines and boilers. Thus was established a small but elite "engineer corps" whose members not only were separate from the "line" of the Navy—they considered their only responsibilities to be in the engineering realm, and that they need not carry out orders from anyone except a superior engineer if, in their judgment, engineering interests were not served thereby. Chief Engineer Stimers, who operated the *Monitor*'s engines in the battle with the Confederate *Merrimac*. and *Merrimac*'s own engineer, Ramsay, were both members of this corps (and, in fact, had served together in the *Merrimac*, Stimers as Chief Engineer and Ramsay as Assistant, before the Civil War). This system had remained in effect through the "doldrums" of the post-Civil-War period when public interest in our Navy was at its lowest ebb, and when new modern warships began to be built, they also inherited this organization. It became evident in a few years, however, that the complete autonomy of the engineering department, in which the chief engineer might sometimes be both older than and senior to the captain, led to frequent differences between them and their personnel and would not do in a modern navy. Shortly after the turn of the century, therefore, the Engineer Corps was amalgamated into and combined with the Line of the Navy. Father, who by this time held the rank of "Assistant Engineer," was thus some years later converted into a Lieutenant of the Line and given charge of one of USS *New York*'s eight-inch turrets, while erstwhile "deck" officers were given duty among the engines and boilers.

The change was all to the good, but not a little of its success was due to the determination of all hands to see that it worked well. Among the hoped-for results was a fuller appreciation by all concerned of the problems and conditions above and below the water line. A more subtle one was that there still remained a great deal of respect for whoever might be assigned as the chief engineer, for it was recognized that he dealt with circumstances and situations very different from those of wind and sea topside. The happiest arrangement, and the most successful, existed when the dictums of the Chief received the Captain's full support whenever possible. Such was Father's outlook and the guidelines of his conduct of his command.

But now he—and his whole philosophy—were at full stretch. At 4:35, he had been told, the ship would be ready to go. Repeatedly his engineers had assured him that this would be the case. To honor this, and not seem to be interfering with the operation of the Chief Engineer's department, he had been forced to contain himself on the bridge, doing what he could to prepare his ship for the elemental onslaught so soon to be upon them, but otherwise only waiting for his engineer to report ready. To the skipper of a ship, schooled in the time-tested ways of running one, there can be no more difficult duty than to stand by idly, waiting for his officers to perform the duties for which they have in their turn been trained, resisting the natural, basic impulse to get into the situation in detail himself. Especially when an emergency situation is at hand!

Even so, Father might have gotten into it, had he not learned another basic truth: At this stage of any game, this would be the very worst thing he could have done insofar as expediting preparations was concerned.

But, at 4:35, there was no more time left. Events had moved at unprecedented speed. One hour previously *Memphis* had been at peace, her only concern the safe operation of her boats; now she was in mortal danger. No one—not the Captain or anyone— could have anticipated that now, only an hour from the very first sign of trouble, she would be menaced by that most fearsome of natural phenomena, a raging, all-destroying sea arisen against all reason, a sea contrary to all predictable behavior of oceans and of centuries of sea lore!

It so happened that the stated time the engines would be ready coincided with the moment when the great yellow wave menacing to seaward would be almost upon them. No man could live on the forecastle, so it was already too late to drop the other anchor, too late to slip the starboard one. One by one these plans had been set aside because of the expected imminence of having the engines. And then the size of the seas had rendered them impossible of accomplishment. Now, all that could be done was to swing *Memphis* to face the careening wave head on and steam to the anchor—that is, reduce the tug of the ship on the anchor by steaming toward it as the sea tried to drive her in the other direction. Then, if *Memphis* could in this condition ride over the sea, beyond it she might find calmer water; there it might be possible for a man to get on the forecastle with a sledge hammer to knock out the pin and link holding the chain stopper and thus slip the shortened length of anchor chain which the men in the chain locker had detached.

Even very reduced power would be adequate for this purpose. There was no longer any doubt that the very survival of the ship, perhaps of hundreds of her crew, was in question. In this, his greatest trial, a trial of command put upon but few captains of our Navy, Father followed through according to his principles. In my opinion (and this is the son speaking, for he never so intimated to me in any way), Father intuitively had sensed that all was not to his engineers' liking below and had resolved that they must be forced to operate the engines anyway. After all this time there must be *some* steam available, enough, at least, to drive the ship around to head into the sea!

At exactly 4:35 he again took the speaking tube to the engine room: "Engine Room, this is the bridge. How soon can we have the engines?"

There must have seemed an interminable wait before the voice at the other end of the voice tube, well recognized as that of Machinist George, an old friend whom he held in high regard, answered. There was a discussion which Dad could not hear, and then George said, "Request five additional minutes!"

Along with the deep feeling of professional failure which swept over him, Dad simply could not accept any further delay. Every request for an engineering prognosis up to this point had been answered uncompromisingly with the statement that the ship would be ready at 4:35. Nothing would budge the engineers from this prediction. The immutable laws of steam and machinery were sacred, they were telling him; they had evaluated the situation, propitiated the necessary gods, set the unchangeable events in motion. Four thirty-five had been a guarantee, a promise; between himself, representing the entire non-engineering portion of the cruiser, and her engineering department, those men of a world apart. He, too, had once been an engineering officer; he well understood the store set by such a promise, both by the bridge and the engineering personnel, and he had abided by it, albeit with some difficulty in the face of the onrushing sea-wave now only a mile or so away and commencing to mount the shoal into the shallow water. Now this promise, to which he had clung while all other recourses were being foreclosed, was also being denied. *"Request five additional minutes!"*

Even as he watched it, the approaching hill of yellow-red water grew higher, the face of it steeper. An iridescent hue had developed just below a now-forming crest, and the barest suggestion of ribbing—striated strain lines in the now slightly concave surface of the wave face—had begun to become apparent. In the meantime, *Memphis'* forecastle and quarter-deck had been almost continuously submerged since about 4:15, and seas were now sweeping regularly over the boat deck. Water could be seen splashing into the fireroom blower ventilators—those rabbit ears—where it was sucked below, proof that at least the force-draft blowers were running, and some of it cascaded high enough to splash into the stacks. Of recent moments, several thudding shocks throughout the entire ship's structure were evidence that she was striking bottom at the lowest point of the troughs between rollers. It was evident that whatever time Father might have had to meet the emergency had completely run out.

No skipper could temporize any longer. The wave would strike within minutes. Even if the engines were not fully ready, surely they must have enough steam to turn them over at some reasonable speed, enough even now to enable *Memphis* to take the anticipated blow head on instead of broadside. He had progressively been reduced to the last extremity. Now urgency possessed him, even affected the timbre of his voice. *"Engine Room, this is the bridge. We must have the engines! The ship is in danger! Stand by to answer all bells!"* He waited a moment for this to sink in. He knew that George would get the message in all its nuances, and that he might have to alert certain persons, make certain arrangements. Then, his mouth still at the uncapped voice tube, his eyes on Chief Quartermaster Rose, who was hovering near the bridge annunciators, he bellowed, "Right full rudder! Port ahead full! Starboard back full!" Rose instantly shifted the handles of the engine-order telegraphs to the desired positions.

Memphis, unlike *Castine,* could not turn by merely going ahead with hard over rudder, for she had a larger turning circle and dead ahead was Torrecilla Point. By reversing the starboard propeller Father intended to apply a twisting force to assist the rudder, as well as capitalize on the anchor's own tendency to drag the ship's head to the south. Once he had *Memphis* pointed fair, he would go ahead with both engines.

Immediately the answering indicators on the bridge engine-order telegraphs switched to "Port Ahead Full" and "Starboard Back Full."

Chapter 6

Private Charles R. Christian of the U. S. Marine Corps, a member of the Marine Corps Signal Company, was an expert in wigwag signaling, semaphore, and signaling by flashing light. On August 29 he had been assigned the afternoon signal watch duty in the signal tower, a temporary wooden enclosure with a canvas awning, which had been hastily built on short stilts upon the highest part of the old Fort Ozama battlements. His duties in the tower were to watch the Marine outpost to the north and the ships in the anchorage for signals, and occasionally he transmitted a message originated by Major Bears, the Marine commander in the fort. The ships almost always sent their messages by powerful signal searchlight, even during daylight, and because of its speed Christian preferred that method over the more laborious wigwag. He himself was able to use a light only during darkness when his feeble lamp was visible over adequate range. Because of the lack of an adequate source of electricity, he had only a "field pack," a battery-powered signaling lamp, and during daylight he was forced to use the wigwag method for his own transmissions and for receipt purposes.

The things of interest within the view of his signal glass were the signal tower at a Marine outpost two miles to the north, on the main road near the northern border of the city of Santo Domingo, the two ships anchored in the harbor, and the Ozama River, which swept by the fort and curved to the west as it discharged into the harbor. He was alone in the signal tower and was not permitted to leave it during his tour of duty. Messages to be sent were brought to him written out on a dispatch form. He would then wave his signal flag and make the call of the station to which the message was addressed. After attracting attention he would laboriously transmit it by Morse code, waving the signal flag to the right for a dot and to the left for a dash. The same procedure, in reverse, was followed for messages sent to the Fort, after which he would shout over the railing into the courtyard below for a messenger.

Not much had been happening during his watch on the twenty-ninth of August. It was a slow, sleepy watch, but conscientiously Christian observed each of his specified points of contact in turn. On a regular round he would swing his telescope from the outpost to the north, to the baseball field, to each of the ships in the harbor, and around again. Whenever a Navy or Marine boat passed in the river he watched it also. He alternated his sweeps with normal lookout duties, inspecting the river and the streets of Santo Domingo through his lookout glasses for signs of unusual goings on, occasionally pausing, for want of better occupation, on any normal activity of the populace.

Action began slowly for Christian, as it did for all other participants of that day. At 3:25, from among the boats milling around the *Memphis,* one detached itself and proceeded to the *Castine.* A few minutes later another one headed for the mouth of the Ozama River and was approaching it—a fifteen-minute trip—when a light began to flash from the bridge of the *Memphis.* He answered the signal by waving his flag. The time, as he recorded it in the log of the signal tower, was 3:39.

"CA NUMBER TWO" spelled out the blinking light. After each word it paused, and Christian indicated comprehension by waving his flag. "FOR COMMANDING OFFICER FORT X SEND WORD TO AMERICAN CONSUL TO TELL ADMIRAL HE CANNOT RETURN X SEAS BREAKING ACROSS BAR X SEND ACROSS RIVER FOR MEMPHIS RE-

CREATION PARTY X KEEP THEM IN FORT DURING NIGHT X DO
NOT LET MEMPHIS MOTOR SAILER RETURN X SIGNED BEACH."
The total message, including heading and signature, was forty-four
words. The signalman on the *Memphis* signal bridge was expert in
his craft. So was Private Christian. Actual transmission of the message occupied six minutes. When it had been completely received,
but before receipting for it, Christian put down his signal flag
and carefully read the message, counting the words and compar-
ing them to the group count sent in the message heading. The
message made sense and the group count checked. He picked up
his signal flag, waved it to the right, to the left, and to the right,
thus transmitting the letter "R," signifying receipt. The time was
now 3:45, and he so wrote on the message blank in the printed
square provided by the form.

Christian leaned over the guard rail of his tower. "Sergeant of
the Guard!" he shouted, "Sergeant of the Guard! Signal messenger!"

Sergeant Arno O. Grimm was on watch as Sergeant of the
Guard in the guardhouse near the base of the signal tower. It was
a warm, humid day and it had been so far a boring watch in his
hot, poorly ventilated office. A call for a messenger to the signal
tower was not much of a break in the monotony, but it was
something. His messenger, too, had heard the call. He rose to his
feet.

Grimm motioned with his thumb. "Go see what he wants," he
said.

Grimm knew what Christian wanted. A message had arrived,
and he would send it to the Officer of the Day, who would decide
what else to do about it. Grimm expected to hear nothing further
about its contents, but would question the messenger when he
returned to elicit any possible tidbits of interest.

It was probably about 3:48 that the Sergeant of the Guard's
messenger arrived at the upper level of the signal tower and
received the message from Christian. "Take this to the Officer of
the Day right away," said Christian, handing him a message
blank upon which he had transcribed the message just received.
"Give it to him right away. It's for the Admiral, and it's marked
'Rush!' "

The Officer of the Day was Second Lieutenant Philip T. Case,

U. S. Marine Corps, an earnest young man who had been in the Marines a very short time. At 4:00 that afternoon he was scheduled to leave the fort on horseback to inspect the Marine outposts in the city. He was at the main gate of Fort Ozama about to depart when the messenger from the signal tower found him. Carefully, Case read the message.

It was clear that he had two duties to perform. He was to inform the Admiral that he could not return to his flagship, and he was to stop the recreation party, which was then ashore, from returning to the *Memphis*. He was aware that a boat had just come from the *Memphis* to the recreation field, but could not have known that it had been sent with instructions to return the recreation party immediately to their ship. Realizing, however, that it would shortly set forth on its return trip, he directed the messenger to return to the Sergeant of the Guard with instructions to proceed to the boat dock below the signal tower and stop any Navy boats from going downstream. Then Grimm was to cross the river and deliver a copy of the message to the senior person in the recreation party on the eastern bank.

Case then swung into the saddle and, accompanied by an orderly also on horseback, cantered out into town. His first stop was at the United States Consulate where a uniformed doorman informed him that the Admiral was across the street in the cathedral. "Take this in and show it to the Admiral," said Case to his orderly, handing him the folded message which he had carried with him.

The marine orderly dismounted, strode into the cathedral, and Second Lieutenant Case found himself with nothing to do but think. Several minutes passed during which an uncomfortable feeling began to grow in the back of his mind. Here he was sitting on horseback, waiting passively in the street, while he also had the duty of preventing the possible passage of a Navy boat into unsafe waters. Whether the Admiral got the message now or or half an hour from now made very little difference, but if there was any danger to the boat returning the recreation party he ought to ensure it received the message. Uneasily, he reflected that the message had said, "SEND . . . FOR RECREATION PARTY," and "KEEP THEM IN FORT." Clearly, a command function had devolved upon him. Informing the Admiral, his high rank notwithstanding, was only advisory. Possibly he had inverted the proper order of priorities. As soon as the orderly returned from the cathedral, Case led the way rapidly southward through the streets to the town wharf, thinking, as he later explained it, that there might possibly be some Navy boat there at the wharf that should be also informed of the unsafe conditions of the sea, and that in any event he would be able to intercept any boat coming past that point from the recreation area, which was on the other bank and farther upstream.

It had taken him about six minutes to get to the consulate from the fort, and approximately five minutes more while he waited for his orderly to return. It was, perhaps, another six minutes, or about 4:10 P.M., before he reached the town wharf. When he arrived, groups of people were looking anxiously to seaward and pointing. Case could see nothing. He dismounted, ran on foot along the river edge to the fort landing, a few hundred feet farther downstream. Arriving there somewhat breathless, he saw Sergeant Grimm in a small boat in the middle of the river.

Gripped with the feeling that something terrible might have happened and somehow he might have failed in his duty, Case cupped his hands and shouted, "Sergeant, did any boat from the *Memphis* go back out again?"

"Yes, sir," Grimm shouted back, "and the seas are so rough out there I am afraid it will be in trouble!"

Fearful now of the worst, and conscious of his failure to put first things first, Case dashed back up the hill to the fort, where he rounded up all men available, gathered ropes, life jackets, and blankets, and raced to the bluff bordering the bay, just to the south of the walls of the fort.

At 4:03 P.M. Sergeant Grimm's boredom had been shattered completely. His messenger came running back from Lieutenant Case. "Sarge," he said breathlessly. "There's a Navy boat just went up the river to get the sailors playing ball. The lieutenant says for you to go over there and tell them not to go back to the ship. They're supposed to come in the fort instead and spend the night here. The lieutenant said to hurry!"

Grimm rose to his feet. "You stay here and man the office,"

said he to the messenger. Stepping outside the guardhouse, he corralled the first two marines he found and walked down a relatively steep path to the dock just below the signal tower. The two privates followed the sergeant without a word. He said nothing to either of them. No boats were in sight on the river. The fifteen-foot wherry used for general messenger duties lay tied to the dock by its painter, its oars nowhere in sight. Grimm had hardly expected to find the boat manned and waiting his arrival, but to get the message to the Navy men he would have to cross the river. Leaving one of his men to cast loose the boat, Grimm and the other entered a small building at the head of the dock where the oars were customarily kept locked in a room. Three other marines, off duty, were standing on the dock idly at this time.

Of this entire group of men on the fort landing below the signal tower, Sergeant Grimm, who had temporarily absented himself, was the only one who knew that there had been instructions for the *Memphis* boat not to return to the ship. Within seconds after he disappeared, the *Memphis* launch appeared from around the bend in the river with a load of men.

Corporal E. W. Garvin and the two other marines had been whiling away a few spare hours between duties. From where he stood on the dock he had a fairly good view of the bay beyond the mouth of the Ozama River. He could see that the sea was running quite heavily and that the breakers at the bar, or beyond it, were larger than any he had seen before. He had no idea what Grimm was about. As the *Memphis* motor launch appeared abreast of them, however, the four men standing on the dock shouted to it. As Garvin later related the story,

I and three others hollered and waved our arms and told them that they could not possibly make it back to the ship. My voice was heard, but I do not think that they heard what I said. Members of the boat waved their hands in answer to my voice for them to go back, but kept on proceeding out into the bay.

Neither Garvin nor any of the other three marines on the dock was aware that there had been an order for the *Memphis* boat not to return to the ship. Their warning shout was a natural human reaction, nothing more.

Still saying nothing, the taciturn Sergeant Grimm returned to the dock with two oars. He and his two crewmen embarked in the skiff, rowed out into the river, and then for the first time Grimm became aware of the *Memphis* motor launch, approximately one hundred yards downstream, heading for the mouth of the river. He hallooed twice: no response from the launch. Incredibly, he took no other action. He continued across the river and a few hundred yards upstream to the landing in a cove on the eastern bank near the recreation field. A light rain had begun to fall, and Grimm found Chief Boatswain's Mate Kasburg in charge of the shore patrol and the remainder of the recreation party, sheltering themselves in an uncompleted house. To Kasburg he delivered his message, and heard, in return, that the launch which had passed him in the river was the one he had been sent to intercept.

There was a larger boat also assigned to the Fort Ozama boat landing, an eight-oared cutter capable of carrying thirty people. This boat had been away on another mission, but now, as the doughty sergeant rowed back across the river from the recreation field, he met it in the river and showed a flash of initiative. He directed the cutter to proceed to the recreation field landing to fetch the remainder of the men waiting under Kasburg and bring them back to the fort landing. The coxswain of the cutter, already heading upstream, nodded as though this might have been his mission anyway, and continued in his original direction.

Someone in naval uniform was running north along the road bordering the east bank of the river, Grimm noticed, but just at this moment Lieutenant Case shouted to him from the dock and asked about a Navy boat. The sergeant, by now aware that something might have gone wrong and uneasily realizing that just possibly he might have done something a little more positive to help the situation, responded that it had gone downstream and that he had fears for its safety.

Corporal L. N. Flatten, U. S. Marine Corps, reported to the Marine Corps contingent aboard the *Tennessee* on May 23, 1916, in Norfolk. He vividly recalls the event two days later when her name was officially changed to *Memphis*, and the foreboding this evoked among some of her crew. Upon arrival in Santo Domingo, the Marines were sent ashore to Fort Ozama, and Flatten at that time left the ship. The vagaries of fortune made him an eye witness of the events of the twenty-ninth of August. As Flatten has told the story, the U. S. Marines ashore in Santo Domingo, billeted within the ancient walls of Fort Ozama and theoretically in "unfriendly territory," were seldom allowed outside the fort and suffered severely from the warm weather and a boring routine. By consequence, when volunteers were requested to ride guard duty on a truck trip during a regular visit to the outpost on the north side of Santo Domingo, Flatten leaped at the proffered diversion and climbed into the truck alongside the driver. They had not proceeded very far from the fort when the two marines noticed an unusual water condition in the bay and so, from pure curiosity, they swung their truck down the next street leading south and headed for the waterfront boulevard. On the seaward side of the boulevard there was a coral reef, a jagged and rough surface which extended about a hundred yards from the road and ended in a rocky bluff twenty to forty feet above the water. As the truck arrived, many Santo Dominicans had already gathered and were staring to seaward from a relatively level spot on the bluff. Heedless of the putative hostility of the people, the two marines stopped their truck and joined the crowd. Immediately they were surrounded, the people making no attempt to conceal their anxiety and sympathy as they pointed into the bay.

Flatten and his companion, whose name was Rogers, saw the *Memphis* motor launch with a load of passengers cross the bar of the Ozama River and head out into the bay. All thoughts of their patrol duties vanished. Flatten's description, written years after the incident, still recalls the immediacy of the moment:

The little craft, like a mere beetle, climbed the perpendicular wall of an oncoming wave, it reached the crest when a roaring, lashing breaker completely swallowed her. We waited. It seemed minutes. Then she reappeared to repeat her perilous climb. Stubbornly she survived four or five such ordeals until finally the inevitable occurred.

A small cluster of heads now marked the spot where the boat had gone down. Each man was hopelessly at the mercy of the vicious waves, to be carried out to sea or perhaps, more mercifully, fall prey to the sharks. They became scattered with each succeeding wave while we waited in suspense in the hopes that at least some would be driven into shore. We were the only Americans among the so-called hostile people. They gathered around us. The language barrier didn't conceal their anxiety and their mutual sympathy as they pointed out into the bay. The women were weeping and the men were shaking their heads.

Suddenly the people began to shout, *"Mira! Mira! La Castina!"* The *Castine* lay off-shore about half a mile, and black smoke was pouring from her funnel. She was underway. Her forward course would bring her in the midst of those unfortunate victims in the water. Would she stop and rescue them must have been the concerted prayer of us all. Now, free from her mooring, she struggled to make headway and for the next twenty minutes or so we witnessed what was declared the most brilliantly executed seamanship ever performed in the U. S. Navy.

It was amazing that a ship of that size or any size could survive under the relentless pounding which she was receiving. Her margin of maneuverability was lessened several yards as each wave carried her shoreward. It was horrifying to see her literally stand on end, her propellers turning idly a hundred feet in the air. A short pause, the next instant she heeled over with the suddenness or agility of a cat. Righting herself for an instant, her bow now shot upward. It appeared her entire length. One was reminded of a frightened monster attempting to leap bodily out of the water. Again she slid, this time astern, then flipped over on her side. This continued as she attempted to move forward as well as to turn to starboard to gain deeper water, but with her propellers out of the water nearly fifty per cent of the time, her progress was slow.

Eventually she came to the area where the victims of the motor sailer were floundering. I marvelled at the courage of those men aboard the *Castine* who dared to come on topside to throw lifebelts and rafts over the side, but more than that they could do nothing. The commanding officer had but one choice; that was to save the ship and crew. Her steering gear had become so stove in as to be useless, but by the grace of God she reached the current of the Ozama River which, as it appeared to us, assisted her in turning to starboard and out to sea. We watched her loping like a deer over the waves until she became a mere speck on the horizon.

The alarm had now been given at the fort and several Marines came rushing to the scene. Our attention now turned to the *Memphis*. It was quite apparent that she was in distress, but why, we wondered, didn't she break mooring and follow the *Castine?* We weren't to know until later. In the meantime, wave after wave struck her broadside, first lifting her up and then pushing her to port.

Chapter 7

THE RECREATION PARTY

Lieutenant (j.g.) Horatio J. Peirce had been at the recreation ground on the east bank of the Ozama River just a few hundred yards upstream from Fort Ozama since shortly after 1:00 P.M. He had a duty section of ten men to assist him in keep in order, under the general charge of Chief Boatswain's Mate Kasburg, and they were mostly employed in patrolling the grounds to prevent any members of the recreation party who might have been so inclined from straying into the city. There were a total of fifty men from the *Memphis* ashore in addition to Lieutenant Peirce.

Peirce had neglected to bring his watch with him and so the times of occurrences in his account are only approximate. To the best of his recollection, Boatswain's Mate Lindsay came to him sometime between 3:30 and 4:00 P.M. that afternoon. In correlating all other times specified, it appears that probably the conversation with Lindsay took place at about ten minutes before four. Lindsay reported to Lieutenant Peirce that he had been sent with instructions to have the recreation party, baseball party,

and shore patrol return to the ship in two boats, and that the
second boat would follow him in shortly.

"Why is the recreation party being called back now instead of
at five?" asked Peirce. "When I left the ship I was told that we
were to remain until five P.M. and that's what the men expect,
too. Is it the weather again?"

"It looks like it's getting rough outside, sir, like last week,"
replied Lindsay. "All I know is that the Captain and Exec had a
conference, and the Exec called me and sent me to tell you about
the two boats and to come back right away."

"Very well," said Peirce. He raised his voice, called Kasburg,
who was some distance away, directed him to pass the word to the
patrol, terminate the ball games, and assemble the recreation
party in readiness to march down to the landing, only a few
hundred yards away.

"What about the other boat, Lindsay?" asked Peirce. "Didn't
you say it was following you in?"

"Yes, sir," responded Lindsay, "but I never saw it. It hadn't
started from the ship by the time we passed out of sight up the
river."

"How about it, Smith?" said Peirce to the coxswain of the
boat. "Did you see the other launch?"

"No, sir."

Lieutenant Peirce hesitated. Lindsay spoke up. "Mr. Peirce,
Mr. Williams said there would be another boat coming and he
said that under no circumstances were we all to come back in one
boat. I am supposed to make sure that you split the party in half
and send only half of them in each boat. Those are my orders,
sir."

"I know, Lindsay," said Peirce. "You go back in this boat,
now, and find out about the other boat right off, while the passengers in this one are still disembarking and before they shove it
off from the gangway. If the other boat has not shoved off from
the ship yet, or has broken down, ask the officer of the deck to
have one sent immediately. I'll wait behind with the rest of
the men. It's only a fifteen-minute trip and maybe you'll have to
come back for us in this boat."

So saying, Peirce measured off the first half of the column of men and, indicating with his outstretched arm, ordered, "All you men from here on forward get in the boat."

As the men clambered in, Peirce stood on the dock alongside and supervised their seating. Mindful of Lindsay's warning regarding the increased roughness of the sea, he specified where each man was to sit ·in the boat so as to maximize its ability to ride over any seas likely to be encountered. The boat landing was in a little cove on the eastern bank of the Ozama River, so located that Peirce could see only the western half .of the river mouth. He observed, as he stated later, that it was a little rough over the bar at the mouth of the river but not excessively so, and since there was no wind nor any indication of approaching bad weather from the sky, there was no reason for him to believe that the boat would experience any difficulty in returning to the ship. Nevertheless, it had been the ship's experience in the exposed anchorage off Santo Domingo that boating conditions could quickly become hazardous. Besides, there were the categorical orders of the Executive Officer to consider, as well as his duty to his men.

"Men, hear this," he called, speaking slowly and emphasizing his words. "You have been seated so as to equalize the load on the boat. It may be a little rough outside. Do not move about. There are plenty of life preservers in the boat, and if you start taking spray aboard, put on a life jacket and get down in the bottom of the boat, under your thwart. Do not climb into the after part of the boat."

Peirce had seated three men on the fore-and-aft seat in the launch's engine compartment and two on each thwart, but now he was surprised to see three men on two of the thwarts. "Sir," said Lindsay, "two more men got in the boat."

"None of that!" said Peirce. "You two men get out! You, Hull, and you, Barsuch! There will not be more than twenty-five passengers in this boat! You'll both go back in the second boat, with the rest of the men!"

Barsuch and Hull stepped out. Barsuch was somewhat disappointed. There might be a long wait for the next boat, as he, a member of the crew of number one steam launch on his duty days, had good cause to know. Suddenly, a third man got up from his seat and made as if to step out of the boat also. "Nothing doing, Teshack," said Peirce. "You stay where you are!"

Impassively, the man sat down again, the impulse which had caused him to try to leave the boat unexplained, unreleased. The incident happened so quickly that it did not occur to Barsuch to offer to exchange with him—a suggestion which Lieutenant Peirce would have undoubtedly disapproved in any event. Peirce later said that it had been his impression that Teshack might have anticipated the possibility of there not being a second boat and that, therefore, this group might have a routine-breaking night ashore.

With everything in readiness, Peirce spoke to Lindsay, being careful to speak in a loud voice so that everyone could hear. "Lindsay, you are in charge. Have life belts broken out and ready for all hands in the boat. Put them on at the first sign of bad weather. There is to be no skylarking or moving about in the boat. Is that clear? . . . Shove off and return to the ship!"

Lindsay, standing in the stern of the boat, saluted, said, "Aye, aye, sir," and sat down. The Boat Engineer started the engine and Smith, the Coxswain, backed the half-loaded launch out of the inlet and headed south downstream. In a few moments it had gone out of sight behind houses and buildings along the shore.

Peirce intended to remain on the dock and watch for the reappearance of the boat as it followed the bend of the river to the right around Fort Ozama, where he might be able to see it cross the bar at the mouth of the river. At this moment, however, it began to rain lightly and Kasburg interrupted his chain of thought. "Mr. Peirce, it's raining and we don't have any rain gear. Would it be all right if we go and wait it out up in that house up there?"—indicating with his hand an uncompleted building near at hand.

"All right, Kasburg," said Peirce. "Permission granted. You will be in charge and responsible that everybody stays together. I don't want any stragglers from this group. You understand?"

Kasburg, a veteran of many years in the Navy, understood perfectly. The men had been aboard ship approximately a month, without an opportunity to get ashore except for recreational visits of the sort just prematurely concluded. Beer had been available at the recreation field, and it was entirely possible that some of the men, having had a beer or two, might wish to seize the opportunity to go in search of more, or possibly some livelier entertainment.

Peirce continued, "I don't see any sign of the other boat yet, so I'm going to walk down to the sugar wharf at the mouth of the river on this side. If the boat comes in, I'll see it and come back right away. Don't let it shove off until I get here."

Peirce headed south, striding swiftly along the dirt road a few yards from the east bank of the river. It was now about 4:03. As he left his men he heard Kasburg shout, "All right men, we'll wait it out up in that house up there and don't nobody try to jump ship on me!"

At about 4:15 Peirce arrived at the sugar wharf at the mouth of the river on the east side. To his consternation he found the sea very rough, much rougher than he had had any idea of, though it was not very rough at the bar at the river mouth. Here, the sea appeared about the same as he had been able to see when he allowed the boat to depart, but there were huge breakers about halfway between the mouth of the river and the *Memphis*. He looked in vain for the boat, a growing feeling of uneasiness beginning to rise in his mind.

Some Santo Dominican natives on the end of the pier were gesticulating among themselves and looking toward the sea. As he approached, several detached themselves from the group and came running toward him. To Peirce's ears what they said sounded like, *"El canoe delfundo! El canoe delfundo!"* The meaning was clear enough. They were so insistent that Peirce had no choice but to believe them. Nearby was a tank of some kind belonging to the sugar mill; so, hurriedly, the lieutenant climbed on top of it to get a better view. He could see nothing, but in a moment he was surrounded by nearly a dozen natives, all pointing in the same general direction and all trying to communicate to him that it was the boat belonging to *El Quatro Vapor,* the four-funneled *Memphis,* which had become *delfundo.* A deep disquiet possessed him.

From where Peirce stood, he could see the signal tower of the fort; hoping that someone might be watching him, he waved his arms semaphore fashion. No answering signal came from the tower, but in a few minutes a rowing cutter with marines pulling on the oars came across the river. A U.S. Marine officer in the boat, wearing the insignia of a captain, shouted that his name was Low, and that he had been attracted by Peirce's uniform and his attempt to signal. Peirce shouted back his fear that the *Memphis* boat had been swamped, since it was no longer in sight. He could not see any men in the water, but most likely they must be farther along the coast to the west. "Please pass that word to the fort commander," concluded Peirce, "and then send a boat over to pick up the rest of my party at the recreation ground."

Not even touching the shore, Low reversed the direction of rowing on one side of his cutter, spun the boat on her heel, and the marines sent her flying across the water to the dock under the signal tower of the fort. Peirce saw Captain Low jump out of the boat and dash up the hill, and shortly thereafter a number of men with ropes and other paraphernalia left the fort and began to run toward the bluff to the west and just south of the fort. The cutter, in the meantime, got under way again and began to row upstream to where the remainder of the recreation party was waiting. Peirce kept pace with it, running along the bank, and in a few minutes a somber group of *Memphis* sailors got in the cutter, were rowed across the river, and disembarked at the fort landing.

Upon arrival at the fort, Peirce's first move was to attempt to find the Officer of the Day. In this he was not successful. The Officer of the Day had left about twenty minutes before to get a message to the Admiral. Inquiring then whether rescue parties had been sent out in response to his request to Captain Low, he was informed by Sergeant Grimm that rescue parties had indeed been sent out, both by Captain Low and Lieutenant Case, and that it was probable that both officers were with these parties.

Peirce's next impulse was to go and help look for them with the remaining men in the recreation party, but first, he thought, he should send off a signal to the *Memphis,* relating what had occurred and giving the names of the men who had been in the boat. But he had no idea of who had been in the boat. In fact, he now realized that he had only a count of the men who had come ashore, not their names. The best he could do was to muster the men still with him and transmit the names of the men who had not been in the boat. Grabbing a piece of paper, he began to write a message.

Chapter 8

With only half her boiler power available, *Castine*'s engines could drive the ship at about 9 knots. During the first few moments after the anchor was hoisted clear of the bottom, she had as yet no momentum, however, and consequently the effect of her hard-over rudder was scarcely felt. The pull of the anchor chain had swung the ship's head around a little to south of an easterly heading and she was just beginning to answer her helm when suddenly the sea seemed to recede from before her and a menacing hollow formed, in cross-section wider than the length of the gunboat, with a steep front on the far side which rose many feet above the level of *Castine*'s bridge and was marked along the top with foamy white frosting. *Castine* leaned slightly to starboard and perceptibly increased speed as she lurched downhill into the hollow.

"Hang on," shouted Commander Bennett, gripping the railing of the bridge himself as he did so. He had seen precisely the same wave formations many times before, in much reduced size to be sure. This was nothing but a huge breaker! More than once he had had occasion to disport himself in the surf of a bathing beach and, of course, he had many times seen breakers from the seaward side where they marked shoal water or rocks to be avoided. But never in his experience had a breaker or comber been so large! The rule of thumb is that the height of a curling sea is roughly equal to the depth of water in which it breaks. Here was a comber actually breaking at *Castine*'s anchorage! Bennett noted, with secret pleasure at his ability to be objective at such a time, that the old rule was not far off. As best he could measure it, the crest where the huge wave started to curl over was approximately forty feet high, nearly the same as the depth of water in which his ship had anchored.

Neither Commander Bennett, Lieutenant Schuirmann, nor Quartermaster Michel later recalled any feelings of fright. There simply was not time for this. With straining muscles they gripped the railing of the bridge and nerved themselves to face the on-sweeping sea. There was a salty, sinking sensation as *Castine* dropped into the trough and then, in a moment, their feet were pressing heavily against the deck as her bow rose and her stern dropped. The gunboat was by now at an unusual angle, much like a whaleboat quartering through a heavy sea, with bow high and stern low, almost buried to the water's edge, the ship in approximately a 15-degrees-up attitude, heeled well over to starboard.

With a rush and a flurry of spray, *Castine*'s bow rose clean out of water; then the crest of the wave was amidships, boiling over the gunwales onto the main deck, and suddenly the bow began to drop with increasing speed until the ship was again reversed, her bow digging deeply into the back of the comber as it swept past, her stern high, her propellers completely out of water and spinning in air. *Castine*'s forward motion had increased as she slid down into the comber, but it had been brought to a standstill when she encountered the face of the breaker. Now, in a reversal of this effect, she again increased speed, sliding downhill on the back of the comber into the next huge breaker forming just beyond. There was a desperate clanking from the engine room— the engines were racing again. Unless the throttlemen were unusually quick of reaction every time the propellers came out of water, they would tear themselves apart.

There was no roar of wind, no whistling of air through the rigging. The Union Jack on the jack staff forward—which there had not been time to take down—hung almost limply. The only elemental noise was the protest of the churning waters and the confused roar astern when the comber broke. Superimposed on this was the rhythm of the engines, and Bennett thought he could hear them begin to reduce speed as the throttlemen closed down on the main steam throttles, and the next instant they slowed down precipitantly as the propellers re-entered the water. There was another sound, too, the straining and creaking of his little ship's twenty-four-year-old hull. Quick glances forward and aft gave Bennett the instantaneous impression—later neither to be proved nor disproved, for there was no way of reproducing the situation—that the bow and stern of *Castine* were not moving solidly together with the accustomed rigidity of a ship's structure, but were instead working in slightly different cadences as though the ship might be bending and twisting along her keel. Bearing this out was a periodic high-pitched, screeching protest of her keel and the strength girders where her main deck joined her sides.

But Bennett had no time to consider these simultaneous impressions, for with her bow now deeply buried, her forecastle almost scooping up the sea, *Castine* gained speed and literally rushed into the hollow of the next wave; again reversed her inclination; again was brought nearly to a halt; now mounted up, seesaw like, her bow, now reaching high, still buried almost to the main deck. The face of this wave was smoothly curved, like the first, but much more vertical, even leaning toward her, even higher than the first one. The second great comber was beginning to break right here and now.

"Hang on!" again shouted Bennett. The breaker towered above them, its face a smooth and beautifully ribbed curve of tunnel-like symmetry from the bottom of the trough up to the leaning-toward-them surface just below the crest. The top moved toward them. The impression afterward remained in Bennett's mind that the sea had actually curved completely over them, that for some fantastically long instant of time he and his ship were buried in an immense underwater tunnel with beautiful curved sides, stretching an infinite distance both forward and aft.

And then, toppling from its impossible position, the sea landed a crushing blow upon *Castine,* covering the bridge with white water, smashing the railing to which Bennett, Schuirmann, and the other bridge personnel were desperately clinging, inundating the main decks, smashing all lightly built topside gear, swamping forecastle and after deck, and pouring through imperfectly fitting hatches.

No one on the bridge later had any conscious recollection of having ordered hatches shut, but it is the fact that they were shut—that some instinctive seaman's reaction on the part of someone, or several persons, perhaps the First Lieutenant on the forecastle, possibly a quickly forgotten order from someone on the bridge, had caused them to be shut—which prevented *Castine* from being sunk then and there.

On the main deck, however, the space between the raised forecastle and poop, known as the "well deck," was enclosed on either side by high bulwarks, which formed the continuation of the sides of the ship. It was through an opening in these bulwarks that Commander Bennett had come aboard only a few minutes earlier. The gangway openings had been closed and bolted, and now the space where the well deck had been could be likened to a tremendous bathtub, equal in width to the beam of the ship and filled to the very brim. Water trapped in this space covered the engine-room hatches, and some got into the after parts of the ship. Again, fortunately, all these hatches had been shut, but they had not been designed to be submerged under water for any lengthy period. Under the poop deck, in fact, they were really nothing more than light partition doors, and water entered the cabin area almost freely. *Castine* lay well over on her starboard side under the combined weight of water on her decks, pressing her down, and the tons caught in her "bathtub." Her forward motion stopped again—her throttlemen were being very cautious after their scare the first few times she heaved her propellers out—and as she struggled to free herself, the weight of water she had taken aft held her stern down. Her bow correspondingly rose, a fortunate event, for the seas were coming with such rapidity that *Castine* could not have survived plunging into them in her former attitude. The next breaker was not so high, possibly it also came before the ship, inanimate fabric of steel plates and girders that she was, could react by plunging her bow again into it. In any event it broke against her high, exposed bow, swung her around again to a northeastern heading, and the whole ship was pushed bodily to leeward toward the rock-strewn shore.

It was virtually a momentary lull, giving Commander Bennett the opportunity to take hasty stock of the condition of his ship. The bridge rail was bent in, and the starboard engine-room tele· graph had been smashed so that it was jammed in the ahead position. Her little chart table, with its protective canopy against rain and heavy weather, had been torn from its bolted-down legs and completely swept off the bridge. She had lost what ground she had gained in trying to claw around to a southerly heading and was now again heading a little north of east. Part of her difficulty was that her engines were going at reduced speed for fear of damaging them when the propellers rose out of water, and this reduced maneuverability. A few days later, describing the incident, Bennett said, "I felt then that it was impossible to go out the way we were trying as the seas struck the bow so solidly that we were thrown to leeward with every breaker."

The time was now about 4:10. In addition to the safety of his own ship, Bennett was concerned with the condition of the *Memphis* motor launch, which had been observed coming out of the Ozama River some minutes before. It must be very near his own ship now, ready to pass close by en route to the *Memphis*. After a momentary search in that direction, he realized that the launch had swamped; the men who had been in it were swim-ming or floating in the water.

Castine herself was now in imminent danger of being swept ashore. Her bow had been thrown back inside of the point of land she had been trying to weather, Point Torrecilla, and there appeared to be no reduction in size of the seas closer to the bluff. Furthermore, from the rise and fall of the ship already experi-enced, Bennett knew that if she were to be driven much closer to shore, there would be danger of striking bottom during her wild gyrations, even though the nominal depth of water might be double or treble *Castine*'s actual draft.

With every wave that struck her, *Castine* was, however, drift-ing nearer to the men struggling in the water. The sea was far too wild to attempt to pick them up by boat, even if one could have been lowered, and permitting the *Castine* to get among them would have been disastrous. Bennett let her drift as long as he dared and then, being only a few yards directly to seaward of the men in the water, he directed that all life preservers and all floatable objects on board be thrown overboard to drift toward them. A number of *Castine*'s crew took off their own life jackets and life belts and also threw them into the water. One man on the forecastle, with his left arm and leg entwined tightly in the rigging, wound up and let fly with a heaving line. This, however, came nowhere near any of the men in the water.

In the meantime, Commander Bennett was taking desperate stock of the situation of his ship. In another two or three hundred yards, if she continued to drift toward shore, she would be striking bottom and this would undoubtedly result in her total loss. Being a small and very light vessel and still buoyant despite the large amount of water which had gotten below, she was rising and falling bodily a distance of twenty feet or more as the succeeding rollers swept past. Recognizing that it was impossible to drive *Castine*'s bow around against the sea, Bennett weighed the courses open to him. He could drive the engines ahead with the maximum power available and hope that, when the propellers heaved out of water, his throttlemen would somehow be quick enough to prevent damage. If he could get up enough speed, obviously, *Castine*'s head must eventually come around to the south. The question of judgment was simply how much speed was necessary, and how much sea room was needed. It only took one sea, hitting the little gunboat's bow when it was raised so vulnerably, to undo everything laboriously gained during several minutes. He had already seen this.

The alternative was to go astern. Even though no ship maneuvers as well when going astern as when going ahead, there was far more sea room in that direction. The whole question really revolved about whether or not it was possible to gain even a little distance to seaward. He had not gained any so far. Just possibly, if she were backing into it, the location of the propellers at the stern might tend to reduce the effects of the seas coming upon his ship. It was also possible that they might tend to be out of water less of the time and therefore, under these particular circumstances, more effective.

Quartermaster Arthur Michel, on the bridge of the *Castine*, helped him make up his mind. Born in Tahiti, he had knocked about the seas of the world in all kinds of ships since childhood. His English was still strongly tinged with his native French, but he was enough of a seaman to recognize the full seriousness of the situation. He also knew that the best advice is that which is given in time. "Captain," said Michel urgently, "I was in a sea like this once before. Not this big and we had a lot of wind, too, but it was pretty big. We couldn't turn the ship around either, so we backed out. That's what we ought to do here, sir." Michel's thick French accent only heightened the stress he placed in his words.

Bennett had about reached the same conclusion, though without the benefit of the equivalent prior experience. "I think you're right, Michel," he said. "Take the wheel. We need your experience right now!"

Gripping the damaged rail on *Castine*'s bridge for assurance against the violent tossing and twisting of the ship, Bennett pulled himself over to the engine-room voice tube, cupped his hands to his mouth over it. "Engine Room," he bawled. "Disregard the starboard telegraph! Give me all you can make astern on both engines!" Then he threw the port bridge annunciation lever to Back Full.

Initially this move met with success. *Castine* slowly gathered sternway and, with her rudder held at hard right, slowly her stern twisted around to the south. A ship going backward is, however, extremely difficult to steer, particularly in bad weather. Michel's seamanship and versatility were taxed to keep the bow of the careening little warship on a northerly heading so that she could continue her southward movement. Alternately he applied full rudder one way or the other, always reversed its position long before it seemed to be necessary. After watching him for a few minutes, Bennett knew that giving his Tahitian quartermaster full rein had been an excellent move. Slowly, *Castine* began to gain ground to the south.

The precious yards thus added to her safety margin proved of crucial importance almost immediately, for now this lull was over. The seas continued to increase, the breakers continued to form farther from shore and grow larger at the same time. As Commander Bennett recalled it:

In a few minutes we were struck by a number of the largest combing seas I have ever witnessed. These smashed down the after awning, which we had not had time to furl, carried away the cabin and wardroom hatches, flooded the cabin completely, ran down the hatch into the wardroom country, filled up the steering engine room and the tiller room. A great deal of water got into the magazines and it also backed up through the drains into some of the storerooms aft. The two whaleboats were filled with water and carried away, the starboard boat taking both davits with it. The second motor sailer at the davits filled with water, the dinghy amidship at its davits filled and carried away, and the wherry was smashed in fragments and washed clean off the upper deck. The ship again took a heavy list; the sea room which we had gained at first to the southward was lost, and we were being forced bows-on to the beach. I directed that the motor sailer be cut away, but before this could be done it broke in two and shortly afterward both ends dropped clear.

The well deck had water up to the engine-room hatches, which fortunately had been battened down, but, notwithstanding this, water got into the engine room and the engine crankpits were filled. The seas filled up the fireroom to the level of the lower furnace.

The large amount of water in the steering engine room put the steering engine out of operation and the hand gear was thrown in. It did not give us control for very long, however, for the rudder chains securing the steering quadrant or tiller to the drum of the steering engine parted under the heavy strain of the seas beating upon the rudder from astern, and the rudder then jammed hard left.

It now looked as if the ship was about to take the ground. What wind there was had been pushing the ship to the westward, however, and it seemed that if we could get two hundred yards west without touching, we might win clear. For some reason or other the breakers did not appear to be so heavy there. Again we seemed to have a lull, and by slowing on the starboard engine and backing full on the port engine, the stern of the ship was thrown around to the eastward. We then must have been heading west-northwest and the Santo Domingo slaughterhouse was approximately north of us. Both engines were then put full speed ahead and, due to the fortunate circumstance that the rudder had jammed on full left, the ship slowly came around. Heavy seas came aboard all the time, but we gathered headway and finally got clear of the breakers, passing out on a course about southeast, passing the *Memphis* close aboard on our port hand. As we passed the *Memphis* I felt that she had touched, or was touching. There was a heavy strain on her starboard chain and her starboard propeller was turning over—my recollection being that it was going ahead. This could be seen as she was laboring very much, her propellers coming out of water, and the seas breaking clear over her at times. The time then, as nearly as could be judged, was about 4:30 to 4:45.

Once clear of the anchorage, Bennett maintained a course of approximately southeast, steering the ship by varying the speed of the engines while a crew of quartermasters and engineers labored in the steering engine room and tiller room to bail the water out and then put the rudder back in commission. Their initial effort was to install the emergency tiller, but to their dismay the squared end of the tiller bar had been so badly burred at some previous time that it could not be fitted into the head of the rudder post. It was, however, at last possible to move the rudder and secure it amidships, and the ship was steered all night with her engines.

Out at sea, the seas were no longer breaking, but were very heavy, with great, deep rollers. For a few hours *Castine* was in a precarious position with all the water she had taken sloshing from side to side as she rolled. The "free surface" effect of a large amount of water loose in a ship's hull is that it will always seek the low side and thus accentuate any list or roll to that side. In *Castine*'s present condition, a heavy roll to either side, which the gunboat might well have withstood under normal conditions, might be enough to roll her all the way over. The safest course appeared to be southeast, heading directly into the sea, since this appeared to cause the minimum of roll.

J. Hobart Rockwell, now an attorney in Rochester, New York, was an ensign on board the *Memphis*. He had been relieved as O.O.D. by Ensign Walker at noon, and he gives the following eyewitness account of the *Castine*'s travail, which he was in a particularly good position to observe:

To relate the story of the Gunboat *Castine*, as seen from the Quarterdeck of the *Memphis* on the Day of the Disaster, may create the impression that the observers were idly watching from that vantage point, with little else to do. But this is contrary to the facts. The Quarterdeck of the *Memphis* was the duty station of the Second Division, for work, action and emergency; hence our observations of the *Castine* on that fateful afternoon were made from brief glimpses, while securing our Station for sea; with W. E. Gerhart, BM1c, rigging in gangways, closing hatches and stowing gear; with C. Barnhardt, the Turret Captain or with F. W. K. Mielke, CBM, making ready No. 2 whaleboat as "Lifeboat". The Second Division was all there; all, except W. B. "Whale Boat" Smith, Cox., R. G. Snell, Sea, and others lost in our motor-sailer. Thus I write for all of my division who were at their duty stations that day.

We were holding pointer and trainer drill in No. 2 ten-inch turret, when the word came to secure for sea. When I dropped down from the turret hatch to the deck, Captain Beach and Commander Williams were standing at the starboard gangway, seeing Captain Bennett off to his ship, the *Castine*. There had been no noticeable sea running that morning, but now the waves were considerably higher, but still with little or no wind. Mielke and Gerhart already had all hands busy on the after end of the ship, so that little attention was paid at first to the *Castine*. However, the waves continued to "roll in" higher and higher. Then, belching black smoke from her stack, we saw the *Castine* get underway and start ahead, to attempt a swing to Starboard, and toward the sea. But almost immediately, a giant wave hit her Starboard bow, throwing the bow around to Port, so that she appeared to be heading for the bar near the mouth of the Ozama River.

The next time we noticed the *Castine,* she was heeled over on her Port Side, so that even her spars actually disappeared from our sight for a couple of seconds; then she righted herself. But the next big wave pulled her bow down, and her stern, her propeller, and at least a third of her after hull rose completely out of the water, with a screw churning the air like a wind-mill. We could see that her engines were backing. The *Castine* had been lying about 500 yards inshore of the *Memphis* and to the Eastward toward the mouth of the river. Now, as her stern settled back into the water, she moved slowly Westward and astern of us, as she backed parallel to the shore so as to get around our stern.

Since the waves were rolling in from the southwest, she was taking them on her Starboard quarter; possibly for a brief period, we may have given her some protection while she was in the lee of the *Memphis*. As the waves grew even higher, the *Castine* heeled first on her Starboard side, then to Port, each time practically on her beam ends, and often completely out of sight. At this time, few of us on the

Memphis quarterdeck realized that our own, and much larger ship, was in real danger, and we were fascinated as we watched the *Castine* begin to swing slowly around our stern, passing us on our seaward side within less than fifty yards, her stern eventually heading South toward the open sea, still rolling and pitching so that her propeller was out of the water much of the time. When we had seen the *Castine* lying way over on her Port beam ends, we never expected she would get safely out to sea. However, get out she did. Probably it took about 15 minutes from the time the *Castine* was underway until she passed us to Starboard, and was well to seaward, still going astern, rolling and pitching.

I have often wondered how the men on the *Castine*'s bridge and deck, and in her engine and fireroom, could hold on with the ship rolling thru an arc of almost 180 degrees. To move the *Castine* from where she had all but foundered on the reef, to the relative safety of the open sea, was a feat of superb seamanship, and it demonstrated the highest degree of courage and devotion to duty by the entire crew.

Thomas Moran, Captain, U. S. Navy, retired, was Chief Engineer of the old gunboat—*Old Cast Iron,* as she was termed by her crew—and his account follows:

We had one (of our two) Scotch boilers steaming for auxiliary purposes, and were waiting for high tide on 30 August (when our river berth would be available) to cross the sandbar at the mouth of the Ozama River and moor to our old berth on the East bank of the river, opposite the Fortaleza. About 1 P.M. our Skipper, Commander K. M. Bennett, went to the *Memphis* for some dental work. At 3 P.M. our Executive Officer, Lieutenant Fred F. Rogers, went ashore in our No. 1 motor sailer to play tennis, and I became temporarily the Commanding Officer as well as the Chief Engineer. Lieutenant (j.g.) R. E. Schuirmann, a good man to have around, was Officer-of-the-Deck with the Day's Duty.

About 3:15 P.M. the ground swell from the South had increased and big waves were breaking between us and the cliffs. I had our large forecastle awning furled, and had just veered chain on the anchor to 60 fathoms, when Captain Bennett returned in a *Memphis* boat at 3:35 P.M. and told me to get the ship underway as soon as possible. The Boatswain's Mate passed the word; the Captain and the Officer-of-the-Deck went to the bridge; and the entire "Black Gang," as they called the Engineer's Force in those coal-burning days, went below to the Engineroom and Fireroom. We did very little warming up. At

4:00 P.M. I reported "Ready" to the Captain and at 4:04 the anchor was aweigh and we were underway, heading East with about 100 pounds of steam on one boiler. Heavy seas from the Southwest washed across the ship, filled the boats in their davits with water, and made the ship roll heavily.

At 4:04 P.M. when our anchor broke ground, we were underway heading East and about a mile from the elbow of a pocket formed by two coral cliffs radiating from the mouth of the Ozama River. One cliff ran West from the West bank of the Ozama River; the other cliff ran South from the East bank of the river. The open sea was to the Southwest on our Starboard beam, the heavy sea was from the South, and with the rudder jammed amidships, the Captain could not turn the ship's head with the engines far enough to the right to head out to sea. Off the mouth of the Ozama River it was very bad—we had no boats—we were in a dangerous spot, and the only help that could be given swimmers from the *Memphis* Motor Sailer was to toss over life preservers. Unable to turn the ship to get to sea, the Captain backed both engines, and by some miracle the *Castine* retraced its course stern first, passing close aboard and inshore of the *Memphis*. Probably the lee of the *Memphis* helped the Captain swing the *Castine*'s Stern around to the Southward and a short lull in the storm allowed him to turn the *Castine* with engines and she stood out to the Southwest to clear away the wreckage and to make repairs. This was close timing.

Down below in the engine and firerooms of the *Castine,* the bilges were flooded and water sloshed across the floor plates. The entire "Black Gang" was down below (usually there is only one of the three watches), so we could station a man at every valve or pump where he could hang on with one hand and work with the other. We received reports that all the after compartments were flooded so the fire and bilge pumps were kept running on the main drain, although we needed all the steam possible for the main engines. When the Captain rang up "Full speed ahead" or "Full speed astern" on the annunciators, we gave him all we had until the steam pressure dropped to 82 or 83 pounds, and then we had to slow and build the pressure again.

A heavy list to Port righted itself when the 2nd motor launch carried away. Water coming down a ventilator soaked the generator and the lights went out, but we rigged oil lamps and candles in the engine room and fireroom, where to further complicate matters, the water gauge on the steaming boiler had broken. Boiler-maker Dennis J. White, one of the best, would open a pet-cock occasionally to make sure there was enough water in the boiler.

When the glass sky-lights on the poop-deck were broken, the big waves washing across the ship flooded the wardroom and the officers' staterooms as well as the steering engine compartment. Luckily the rudder was amidships when the steering engine was jammed by clothing from a scrub-and-wash-clothes line that got adrift on deck and was sucked into the steering engine compartment and wrapped itself around the wheel ropes. We told the bridge via voice-tube, and after that we had to steer with main engines—to go left, "Stop Port engine" and "Full speed ahead Starboard engine." The deck force under Ensign Jack Lenny tried to rig a tiller arrangement on the rudder head but had no luck. Then he had a bucket brigade bailing out the flooded steering engine compartment, and finally when we were well off shore the water was gone and the impedimenta cleared away and we all felt much better with the steering gear in operation again.

On deck, the crew not "on watch" took to the masts and rigging, or the bridge area. Paymaster Tudor reported later he had climbed to the top of the foremast and thought he was "high man" until he looked up and found a young Seaman holding on to the lightning rod. The *Castine*'s Deck Log for 29 August 1916 includes the following:

Meridian to 4 P.M.

About 3:35 Commanding Officer returned on board and prepared to get underway. Sea making rapidly and breaking in 5 fathoms of water. About 3:40 1st. sailing launch returned to ship and was ordered to join *Memphis* boats which were lying to seaward beyond long rolling seas. About 4:00 P.M. sailing launch from USS *Memphis*, while attempting to come out of river, capsized. /Signed/ R. E. Schuirmann, Lieutenant (j.g.) USN

4 to 8 P.M.

At 4:04 got underway with one boiler and attempted to stand out. Seas breaking on all sides of ship. All boats except motor whaleboat washed away and ship filling through Poop hatches. Wire on quadrant of steering gear carried away. Stood (East) toward Torrecilla Point and as impossible to turn, backed. When (Santo Domingo City) lighthouse bore about 30 by estimation, ship passed first line of breakers and turned with engines during lull, stood out to Southward.

Turned all hands to clearing wreckage and bailing water from after compartments. Relieving tackles on steering gear rigged but emergency tiller on rudder head would not stay on. About 5:30 passed breaking seas—, at 7:15 lighted fires in No. 2 boiler. Impossible to cat the anchor, and as anchor stove holes in the bow, slipped it with about five fathoms of chain attached. Assistant Paymaster, H. P. Tudor, injured by falling rigging and debris, received lacerated wounds in scalp, lacerated wounds right ankle and numerous abrasions about body. (Others with lesser injuries). Steaming at one-third speed into heavy head seas on course S. E. steering with engines.

/Signed/ R. E. Schuirmann, Lieutentant (j.g.) USN

8 P.M. to Midnight

Steaming under one boiler at one-third speed, standard speed 90 RPM on South-easterly courses. Sea increased considerably accompanied by heavy rain squalls and wind which at times was of force 11 to 12. The ship weathered head seas very well. Steering with engines. All hands securing wreckage and bailing water. Ensign Lenny repairing steering gear. At 10:20 connected up No. 2 boiler.

/Signed/ G. L. Greene, Ensign USN

At about 6:00 P.M., after *Castine* had cleared the anchorage, it was reported to Commander Bennett that a boat was in sight to the southwest. Fearing the possible consequences of changing course, particularly to a new course which would put the sea on the beam and result in maximum roll, Bennett held on to the southeast. The sea was still tremendous, running, in Commander Bennett's own words, "as high as I have ever seen it." Men could not have been rescued from any boat without great danger, even were it possible to handle *Castine* in such a manner as to approach safely.

Bennett, exhausted from the elemental battle he had just won, was simply unable to entertain any other thought than to restore damage and ensure the safety of his ship. With hardly a thought for the men in the boats and their prospects under the fantastic weather just experienced, he figured to search for them next day. All night long, *Castine* stood off to the southeast, repairing damage and restoring the forces of her officers and crew by rest. But during the night it became very dark with frequent heavy rain squalls and at times strong winds, and as the hours passed and it became clear that physical exhaustion must be considered, *Castine*'s skipper began to have some fear for the safety of the three boats at sea. The weather was warm, so exposure was not a problem; but the heavy rain and the spray being whipped off the seas during the squalls might easily put an engine out of commission. Bennett's concern, however, caused no change in plans. Despite the seas and the rain, rationalized he, the boat's crews needed only to drift around until someone picked them up the next day.

At first light the sea had gone down considerably, the wind had fallen, and *Castine* began her search. Considerable debris was found in the water, including the wherry which had been smashed and washed off her deck the night before.

But the search was cut short. As the gunboat came within sight of her anchorage of the day before, her radioman recognized her call being made by radio. A short time later he had received a short message, transmitted uncoded, in plain language:

FROM COMMANDER CRUISER FORCE TO CASTINE X PROCEED IF ABLE TO PORT PALENQUE X SEARCH FOR AND ASSIST POTO-MAC

Surely, thought Bennett, the Admiral would know that he was searching for the boats he had been unable to pick up the night before, and this message must mean that they were already safe. Doubtless they had gone back to port when the seas had subsided, possibly at daybreak. He dismissed them from concern, swung *Castine* about, headed west.

The U. S.-owned schooner *Daylight* had gone aground some days ago in Port Palenque, and it was this vessel which the tug *Potomac* had been sent the previous day to assist. *Castine* arrived shortly before noon; so far as could be seen, the events at Santo Domingo had had little or no counterpart in this smaller, but more sheltered harbor. There was no sign of the tug, but as the gunboat's remaining anchor splashed into the water, the *Daylight* signaled that, after pulling her off, the *Potomac* had gone to another small bay, farther to the west. A short time later a radio message brought the information that *Potomac* was en route back to Santo Domingo.

While Bennett waited at Port Palenque, uncertain as to his next move, his feeling of uneasiness returned; as soon as he had read the message from the *Potomac* he ordered the anchor hoisted and set course once more for Santo Domingo. During the return trip a sharp lookout was maintained, but only some un-identifiable pieces of debris and a wrecked motor launch, floating belly up between the anchorages occupied by *Castine* and *Memphis* the day before, were found. The boat had lost its propeller and rudder, and several bottom planks were badly stove in. Affixed to the bows, upside down in the water but discernible, were the bronze letters MEM and the figure 3, identifying it as the number 3 motor launch of the *Memphis,* the same which had been picking up gear from the capsized dinghy the day before and which Yancey Williams had, for a time, planned to send after the second contingent of the recreation party.

Late on the afternoon of the thirtieth of August, *Castine* steamed into Santo Domingo harbor and was able, for the first time, to appreciate the convulsion of nature from which she had escaped. Having lost all her boats and suffered other damage, she went directly to the Ozama River, passing easily over the bar at the mouth, and moored to the municipal wharf a short dis-tance upstream from the medieval stonework of the old Spanish fort. Commander Bennett looked among the faces greeting her at the dock for the members of the boat crew which he had sent out to sea the day before, but they were not there. Lieutenant Rogers, his Executive Officer, was the only one he recognized.

Chapter 9

When Chief Machinist George asked the bridge for five minutes' additional time, he fully appreciated the significance of the request. He was therefore not unprepared to hear the voice at the other end of the voice tube respond immediately and emphatically: "We must have the engines now! The ship is in danger! Stand by to answer all bells!" Despite the distortions caused by the long voice tube, there was no longer any doubt in George's mind that he was then—and might have been for some time—talking with Captain Beach. There was a never-before-heard urgency in the tone of the Captain's voice.

Awareness of the emergency had also been growing upon George for the past half hour. During the period since he had reported the engines ready to Lieutenant Jones he had been essentially idle, transmitting information and orders to and from the bridge—directly from the Captain, as it now appeared—but otherwise not occupied except in assuring the continued readiness of the engines. Thus there was ample time to consider the situation. There was by this time no question but that the ordinary requirement to await full steam pressure before operating the engines must go by the board. "Engine Room, aye, aye," he shouted into the voice tube, and swung about to communicate the information to the chief engineer. But Lieutenant Jones was no longer beside him. George saw his back disappearing from the forward part of the engine room as he hurried toward the firerooms.

"Stand by to answer bells!" shouted George to the starboard throttleman. "Stand by to answer bells!" he shouted again, this time directing his voice through the watertight door into the port engine room so that the port-engine throttleman could hear the command clearly.

Anxiously, both engine throttlemen stood at their stations, both aware that conditions entirely beyond knowledge or comprehension had suddenly brought a condition of extraordinary emergency upon them, and both also aware, as well, that the firerooms were having difficulty in producing adequate steam.

The annunciators tinkled. The telegraph for the starboard engine, attached to the bulkhead above George's watch desk, switched to the "Back Full" position. Its mate, for the port engine, a moment later went to "Ahead Full."

In the columns of the Engineering Log Sheet, George wrote: "4:35 P.M.—SBF. PAF." He had always prided himself on neat logkeeping, and his figures were meticulous. The steam-pressure gauge, centered on the bulkhead above the engine-room telegraph telltales, registered ninety pounds per square inch, but as the throttlemen slowly opened their throttles, George saw the pressure begin to drop. This could only mean that the boilers were not yet generating enough steam. In the emergency he had to make a quick decision. To Rudd, standing worriedly just inside the open door to the port engine room, and Stillman, also nearby and equally concerned, George shouted, "Hold her to thirty turns!"

Full speed was 120 r.p.m., but opening the throttles wide might expend all the steam immediately and drag the steam pressure down to zero. It was first necessary to establish equilibrium between steam generated and steam consumed. Then, watching the pressure carefully and adjusting the throttle openings accordingly, it might be possible slowly to increase speed. Now, however, with engine throttles only very slightly opened, steam pressure continued to drop until it reached sixty pounds. To George's relief, it remained at that level. On the same line as his previous entry in the log sheet, he now added the carefully lettered phrase: "HELD TO 30 RPM."

The motion of the ship had become quick and violent, making it hazardous to walk about in the engine rooms now that the ponderous machinery had begun to operate. Loosely secured articles were becoming displaced, to add a missile hazard on top of other problems. It was necessary to shout to be heard over the roar of the water pouring into the engine rooms through the boat-deck hatches and the intakes to the engine-room ventilating system on the quarter-deck. At approximately this moment, Newton George felt an unusual twisting motion in the ship, accompanied by a resounding, drumlike roar which, growing from nothing, rapidly overtook the noise of the engines, the crashing of the seas on deck, the water pouring in through the ventilator ducts and boat-deck hatches, and the crashing of broken lockers and other gear being hurled about the engine room. The noise rose until it was the only noise extant in the world—a great, hollow, reverberating noise, high in pitch, composed of a thousand different notes discordantly joined into one, to which the great, steel-lined cavern of the ship vibrated in tune.

Memphis, starting a violent roll to starboard, suddenly reversed the direction of her motion with horrifying speed and heeled far over to port. Instinctively George braced himself against his desk, itself well bolted to the bulkhead, and half-cringed with the expectation of something falling upon his exposed back and head. Stillman, he noticed fleetingly, had gripped the railing of the walkway around the engine, and the suddenly thrown weight of his body was causing it to bend several inches out of line. If the rail gave way, it would catapult Stillman into the vicinity of the ponderous, reciprocating motion of the connecting rods of the starboard engine and its slowly turning shaft and cranks.

Faintly from somewhere up above there came noises of the smashing of equipment. Something heavy was carried across the boat deck, crashing and banging on the way, and George was aware, without consciously hearing them, of shouts and cries of men and hundreds of confused footsteps emanating from the general vicinity of the berth deck.

A fortunate quietness sometimes accompanies emergencies: the mind seems to blot out all extraneous impressions, while nevertheless recording them, and remains aware only of those directly pertaining to the situation of stress then at hand. Professional men, if they know their environment—be it ship, railroad train, automobile, or aircraft—become instantly aware of the unusual; all usual or expected noises, signs and signals fail to register upon their minds, and they are free to devote full attention to matters demanding it. Feats of superhuman strength, as well as feats of superhuman acuity, take place at times like this, even to such a degree that the individual may be unable later to reproduce them, and must be forced to believe that things cannot have occurred quite the way he remembers them. In this instance, the recollection of all hands in the engine rooms was that their ship had rolled 60 or more degrees to port, nearly on her beam ends, as the nautical expression goes.

But time does not stand still, even though it sometimes may seem to, and in a few seconds the staunch cruiser surged upright once more. During this titanic heave, which covered an arc of more than 90 degrees, engine-room personnel became aware of a new noise, a new danger: the heavy battle-bar gratings above the engines had begun to shift. At least one was flung out of its socket, and they heard the deep crash as the armored beam, weighing several hundred pounds, struck some part of the structure of the ship. Luckily, with *Memphis* nearly on her beam ends, the heavy piece of steel fell against a bulkhead instead of straight down.

As *Memphis* came back to an even keel, another deluge of water roared down from the boat-deck ventilation hatches past the disarranged battle bars and into the engine room. George heard the clink of the engine-order telegraph again and saw the port-engine telegraph switch from "Ahead Full" to "Back Full."

It was within a minute, hardly yet 4:36, when Claud Jones, gripping the rails alternately on both sides of the narrow walkway beside the engine for support, returned to the starboard engine room. As they braced themselves, wide-stanced, George gave him a rapid report. "Mr. Jones, I tried to tell you a minute ago, but you had gone forward. Bridge called and said that we must use the engines—that the ship is in danger. It was the Captain on the voice tube, sir. He rang up full speed astern on the starboard engine and full ahead on port. Now they have just switched the port engine to full astern also, both full astern, but I am not able to give it to them because steam pressure has dropped to sixty pounds. So we're running the engines at thirty r.p.m.'s, and that's all we can do, I think."

Jones, his sweaty face covered with coal dust, his once white trousers now sodden with a combination of perspiration and salt water below his stained dungaree jacket, nodded in a defeated way. "We're just cutting number thirteen boiler in on the main line," he said, "but that's not enough. With the ship rolling the way she is, we need more time to get steam on the boilers and get the pressure up." This last was said almost as though he were talking to himself, as though he were making a status report to keep abreast of the kaleidoscopic movement of events. He raised his voice a little more decisively. "Chief, call the bridge and tell them that we don't have enough steam to operate the engines yet."

"Mr. Jones," hoarsely whispered George, "this is a case of life or death! I think I can feel the ship hitting bottom. We must use the engines now or never!" He uncapped the mouthpiece of the voice tube, cupped both hands to it, leaned forward and cupped his mouth into his hands.

"Bridge," he shouted, "this is the engine room. We don't have enough steam to operate the engines at this time!"

The voice that came back down the voice tube—undoubtedly that of the Captain—sounded clipped, terse, betrayed. "We *must* use the engines!" it said.

"Tell them," said Jones, "that if they must use the engines we recommend they only use one engine."

Cupping the voice tube once more, supporting himself by its sturdy structure against the heavy rolling of the ship, George shouted. "Bridge, this is Engine Room. Recommend we use only one engine!"

"Bridge, aye, aye," the Captain's voice instantly replied. "Which engine?"

"Starboard engine," promptly replied George, not waiting for

his own chief. As he spoke, he remembered the night in a lonely
foreign port when he had arrived at the boat landing, with several hours of waiting ahead of him, to find only one other person
there—his skipper, also lonely. And he remembered how, in a
moment, instead of Captain and Warrant Officer, there were only
two engineers there, talking shop talk, meditatively sipping a last
nightcap, and how shortly thereafter he rode back to the *Memphis* sitting beside her Captain in the Captain's Gig. And now
that ship—and that Captain—were totally dependent upon him,
and his engines. He felt an upsurge of kinship, of understanding.

The Chief Engineer's eyes stared at nothing. Only he could possibly know the agonizing, slowly losing battle which his men had
fought to make steam within two black, dusty compartments with
fire on either side and water pouring in from ventilator shafts,
and the whole gyrating madly through arcs of sixty degrees on
each side of the vertical. It had been considerations of the best engineering judgment, thoroughly discussed with the Captain,
which had led him to recommend and the Skipper to agree that the
emergency under-way procedure would specify lighting off four
more boilers, for a total of six. While four boilers steaming at full
capacity would be sufficient, the new fires would not immediately
be in the best of shape and this would be compensated for by additional capacity. But for a short time this would place an extra drain
on the two boilers already steaming, in that their fires would be
further depleted to start four instead of two more fireboxes and
their steam employed to start and run twice as much more cold
auxillary machinery.

On the other hand, in some quarters it had been held that in
emergency two boilers, pushed to the utmost, could move the ship
if all unnecessary machinery were secured. While this was possibly
true, he would never have agreed, as Chief Engineer, willingly to
get under way in such precarious condition. But almost anything
would be better than the situation *Memphis* was now in. Conceiv-
ably she might have been able to gain a few miles of precious sea
room by such a maneuver, might even now be well off shore, lighting off her other boilers at leisure.

But who could have predicted conditions like these? Less than
an hour ago punctilious quarter-deck routine was being observed, a visiting skipper was being piped over the side. Difficult

as international relations might be, the ship was peacefully at anchor in a peaceful port. Only an hour ago, he himself, in full uniform befitting the occasion, had been seated in the wardroom gravely considering the case of Coxswain Potter. And now, deep in the bowels of his own private Hell, he was fighting for the life of his ship, for his own life and the lives of his men in the midst of a set of circumstances which no one in his wildest imagination could have predicted.

His machinery plant, his boilers, and auxiliary machinery, the engines which had recently driven the ship around South America and had made through the Straits of Magellan the fastest sustained full-speed dash ever recorded by any ship, his engineer's world which had upon so many occasions demonstrated its capability and utter reliability, had become converted within one hour into a rendition of Hell itself, with leaking steam joints, violent wracking of the basic structure and an utterly insane—fantastic—heaving and jerking of the decks, walls, and overheads. The fight to keep fires going—while water constantly came into the firerooms through the forced-draft blowers and even, incredibly, entered the tall funnels at their upper ends and had poured down through them into the fireboxes—had become a fight for survival itself. Sliding and stumbling on the mixture of water, coal dust, and small lumps of coal on the floor plates of their hot, roaring caverns, bracing themselves against wild shifts in the direction of gravity, the jangled uproar of tortured machinery stressed beyond stress and beyond the extra capability built into it by dedicated designers and builders, his firemen were devoting their all to the god of fire. Figuratively they were jumping into the flame every time one of the firebox doors was opened, braving shriveling heat as they tried to select dry coal with their shovels and reached into their furnaces to place it—contrary to the normal practice of tossing it with a skillful heave of the shovel from a greater distance—at the spots where the fire seemed most in need.

But Jones recognized that they were losing the fight. The fires were not growing stronger. They were, in fact, becoming weaker. Heat had been created, put into the water, and steam was forming, but now the fires were progressively being put out, instead of becoming stronger, because of the heavy spray coming down the stacks.

Uneasily, he realized that his estimate of only half an hour longer to wait, given after he had been some twenty or so minutes in the engineering spaces, had been based subconsciously on a continuance of conditions as they then were, or as they appeared to be from below decks. At that time, 4:05, they were not very different from those encountered a week previous when *Memphis* had been ready within forty minutes. But upon that occasion the ship had continued to lie relatively quiet at anchor, only, for a short time, rolling a little more than usual. Now he must face the despairing knowledge that this time, in some way, he had failed his Captain and his ship.

The voice from the bridge which answered George was that of the practiced mariner who must make the best of a bad situation. There was no time to ask what or why. "Very well," it said. The emergency had wiped out all organization, all protocol whereby the Officer of the Deck relays the Captain's desires to the Engineering Officer of the Watch—neither principal speaking directly to the other. Distorted by reverberation in the lengthy piping required to run the voice tube from engine room to bridge, the Captain's voice was nevertheless fully recognizable. That Captain Beach had in turn recognized *his* voice, George was certain.

"Port Engine Stop!" George yelled. No answer. Probably, in the noise now going on, he could not be heard. He waited no further. Bending double, he jackknifed through the low watertight door into the port engine room, took hold of the port-engine telegraph, swung it to "Stop." Customarily the telegraphs in the engine rooms are used only to answer signals from the bridge, thus to indicate they have been received and understood. Only in emergency or when there has been some prearranged evolution does the engine room initiate signals itself.

The annunciator clicked, the bridge-controlled indicator went also to "Stop." "Rudd," shouted George, "We're stopping your engine; answering bells on the starboard engine!"

Though Rudd was only a few feet away, George had to yell at him. Rudd nodded his understanding, and his superior stooped swiftly through the connecting watertight door back into the starboard engine room. The time was now about 4:37.

Lieutenant Jones turned and proceeded back into the fireroom
in the same manner in which he had come, staggering with the
motion of the ship, using the passageway rails as walking guides.

For some time, perhaps as long as five minutes, George had
been increasingly aware that the ship must be striking bottom.
This was at first gentle as the ship merely settled into the ooze of
the harbor bottom at the extreme lower limit of some of her
surges, but rapidly it became more noticeable, each jolt more
severe, and at about 4:40 the *Memphis* began to land on the
harbor bottom with an extremely heavy impact which shook the
ship's structure and added the screeching protests of distorted
metal and twisted keel to the bewildering cacophony of noise
already going on.

At about 4:45 P.M. there was a particularly heavy series of
crashes and the port engine room, as seen through the open
watertight door, seemed to fill with a white cloud. This could not
have come from the main steam line, however, since there was no
appreciable drop at that time in main-line pressure which was still
about sixty pounds. George says:

It was my opinion that it was a branch of the main or auxiliary
steam lines and not too serious so far as operating the starboard
engine was concerned. I reported on the casualty to the senior engineer officer, who, after inspecting as closely as possible, decided that it
was not serious enough to warrant cutting out the port engine room at
that time. It would in any case have been impossible to get to the
forward end of the port engine room to reach the steam-line cutout
valve, and to get at it from the fireroom side would have involved
cutting out number eight fireroom also.

At about this same time the starboard main air pump—being
used for pumping condensate from both main condensers in
place of the normal condensate pump which, being larger, would
have required more steam to run it—suddenly stopped. George
sent an oiler over to the pump to try to get it back in commission
again, but the man soon returned stating that it was impossible
to get it started since, as he put it, "The main engine was falling
down."

This was not strictly true, for the engine was still operating at
the time, but it is illustrative of the conditions that had devel-

oped. The consequence of striking repeatedly against the coral-based floor of the Caribbean Sea had to be huge dents in the ship's bottom. By now she must have suffered severe distortion of her hull and frames. The main hull members formed the principal foundation for the machinery bed plates, and these, inevitably, were also distorted.

At 4:46 the starboard engine-room telegraph rang again and the annunciator shifted from full speed astern to full speed ahead. The signal was answered immediately and the reversing link was thrown. The engine came to a quick stop and then began to turn in the ahead direction. It responded very slowly, however, picking up speed in an extremely sluggish manner. It was the Chief Machinist's impression at this time that the sluggishness of its response to the change in direction was as much due to its having been forced out of alignment from changes in the ship's structure as to any other cause. In the meantime, water was still dropping from the ill-fitting boat-deck hatches far above, and loosened battle bars from the disoriented battle gratings over the engines were falling, doing damage to lockers and other unimportant equipment, but luckily striking no one. Prudently, Rudd and Stillman had defined the probable danger areas and kept their men away from them.

The ship was now rolling madly, crashing on the harbor bottom on every roll and the resultant distortion of her hull could be seen as well as felt. Steam pressure had been slowly dropping for some time and was now approaching forty pounds. Since the port engine was not in use, at 4:48 Machinist George decided that it might be useful to shut off the port engine-room steam lines in order to conserve all possible steam for the starboard engine. Lights had by this time begun to grow dim. George himself closed the port engine-room steam crossover and bypass valves, and sent a messenger to number eight fireroom requesting that they shut the main steam cutout. Lieutenant Jones followed to see that this was properly done.

At 4:55 the starboard engine, which had been laboring and gradually reducing speed as its shafting was progressively thrown out of line, stopped entirely. Steam pressure was now thirty-five pounds per square inch.

The ship continued rolling very heavily, and tremendous

quantities of water had been coming into the engine room. Pumps were running constantly to keep the water level in the bilges down below the main crankcase level, though the violent motion of the ship made it almost impossible to keep a constant suction on the bilge pumps.

George's private report to the Navy Department stated:

Up to this time I had received no word from the bridge as to what was going on topside. I didn't know whether the ship was being driven ashore or being engulfed by heavy seas at her anchorage. I did know that the ship had been rolling violently—dangerously—and was being tossed about by titanic seas that continuously swept over the ship to the extent that at times it seemed the ship would capsize. Officers appearing before the Court of Inquiry following the wreck who had observed the rolling of the ship from on shore and on deck, testified that the ship rolled ninety degrees.

Shortly after the engine stopped, I went to number seven fireroom to learn first hand what conditions were there and what the prospects were for more steam. The fireroom was in darkness but from some fire in the furnaces I could see that the fireroom had been abandoned. Most of the furnace doors on boilers number thirteen and fifteen were open and there were some live coals in the furnaces, but certainly not sufficient to be generating any steam in either of these two boilers. I also noted considerable steam escaping from seams about the boiler casings near the side boxes, indicating that these two boilers were breaking up due to the ship's structure changing under the stress of the vessel pounding on the rocks. The watertight door leading from number seven to number eight fireroom was closed and from conditions in number seven fireroom it was apparent that this fireroom had been abandoned for some time. In any event there was so much steam in number seven fireroom and it was so hot there, due to the fact that the forced draft blowers and ventilating system had been shut down for some time, that I retraced my steps to the starboard engine room without having contacted anyone in the firerooms.

I now felt certain that everything had been done that was possible. At the time the pounding of the ship on the rocks had grown much worse. Floorplates were being displaced and thrown into the bilges, making it practically impossible to get about the engine rooms which were also filled with steam and practically in darkness.

The hopeless, rending pounding on the bottom and the violent heaving rolls of the ship from side to side were now the main source of noise. The bottom of the ship was perceptibly bulged upward underneath the walkways, condensers, and main engines, and at about 5:00 P.M. George received a second report about an engine—this time the port engine—being so far displaced out of line that it was in danger of falling over. This was not credible, since the engines were securely fastened to the ship's structure. It was, however, possible that displacement of the engine, resulting from distortion of the hull, could give this impression.

Since nothing further could be done in the engine rooms, the men in those two compartments had gathered about the control station.

"Has anyone seen the Chief Engineer?" called George.

It so happened that Lieutenant Jones had just re-entered the engine room from the firerooms. Now he made his way aft to the bedraggled group of oil-and-water-soaked main engine personnel.

"Here I am, Chief," said Jones.

The warrant officers in the Navy are professionals in their business and Navy men through and through. During the progress of the catastrophe, leadership in the engine rooms had subtly passed from Lieutenant Jones to Chief Machinist George, a man some years older who had spent his entire service life in the engineering departments of big ships, in contrast to Lieutenant Jones for whom this was only a present assignment probably to be followed by one of a totally different nature. During the emergency, Jones, of course, had responsibility both for engine rooms and firerooms. He had rightfully concentrated his efforts where they were most needed, and had left the entire responsibility of the engine rooms to George. Now that a different sort of decision had to be made, the professional engineer retained the responsibility almost by common consent. He spoke slowly and carefully. "There is nothing more that we can do to operate the main engines, sir. Steam pressure is below thirty pounds per square inch. The starboard engine has stopped and will not turn over. You can see that it is out of line. The port one is worse. There are numerous steam leaks and it will soon be impossible to breathe. We have not heard anything from the bridge for a long time and we don't know what's going on topside. I recommend we abandon the engine rooms, sir."

The Chief Engineer nodded his assent. "Very well, George,"

he said. "I'll go back through the firerooms and see what can be done there." So saying, Jones left the group and went forward once more.

George now took charge of his men. "All right, men," he said, "abandon the engine room. Take it easy, now, so you don't get hurt. Go on up all the way to the boat deck before you go topside. Go up through the starboard engine-room hatch—the ladder's clear—and take it slow and easy. Everybody keep together now and help each other!"

As the men silently started up the ladder, George quickly looked around. There was no one left in the engine room. He stooped, swiftly stepped into the port engine room. It was still filled with the white fog of steam, but the vapor was only warm, not searingly hot. Holding his cap in front of his face and trying to hold his breath, he surveyed the compartment. It appeared empty, and had considerable water, two or three feet above the floor plates. George pulled off his dungaree jumper, held it in front of his face, returned to the starboard engine room, quickly searched it, then ran through the low bulkhead door to the port engine room once again. There was no one visible. Several times he shouted, though it was evident that his voice could not have been heard more than a few feet away. Carefully, as well as he could, he searched the space, sloshing through water above his knees.

Despite the emergency lanterns which had been lighted when the electricity failed, it was difficult to see and increasingly difficult to breathe. In the forward end of the port engine room there was a little-used ladder leading to the berth deck, and this he found by feeling and groping for it. Reaching the berth-deck hatch at the top of the ladder, he opened it; the deck area was completely deserted and under about two feet of water, only a few inches below the hatch coaming. He sloshed his way to the nearest companionway ladder, climbed up to the gun deck and through another companionway to the main deck and thence to the boat deck above. Here, for the first time, he appreciated the enormity of the disaster.

Chapter 10

By 4:35, Charles Willey had been for some time fully engaged in getting steam up in the two standby firerooms, and for some time he had also realized that *Memphis* was in danger. Her motion, her jerking on the anchor, her pounding into the sea and the heavy rolling, not to mention the occasional deluge of sea-water which came in through the forced-draft blowers, spelled but one thing about conditions topside to the practiced antennae by which he maintained his personal sense of conditions affecting the ship.

All four boilers had by this time received fire and were making steam, but the steam pressures as yet were very low, far below the pressure on the main steam line, and they could not, for this reason, be opened to or "cut in on" the line. Among difficulties which slowed down the process was the necessity of using wet coal, since it was impossible to keep coal dry on the floor plates with the constant influx of water from the blowers. The fact that water occasionally came down the smokestack and further dampened the fresh fires helped not at all. This was not yet a problem in number one fireroom where the fires were already hot enough to vaporize the incoming water, but in the four cold boilers the continual heavy spray coming down number four stack was a serious impediment to development of the roaring fires needed. Leaky handhole plates, resulting from uneven expansion of the steam drums under the combined effects of cold sea-water, fire, and violent motion, caused loss of pressure and added danger from steam leaks. Should a complete rupture of a tube or steam drum take place, or an important gasket be blown out, both boilers in the affected fireroom would be lost, not to mention the lives of everyone in it. At 4:35 Lieutenant Jones came to Willey from the engine room. "Willey," he said, "the bridge says that we must use the engines! The ship is in danger! I have asked the bridge for five minutes more."

Willey was no longer the fastidious-looking individual who had answered the call for emergency under-way stations. He wiped his coal-dust-smeared forehead on the sleeve of his jacket. "We don't have enough steam, sir," he said. "These other boilers aren't ready yet. All this water coming down the stacks and through the blower shafts——"

"This is an emergency, Willey," desperately rasped the Chief Engineer. "Whether we're ready or not, we've got to cut in these boilers. Which are the best ones?"

"Number thirteen is farthest along. She has the highest pressure. Number fifteen is next. Both the boilers in number eight fireroom are behind this one."

"All right, Willey, start cutting in these boilers right now. Start with number thirteen. Then cut in number fifteen. Build up your fires just as hot as you can, and keep forcing them. Get the dryest coal you can find—use it straight out of the bunkers if you can. The ship will be wrecked if we can't get steam to the engines—and that damn quick!"

As Willey described later, the situation was enough to make anyone who knew anything about steam engineering cry in frustration. There were as yet only two working boilers, together able to produce barely enough steam to operate necessary auxiliaries to support the engines and the four newly lighted boilers. These were not yet anywhere near the pressure of the first two, and therefore not yet ready to be connected into the main steam line. The normal procedure for cutting in a boiler is to keep it isolated while its steam pressure is built up. When its gauges show a slight excess over the pressure in the main steam line, small bypass valves are carefully opened to equalize the pressure, and then the main boiler stop valves are opened. In this way the boiler comes on the line smoothly, there is no noticeable fluctuation of pressure, and from then on it makes its own contribution to the total amount of steam delivered to the main steam line. In the instant case, however, because of the great disparity between boiler pressure and main-line pressure, main steam-line pressure would enter the boiler, instead of the other way around, and, for a time at least, the boiler would be a drag on the line rather than a help.

With misgivings, Willey carried out the order received. Since the evolution required the highest degree of engineering experience and was hazardous as well, he attended to it himself.

Simultaneously, he felt the rumble and the rhythmic clanking of the connecting rods as the engines began to turn, and within a minute or two of this time he was able to get the first of the new boilers, number thirteen, cut into the main steam line. The temperature of the water in number thirteen was not high enough to support steam pressure above about twenty pounds per square inch, and he noted, as he had expected, that boiler number thirteen actually cooled the main steam line rather than adding to it, and thus subtracted power from it.

Willey's times are not as specific as George's, since he had no log desk and was forced to carry his office more or less in his head. His recollection is that steam pressure began to drop immediately after the engines were started, dropped further when boiler number thirteen was cut in on the line, and more yet when number fifteen was cut in. The greatest drop, however, occurred a few moments later when there was a steam casualty in the port engine room.

Boiler number thirteen was losing steam directly, in the form of a bad leak whistling from a handhole plate in its upper reaches, and Water Tenders Quinn and Porter crawled up on the fireroom upper gratings with a wrench to tighten it down. Steam, if inhaled in any quantity, is a lethal gas. Even when seemingly cool, it can still retain enough heat to sear nasal passages and do incalculable damage to the lungs. From the point of view of safety, as well as efficient fireroom operation, it was important to cut down on serious steam leaks.

All this time, as previously noted, *Memphis* was pounding in the seaway on the end of her anchor chain, rolling through an arc of more than 90 degrees, striking bottom with great, rending crashes about the midpoint of each roll. Her rugged structure was in constant motion, each part relative to all the other parts, either from sympathetic vibration or from the progressive battering of her keel and bottom plating against the rock foundation under the ancient ooze on the harbor floor. There was almost continuous groaning from twisted steel girders, but far louder were the successive, unmuffled reverberations as the 500-foot armored steel hull was, blow by blow, beaten in from beneath. Willey and Lieutenant Jones felt the floor plates of their firerooms being lifted by increasingly violent blows from the ocean floor, saw their boilers shift in position as their foundations were driven in, and recognized the significance of the abrupt changes in motion. The realization that they had lost their battle to save their ship grew more and more prominent in their minds.

At about 4:45 great clouds of steam burst into fireroom number seven. From their origin, it was evident that a steam connection high up over boiler fifteen had given way. Luckily, the pressure was so low that the boiler itself did not burst and the opening was small enough so that the compartment did not at once fill with the deadly white vapor. But to stop the entry of steam immediately was vital to the continued operation of boiler number thirteen, and the compartment would have to be abandoned soon if the leak could not be eliminated. Quinn and Porter did not hesitate, asked for no orders or instructions. They had hardly reached the fireroom floor plates from their first trip into the hot, black upper reaches of the boiler uptakes when they began the climb once again, this time accompanied by Firemen Copius and Farrell, the heads of all four swathed in their own dampened shirts or jackets, their gloved hands carrying tools.

The ladders they mounted were made of steel and were both narrow and absolutely vertical. The thin steel rungs, hot with the heat of fire and stagnant air, pressed painfully through the soles of their sodden shoes and into the flesh of their hands.

Their bodies lurched heavily from port to starboard as *Memphis* rolled, and since the motion of their environment in relation to the force of gravity was invisible, their progress might have been likened to some grotesque monkey dance in a primeval jungle rhythm. The cavernous darkness was lighted at either end by a pair of dim electric lights, now burning more dimly than usual. Surrounding them was a gigantic jumble of large pipes, some of them covered with dirty, coal-dust-and-soot-covered, once-white plaster-impregnated canvas insulation, hot to the touch because of the raw steam carried inside—and the others bare, dark, dusty metal which could burn the skin with the heat of the combustion products they contained. Gauges and instruments were sparse, having been concentrated in the working area below, but there were numbers of valves, jointures, test fittings, and expansion joints which, with their hangers and the shadows cast in the fog of steam by the uncertain light, gave indeed the effect of a hot, stinking, dirty jungle in an area of maximum humidity.

To the four men painfully crawling up the ladders it was an unfamiliar jungle, for though they had each many times before climbed into it, both while under way with the fireroom under steam and during other times when the temperature was more normal, it had at those times been quiescent even though there might have been considerable motion on the ship. But now it was almost alive with ominous, portentous movement in the continual, wracking displacement of parts relative to one another. Additionally, the ship was rolling much more severely now than ever before, and the visibility was poorer, both from the vapor and from the swathings they had placed about their heads. As the force of gravity pulled them first one way and then the other in unrhythmic and unpredictable lunges, with the danger ever present of stumbling against burning hot steel or into the path of the steam leak they had come to stop, they finally reached the highest walkway gratings in the fireroom, those located about the main steam valves and the boiler safety valves—their objectives.

"Cope," said Porter, after a moments' hasty evaluation, "you and Farrell get number fifteen boiler stop valves. Be sure you get them shut tight, now!" His hoarse, shouted words came through his shirt too muffled to be clearly heard by the others, and realizing this, he lifted the shirt away from his mouth.

"Copius, you and Farrell shut the the boiler steam stops. Quinn and I will stand by the safety valves, and as soon as you get the stop valves shut, you let us know, and then get out of here and get below. Be sure you get them tight shut, now! We don't want any more steam backing up into this here boiler from the main line!"

Porter shouted the instructions as loudly as he could, then placed the wet shirt again around the lower part of his face. The purpose behind not opening the safety valves before cutting out the boiler was to protect the main-line steam, which otherwise would flow backward into the boiler and thence be wasted through the safety valves as well as continuing to issue forth into the fireroom through the break in the connection to boiler fifteen. The two firemen dashed to the stop valve, which was located in the overhead near the center line of the ship, and began to turn its great brass handwheel rapidly with their gloved hands, heedless of the heat which it held and which, under ordinary circumstances, would have dictated the additional protection of several layers of rags. Perhaps thirty seconds of quickly turning the handwheel; then, the valve driven tightly home on its seat, the two men scuttled down the ladder once more.

In the meantime, Porter and Quinn had each fitted a wrench to a nut beneath the springs of the two safety valves with which the boiler was fitted, and as soon as it was apparent that the stop valve was closed, they began to release the tension. Another thirty seconds, as each man hurriedly plied his wrench, were followed by the whistling roar of two safety valves venting into the uptake piping leading into the stack.

Both men were by this time noticing some difficulty in breathing, and both made for the single ladder down as soon as they were certain that the safety valves were locked open and would remain so, that all the pressure in the boiler steam drum would bleed off. They had been gone from the fireroom floor for about five minutes, and their descent was slowed by their apparent lack of wind, the motion of the ship, and the fact that the ladder was not a single straight ladder all the way down but was instead broken by walking levels at two different heights, the center ladder section separated by the length of the intervening platform gratings from the top and bottom sections. As they laboriously climbed down, seemingly taking much longer than they had taken to make the journey upward, the lights became progressively dimmer and then went out. The two water tenders reached the floor plates a moment later, panting heavily. Porter felt as if his vision were closing around him. It was almost impossible to draw a deep-enough breath. He tried to remove the wet shirt from around his head, looked around for Quinn, could not see him, and sagged weakly to the floor. The few inches of water felt cool and refreshing, he thought, and after he had recovered his breath for a moment he would roll over in it and soak all his clothes. . . .

According to Farrell, just after he had returned to the fireroom floor, the lights went out and a moment later a tremendous amount of water came down the stack and entirely drowned the fires in both boilers. Steam and scalding hot water poured out into the compartment. It seemed to him that the front of boiler thirteen became disconnected from the main portion and fell out on to the floor plates.

Willey was at the time in the opposite fireroom on the port side, number eight, and it must have been just about the same instant, seconds after the lights had gone out and he had turned his flashlight on the boiler steam gauges, that both boilers in that fireroom let go, nearly simultaneously. The rupture, so far as Willey could estimate, occurred somewhere inside the fireboxes of both, and was accompanied by a great influx of water down the stack. To this day he recalls thinking how fortunate it was that the pressure was so low, only thirty pounds according to the gauge he had just inspected, for otherwise there would have been a catastrophic explosion.

Like Newton George in the engine room, Willey realized that there was nothing further that could be done in either of these two firerooms, and that attention must now be given to the rescue of personnel. The ship's bottom must by now be smashed in throughout its length, was probably holed in a dozen places. She would soon fill with water, and the water in the two after firerooms was already ankle deep over the floor plates. He felt, however, that he could not give the order to abandon the compartments until the Chief Engineer had approved. Lieutenant Jones had been present a few seconds before and had commented that the ship appeared helpless and that it might soon be necessary to abandon the firerooms. No doubt he could be depended on to give the necessary instructions, if, in his best judgment, this was indeed the proper thing to do.

Thinking that there might be some men still in the coal bunkers who might fail to get the word, and since in any event there was no point in passing out any more coal for either of the two after firerooms, Willey started for the nearest bunker. He had hardly got inside of the door when he felt a tremendous shock, the heaviest shock yet, as the ship struck bottom, careened far over to port, rolled back nearly to an even keel and stayed there. Her violent rolling motion suddenly stopped, and there was a great grinding of mangled steel plates on the rocks beneath, and a renewed roar of escaping steam. He waited no longer. "Get out, men!" shouted Willey. "Get out!"

In the adjoining fireroom, Farrell was troubled with no such sense of responsibility for command or protocol. When the great jolt came to the ship and boiler thirteen blew out its face, he instinctively yelled, "Head for the ash hoist!"

The ash hoist and ventilator shaft, with which each fireroom was equipped, were one and the same, a narrow trunk leading vertically upward through all the intervening decks and terminating in the rotatable rabbit-ear ventilators which were so prominent on the boat deck. At the base of the ventilator as it reached above the boat deck, and at a convenient height, a door was cut in the metal for access to the trunk. A pad-eye was attached in the top inner surface of the rabbit ear at the exact center of the trunk to facilitate attachment of a pulley or hoisting block, and the trunk was most frequently used to hoist ashes when fireboxes were being cleaned, hence its name. A narrow steel ladder was also built into the side of the shaft, and it was for this ladder that Farrell ran. He, too, could hardly breathe and felt pain and swelling in his throat. His feet and hands were burned, severely as it later turned out, but the continual drenchings of water coming down the shaft temporarily cooled his burning skin and he was able to climb to the top and out the hatch onto the boat deck. There a wave struck him and knocked him unconscious under a section of the superstructure, where some moments later he came to.

Willey in the meantime had dashed from fireroom eight across the ship—leaving the watertight door open this time—to fireroom seven. He had already inhaled smoke and steam, was beginning to feel the effect, and realized that he could not much longer continue. His conscious thought was to see if Lieutenant Jones was there, and if so to counsel with him. If not, he would make a quick estimate of the prospect of there being anything further his men could do and the dangers to which they might be exposed, and would then take upon himself the responsibility of ordering that compartment also abandoned. The situation in fireroom seven was little different from that in fireroom eight. The men were already starting to climb up the ventilator trunk and had lined up before the ladder leading into it. There was nothing more Willey could do.

He wrapped his dungaree jumper around his head, lay down in the water covering the floor plates and rolled back and forth several times to saturate his clothing with the dusty mixture. He felt the body of someone else lying on the floor plates, but already on the way to losing consciousness, he had no clear recollection of this, nor of whom it might have been. Years previously, however, he had decided what he should do if ever confronted by this or a similar situation. First, he must see to the safety of his men. Like the captain of a sinking ship, he must be the last one out. There would be men in the upper levels as well as on the fireroom floor plates, and once safe evacuation of those below was under way, he must search there also. Moving by instinct born of long planning in advance, Willey groped his way to the ladder leading to the upper walking level in the after firerooms, climbed to the top, felt for and found the dogs of the door leading to the firemen's washroom above fireroom number eight. There were other men present, fumbling for the door, apparently bewildered in the smoke, steam, and heat. Willey heaved up the dogs, wrenched open the door, clutched at the men, and pushed them before him into the washroom. Then he stumbled through himself and lost consciousness.

One result of the failure of the lights and the clouds of smoke and steam in the firerooms was that men only a foot or more apart had no contact with each other, no awareness of the others' presence, unless actually touching. Willey lost contact with Lieutenant Jones when the latter made his final trip to the engine rooms, and when Jones came back, he and Willey might have been in opposite ends of the ship, so far as regaining communications was concerned. It happened that Jones walked into fireroom seven a moment after number thirteen boiler suffered its mercifully low-powered explosion. The space was filled with smoke and warm, wet steam. Visibility was nil, but he was aware of the presence of a number of the fireroom crew evacuating via the ventilator shaft as rapidly as they could.

Intermittent gulches of water were still coming down the shaft, as they had been for the past half hour, but their power seemed lessened, or maybe it was that there was a lesser quantity of water, now that *Memphis'* wildest rolling had somewhat subsided. In any event, Jones received the instantaneous impression that the water coming down through the shaft was probably beneficial in that it swept it free of steam and thus protected the men on the ladder inside. He had not heard Farrell's startled shout, but with the abandonment of the compartment he completely concurred. There was no need to give further orders.

Like Willey, Jones's immediate thought was for the men in the other firerooms. He felt his way to the door to number eight, found it ajar and, not realizing that it had just been left so by Willey, stepped through. Fireroom number eight was in the same condition as number seven: a hot, steam-and-smoke-filled space in which total visibility was not over six inches. Dimly, mainly because of the heat emanating from them, he was aware of open furnace doors to the fireboxes on either side of him, and the smoking half-burned coal inside. No one was present, but again, as in the case of the other fireroom, he had the impression that there had been a recent and hasty exodus.

Holding his arm in front of his nose and mouth, breathing through the fabric of his jacket sleeve, Jones stooped through the watertight door again into number seven, this time shutting the door to number eight behind him. He turned sharply left along the now-buckled amidships bulkhead and dashed to the door leading to number five fireroom, the next one forward. The electrically operated "guillotine" door was closed, but a few quick turns on the emergency hand mechanism lifted it clear and he jackknifed through. A quick check of fireroom five and a look through the door into number six assured him that both compartments were essentially dry and that no one was in either of them. The next two compartments, firerooms three and four, were likewise abandoned, and flooding slowly. Quickly, because of a feeling of faintness which was beginning to come over him, Jones moved to the portcullis door at the end of a narrow passageway between boiler number five and the amidships bulkhead separating the pair of firerooms. He seized the hand gear and began to open the door into number one fireroom.

The story of fireroom one was less dramatic than that of the two after ones, primarily because its boilers were already steaming and there was no struggle to fire them up.

Fireman W. J. Knokey, in the oncoming duty section, had reported to fireroom number one a few minutes before 3:45 to go on the four-to-six watch. Shortly after he arrived the word was passed to man emergency stations for getting under way, and Knokey helped carry fire in a shovel from his boilers to the two aftermost firerooms. The men in boiler room number one worked furiously to build up the maximum possible amount of steam in order to make up the deficiencies existing in the cold boilers, and the sense of urgency grew as the *Memphis'* motion increased and the noises and other signs of disaster became more evident. At about 4:55 the ship suddenly stopped her heavy rolling, and by this time the men in fireroom number one had completely lost touch with everyone else in the ship. They had no electricity, no lights, except from their own boiler fires now suffering also from continual dampening by water down the stack, and it was as though they were dumping all their steam into the open atmosphere, for despite their efforts there was no steam pressure. Nobody had thought to bring a flashlight. To check the water level in the boiler it was necessary to get fire on a shovel, lift it up some twelve feet to the walking gratings on the level above, and hold the fire near the sight glass. The main feed pumps in the engine room were no longer supplying water for the boiler, and Water Tender Kenney directed Knokey to start up a standby feed pump.

Before starting the pump in number one fireroom, it was necessary to cross over into fireroom number two to line up the proper valves. Everything was in total darkness there. No one was present in the compartment, and it was in water up to Knokey's knees. Nervously feeling around with his feet, he came upon the outline of a slimy, cold, pinnacle, a sharp rock which had pierced the bottom of the ship, displaced the floor plates and projected itself into the fireroom. Knokey could feel the cold current of water rapidly entering through the hole.

He ran back into number one boiler room, dogging the door to number two tightly behind him, and realized that water was already above his ankles in this compartment as well.

Under the leadership of Kenney the men linked hands, took a muster by calling their names, and felt around in the blackness for the ladder in the ventilation shaft. Water was up to Kenney's waist by the time the last man preceded him on the ladder, and the fires under the boilers had gone out in great hissing and steaming and the belching of white vapor up the stack. There was no boiler explosion, because there was no steam pressure left.

Number one was an abandoned and flooded compartment when Lieutenant Jones lifted the portcullis door from number three fireroom and let loose a miniature waterfall over the sill against his thighs. Nonetheless he entered, inspected hastily, and then attempted to open the door to number two, on the port side, for a similar inspection. This door, hinged on the other side of the bulkhead, would not open. Jones struggled against it in vain, rapidly growing shorter of breath, unable, in his debilitated condition, to appreciate that the pressure of the water on the other side must be holding it closed.

Finally understanding that it would be impossible to enter the last fireroom, and that, in any event, everyone had departed who was able to, the Chief Engineer wearily began to climb the ladder leading to the berth deck, some thirty feet above. He panted heavily from the climb, rather more than usual, he thought uneasily, and he had no recollection whatever of passing up through the berth-deck hatch and falling flat on his face on the wet, slick, linoleum-covered deck above.

Chapter 11

Chief Machinist Mate George W. Rudd, standing in the center of the port engine room near the port-engine throttleman, had, like everyone, become increasingly aware of the precarious position of the ship. He, too, was conscious of the rapidity with which her motion had increased from normal rolling to the cataclysmic gyrations now taking place. Both engines had long since been made ready. The cylinders were warmed up, steam was on the jackets, all labyrinth packing had been inspected and was holding normally, the oil sumps had been checked, and the engines themselves were being jacked over slowly to insure that everything remained in full readiness. After this he was helpless to add to or detract from the march of events, and as he and the other engine-room personnel awaited the vital steam, he, like all the others, became aware of new cadences in the motion of the ship. In addition to the rolling and the jerking there was a feeling of suddenly dropping, as though *Memphis* had fallen several feet, and then there would be periods of momentary lapses in the rolling during which an ominous stillness, a surcease from the lashing of the sea, was evident. Occasionally there would be a buoyant feel to the ship—the floor plates pressing more firmly against the bottoms of his feet—but these periods seemed to be shorter in extent, less frequent in occurrence, and generally less than their opposite, the lurching descents.

About this time, as in the starboard engine room, great volumes of water began to issue from the ventilating trunk at the after extremity of the compartment.

The large, solid stream pouring into the engine room told Rudd—as it did George—that water was coming up on the quarter-deck to a depth of at least three or four feet, since a lesser depth than this would not reach the ventilating opening. The ship must be half under water, thought Rudd as he wiped the warm but cooling salt spray from his face. The explanation of the falling or sinking sensation he had experienced earlier was now apparent. The sea must be huge. The ship must be in the trough. Seas were sweeping her deck, the added weight of the water itself pushing her deeper, until she managed to free herself of it.

A few minutes before 4:30, great downpours of water began to come through the imperfectly tight engine-room ventilating hatches in the overhead, more than four decks above him. These hatches, located in the boat deck and themselves protected by a coaming eighteen inches in height, were some fifteen feet above the ship's main deck. Everything in the engine room was instantly soaked by the spray thrown up from the sixty-foot drop to the engine-room bilges.

Rudd's action was automatic. It was obvious the ship could not long stand to receive water in the quantities the engine room was now getting. Continued, they would in a relatively short time fill the engine rooms, but most immediately vulnerable were the main-engine crankcases. Though largely enclosed, these had to have openings in the top through which the connecting rods could operate the engine's heavy cranks. At all costs, water must be kept out of the crankcases.

He directed one of his men to start the fire and bilge pumps and to keep them pumping so long as there was water in the bilges, or water continued to come through the ventilation line or open hatches on the boat deck. There was a psychological relief in giving the order. It was at least something he could do. Unfortunately, the pumps were run by steam.

It must have been about this time that another effect intruded itself into Rudd's consciousness. The motion of the ship until now had been entirely a matter of heavy rolling with occasional jerks at her anchor chain, but now, more or less coincident with the great influx of water through the ventilating hatches on the boat deck, there was a bump which Rudd instantly recognized for what it was, although he had never experienced it before.

Memphis was hitting bottom. From here on she continued to hit bottom in staccato punctuation of her great heaving desperate rolls, and Rudd, like George and the other engineers, soon became concerned at the danger of being struck by displaced equipment flying about the engine rooms. All loose items had long since been placed down low where they could not create any hazard in moving about, but now even such items as a strongly secured locker became a matter of concern. Heavily loaded with tools and spare parts, such a locker might easily tear loose from its fastenings, or alternatively burst open under the accumulated momentum of its heavy contents, in either case spewing them forth all over the engine room and seriously endangering anyone who happened to be standing in the wrong place at the right time.

For a moment Rudd entertained the thought of taking a piece of line and securing more tightly any items which seemed to be in danger of becoming loose, but this was quickly forgotten in the shape of a new danger which caused him to look into the overhead apprehensively. There, symmetrically arranged in sockets beneath the engine-room hatches in the boat deck, as well as elsewhere in less visible locations, were the battle bars. As Rudd watched with concern, several of them lifted part way out of their places and then fell back. If the heavy rolling continued, it would only be a matter of time, he realized, until one of these came out completely and fell through into the engine room.

The ship was rolling between 50 and 60 degrees on a side, interspersed with resounding thumps on the bottom of the bay when, at last, Rudd heard Machinist George shout, "Stand by to answer bells!" The ninety pounds of steam pressure then registered on his steam-pressure gauge gave him concern, but he fully realized from the violent motion that an emergency existed and emergency measures were required. Doubtless there would soon be more steam.

The time was 4:35, and Rudd was standing alongside the throttleman when he received the first signal on the engine-room telegraph from the bridge, "Port Engine Ahead Full Speed."

Grasping the engine-room answering telegraph handle, Rudd swung it likewise to the Full Speed Ahead position, thus communicating to the bridge that the bridge's signal had been received and understood. At the same time, the throttleman threw the engine-operating valve-reversing gear into the ahead position, and slowly opened the large valve wheel which controlled the main throttle valve and admitted steam into the engine cylinders.

"Watch yourself," said Rudd. "We don't have much steam pressure!" The throttleman, Raymond Pennell by name, nodded, continued slowly and carefully opening the throttle valve. The black needle in the steam-pressure gauge indicating the actual pressure in the steam line was already far below the fixed red needle which stood at the normal pressure of two hundred and fifty pounds. It commenced to drop rapidly, even before the engine began to turn. Pennell continued slowly to turn the valve, all the time watching the steam gauge, and finally the engine responded with a slow, rhythmic movement of the connecting rods, slowly increasing in speed.

At 4:35, or a few seconds after, Rudd heard George shout through the open door from the starboard engine room, "Hold her under thirty turns."

"Thirty turns," said Rudd to Pennell. Pennell, also having heard the order, nodded.

"Thirty turns, aye, aye," he said. Slowly the engine speeded up until it seemed to be turning about one revolution every two seconds. There being no tachometer, it was customary to make an initial rough estimate of engine rpm by the steam pressure admitted to the high-pressure cylinder. This, however, was only useful under conditions of full steam pressure in the steam lines. With greatly reduced pressure, there was no way of estimating in advance how many revolutions the engine would make. Opening his throttle to what he judged to be about the right setting,

Pennell began to count the plunges of the nearest connecting rod—that of the after low-pressure cylinder. Each plunge of the connecting rod indicated one revolution of the crankshaft. As he did this, he frequently glanced at the clock attached to the bulkhead, and getting his finger in rhythm with the plunges of the connecting rod, counted for precisely one minute.

Rudd also had been counting with his finger and watching the clock. As Pennell adjusted the main throttle, Rudd asked, "What did you make her?"

"Twenty-eight."

"I got the same. Don't go over thirty."

Approximately a minute passed. The engine-room telegraph rang again and the annunciator pointer switched from nearly the full right quadrant position to the full left—from "Ahead Full" to "Astern Full." This time it was Pennell who grasped the engine-room annunciator handle and answered the signal. Then he stepped quickly to the operating valve-control gear, released its spring-loaded ratchet, swung the reversing link to neutral. The engine stopped immediately. As soon as it was stopped, Pennell swung the gear into the reverse position and the engine started up once more, now turning in the opposite direction.

Rudd nodded approvingly. It was customary to reverse the direction of the engine by first closing the throttle, and then after it had come to a complete stop, shifting the reversing gear lever. This reduced torques and other stresses upon the engine and was considered good engineering practice. With the engine turning at only 30 rpm, however, and under the conditions then existing, Pennell was fully justified in dispensing with the intermediate step. Holding the reversing gear lever in the neutral position long enough to permit the engine to come to a stop before throwing it the rest of the way into reverse showed his respect for the engineering equipment in his charge, and cost only a second or two.

Rudd continued to cast anxious glances at the steam gauge, hoping to be rewarded by the beginning of a gradual increase in pressure which might later result in his being able to increase the number of turns made each minute by his engine. Theoretically, 30 rpm should drive the ship about 6 knots in calm water, but the waters in which *Memphis* was laboring at the moment were

anything but calm, and the propellers had as yet been turning
for too short a time to have been able to impart any momentum
to the ship. It was evident that the Captain's first move in going
ahead on the port engine and backing on the starboard was to
attempt to twist the ship in order to head her around to the
right. Although Rudd had spent most of the day below deck in
the engine rooms, he surmised that the open sea lay in this direction. Now, however, with both engines backing, it must be that
the Captain's intentions were to back clear. It would take some
time, Rudd knew, before the slowly backing propellers would
have any effect. In the meantime there were the violent rollings
of the ship, the thumping smash every time she struck bottom,
the clanging jerk on her anchor chain, now less evident because
of the greater prominence of other effects, and the deluges of
water that came below decks when a sea came aboard.

Rudd tried to station himself where he could remain constantly aware of everything happening in his engine room and in
the controlling engine room. He thus knew of Chief Machinist
George's conversations with the bridge relative to the number of
engines that should be used, and was standing but a few feet
away when George dashed into the port engine room, grasped
the port engine-room telegraph and swung it to "Stop." "Stop
the engine!" shouted George. Then, seeing Rudd, he explained,
"We don't have enough steam for both engines. We're answering
bells on the starboard engine. Bridge has the word."

Pennell was already shutting the throttle. Rudd took two
quick steps to the valve gear-reversing lever, swung it to neutral.
The engine quickly slowed to a stop, describing approximately
three-quarters of one complete revolution before it finally came
to rest.

The time was now about 4:42, and at the moment there was
nothing to do in the port engine room except keep the water
pumped down and remain ready to answer any further orders
from the bridge. The rolling of the ship, had, if anything, become worse and *Memphis* was striking on the bottom along her
entire length with great rending crashes. The ship's bilges must
have been bulged up, Rudd noticed, because the walkway alongside the engine which had been flat and regular was no longer so.
Evidently the supporting girders beneath had been displaced.

After one particularly heavy thump which was brought up with a jarring shock, the tall, steel bulkhead between the two engine rooms suddenly showed a crimp nearly the length of the two big compartments: the ship's keel had been beaten in.

Another sound seized Rudd's attention. One of the battle bars had become displaced from its position thirty feet above and came hurtling down between the engine and the centerline bulkhead, missing everything except a cleaning-gear locker, which it struck squarely. The heavy bar smashed in the top of the locker, ripped it from its fastenings and knocked it into the bilges alongside the engine crankcase, where it lay on its side, doors open, completely submerged by the wash of the water in the bilges when the ship rolled to starboard, partially exposed when she rolled the other way.

There would be more battle bars to come, thought Rudd, the first one in effect having left a hole through which it would be easier for others to follow.

There came another particularly sharp thud. Rudd saw the smashed locker move as the bilge plates beneath it were driven upward, and the walkway in the immediate vicinity suddenly heaved six inches higher than it had been. "Stand clear of those battle bars!" he shouted—an unnecessary precaution; everyone in the engine room was aware of the menace of those loose bars in the overhead.

Less water was now coming through the engine-room hatches on the boat deck; someone had finally got to them and covered them with a tarpaulin. They had evidently become distorted during years of service and were leaking badly. By consequence of the elimination of one of its primary sources, the ports in these hatches, there was now not so much light in the engine room as there had been, what there was being supplied by electric-light bulbs strategically located. Peering upward, however, Rudd thought he could still distinguish the outlines of the bars, and if so, it was evident that they had become badly disarranged. One of the last bumps must have knocked several of them loose, and they were lying across the others. Gripping the hand rail in the after part of the engine room, Rudd felt the ship begin one of her sweeping, careening lurches to starboard, her entire 18,000 tons whipping into a deep chasm in the sea. He could only judge how far over she had gone, possibly 50 or 60 degrees. She struck bottom again with a reverberating crash. Two of the battle bars hung poised under the hatches. They would fall in a second. The ship started back, came upright, then swept far over to the port side. His clothing soaked, perspiring heavily, shivering at the same time, Rudd could only hold on and wait.

Both battle bars broke loose and fell into the engine room. One of them struck a glancing blow on the auxiliary steam line in the forward section of the compartment, in the vicinity of the expansion joint. The auxiliary steam line sagged, and steam poured into the engine room. Luckily the break was in such a location that the steam issued in a forward direction, away from the engine control station and away from the locations where Rudd and his crew were standing by.

The cloud of steam filled the forward end of the engine room so rapidly that it was impossible to see exactly what had broken. "Did you see what the break was?" Rudd asked his men anxiously. All shook their heads.

"Auxiliary steam line," said one. "Dunno where."

"Where" was vitally important. The auxiliary steam line, as its name implies, is a steam line of small diameter intended for the operation of various auxiliaries in the engineering spaces it serves. It gets its steam from the main line through a reducing valve and a stop valve. If the break were on the downstream side of the stop valve—or the reducing valve for that matter—it might be possible to close one or the other and thus preserve the integrity of the main steam line. On the other hand, if the break were on the upstream side of these valves, the only way to prevent loss of main-line pressure, as well as to avoid filling the compartment with lethal gas, would be to close one of the two sets of main steam stop valves, either in the firerooms or on the forward bulkhead of the engine room.

"All you men get in the starboard engine room!" Rudd ordered. He jerked off his drenched dungaree jacket, wrapped it in front of his face, dashed into the billowing clouds of steam. Keeping his eyes covered and closed, exposing them only for quick looks in order to orient himself, proceeding mainly by feel along the now unfamiliar, buckled, constantly shifting walkway, guiding himself with his hands along the vibrating railing, he quickly reached the place of the break. The whistle of the escaping steam, the increased temperature, and his own intimate knowledge of the layout combined to assure him that this was the place.

Carefully he lowered his wrapped-up jumper below eye level. He could feel the heat on his forehead. He opened his eyes. He could barely make out the auxiliary steam line through the fog of vapor. The break was downstream from the auxiliary stop valve, but steam was issuing from the expansion joint in both directions, it having evidently been damaged by the impact of the battle bar. To reach it, even from the most favorable position, below and behind the spout of steam, required that his hands and forearms be perilously close to the break in the line.

Within the sanctuary of his curled-up jacket, Rudd took a deep breath. Then, dropping it, heedless of the searing blasts which struck his forearms and hands, he began to turn the valve. It was stiff, stiffer than normal. The valve-stem too, perhaps, had been distorted by the blow of the battle bar. He tugged at it mightily, broke it free, spun it rapidly to the closed position. It seemed to become more difficult to turn as it became nearly closed, and again Rudd exerted all his strength to jam it home.

The steam jets greatly decreased, but did not entirely stop. Apparently the valve had also suffered damage, could not be entirely closed. It was no longer possible to see the valve wheel which he had begun to turn. His hands and forearms felt completely sensationless. He dropped to his hands and knees, groped about for his jacket, found it, put it to his face and started to crawl back the way he had come along the buckled and constantly moving walkway.

The valve wheel had been extremely hot. Although he had soon ceased to feel it, he was aware that he had been forced to take several breaths in the process of closing it, and that the heat and steam had penetrated deep into his lungs. He knew very well the effects of breathing steam, and could only hope that the precautions he had taken would reduce the injury.

It became increasingly difficult to move and his breath became shorter, but there was one more thing he must do. In a few more feet the walkway upon which he was crawling branched to the right, over to the main condenser. With the port engine secured, it would not be necessary to use the condenser; in fact it could only serve to draw away more of the precious steam needed by the starboard engine. Heedless of the stinging pain in his hands, forearms, and face, to which feeling had begun to return, and only dimly aware of the continued wracking pounding of the ship and the violent gyrations to which it was subject, he laboriously turned right, crawled along the walking platform to the condenser, pulled himself upright and climbed the few short ladder rungs to its top, where were located the 30-inch diameter exhaust steam line and the tremendous valve which closed it. It took nearly a hundred turns of the valve wheel to close this valve, but this was facilitated by a collapsible crank handle inset into the rim. He felt around the rim, found the crank handle, pulled it out against the spring and dropped it into its socket. Then he commenced to turn, jackknifing his entire body with each revolution as he drove the yard-diameter valve wheel around, around, and around.

Several times he had to stop for breath and then, with renewed determination, returned to the seemingly interminable task. When the valve wheel finally would turn no more, he continued to try to turn it for several more seconds, not realizing that it had in fact gone all the way closed. Then finally he let go, slowly and painfully eased himself down the ladder, and collapsed again on the walkway plates below. Water was now sloshing over these plates with every roll of the ship and this revived him. Painfully he continued his crawl aft. The ship's motion seemed to have eased somewhat; she was not rolling so far as before, but he recognized now that she must be aground, for every time she rolled there was a creaking, screeching, and howling of tortured steel plating in the bottom beneath him, and the deck plates of the walkway were constantly moving and flexing, opening and closing the joints between adjacent plates, sometimes springing open with a sharp report as a rivet or bolt snapped under the stresses of the bending ship's structure. Along with the hellish creaking and groaning of machinery, he could hear the thudding of additional battle bars falling into the bilges, as well as other less familiar noises of heavy machinery falling or being displaced.

Now he realized that he was back in the vicinity of the throttle station of the port engine. The place was filled with white vapor, and it was impossible to see. He felt around. There was no one else in the vicinity. He crawled to the watertight door. It had been partially closed, but not dogged. Pushing it open, supporting himself on the dogs, he dragged himself over the coaming and into the starboard engine room.

It was dark. All lights were out. He had not noticed this in the port engine room because of the fog of steam. His eyes could barely make out the familiar shapes about him, but the engine was stopped and there was no one there.

Chapter 12

TOPSIDE--4:35 AND AFTER

For thirty minutes the Captain had stood on the bridge, constantly being reassured by reports from the engine room that all would be in readiness at 4:35. He had contained himself as well as he could in the face of a disastrous situation which was getting worse more rapidly than anyone had ever before experienced. To shoreward the great lines of breakers which had been forming outside of the bar had continued to form—though now more in the shape of big rollers—farther and farther from shore until finally, some fifteen minutes ago, they had completely engulfed the *Castine*. It had been a fantastic experience to stand on the bridge of the *Memphis,* still dry and relatively stable in comparison even though she was now rolling quite heavily, and see the *Castine,* only six hundred yards inshore, fighting to remain afloat in seas that rolled and broke over her, completely submerging her out of sight. The waves pouring over the *Castine* must have been thirty feet in height, he estimated. If the receding breakers reached *Memphis,* they would also swamp her decks and throw her about mightily; but this was not the great danger, for to seaward was also coming a huge, yellow mountain of water at least fifty feet in height. It had been traveling at high speed from over the horizon, and it was now near at hand. The rollers already experienced in the harbor would be as nothing compared to the effects to be looked for when this wave which was rushing from the depths of the sea slowed its advance and combined its forces, climbed the steep bank between the 100-fathom curve and the 10-fathom curve, and threw a billion tons of water into the shallow anchorage.

Memphis was still riding to her starboard anchor with 70 fathoms of chain at the water's edge. Preparations had been made to slip this anchor and preparations had likewise been made to drop the port one. But, assuredly, the chain should not be slipped until the ship's engines could move her. On the other hand, dropping the second anchor would complicate the problem of getting under way. Neither had yet been done while there was hope of getting sufficient steam to run the engines.

Since 4:15, however, the rollers had been coming more rapidly, and they had continuously been increasing in size. At about 4:10, as the lifeboat was on the point of being lowered, the first one pushed across the quarter-deck. *Memphis* with her battleship armor had great weight and great inertia; consequently she could not rise as rapidly as *Castine,* and instead remained, submarine-like, beneath the rapid succession of rollers as they swamped her decks. It was noted that there was no actual movement of water to speak of, although once it came on deck, of course, the water ultimately did move; but there was no great wave crashing on board. There was merely the sudden heaving up of the sea on the starboard side, and the water flowing over her main decks. From 4:15 the forecastle had been flooded, and it was impossible for anyone to live on it. All hands had taken shelter in the casemate under the boat deck, and from that moment it was impossible to drop a second anchor.

Now, at 4:35, the view to seaward was catastrophic. The ship, straining at the tether of her anchor, was rolling and pitching like a wild animal. Successive rollers were inundating both forecastle and quarter-deck; frothing high about the turrets, submerging the bow turret until the great twin long-barreled rifles were out of sight, until only the roof of the turret with its canvas-

covered range-finder was visible; completely submerging the after
turret—guns, range-finder and all. And, most important, the
menace from the depths of the sea—an atavistic, primordial convulsion of nature—was now at hand.

Castine, going astern, passed within 100 yards of *Memphis* as
she clawed her way to safety (some accounts say 50 yards). Her
skipper credited the lee afforded by the larger ship with giving
him just enough control over his own vessel to permit him to win
clear. As Bennett passed his consort, he noted that she, too, had
begun to rear and plunge. As *Castine* passed close under *Memphis'* port quarter, the larger vessel heaved her bow high into the
air, and then the bow descended deeply beneath an enormous
roller. The descent stopped abruptly, however, with her forecastle
far submerged; Bennett and Schuirmann both remarked later
upon this fact. It could only be explained by the bow striking the
floor of the anchorage.

At this moment, *Memphis,* which had rolled deeply to starboard, heeled far to port; and the deep hollow of the trough
between rollers precipitantly appeared close under her starboard
quarter. *Castine* was at the moment just clearing her stern and
descended into the hollow, likewise heeling, but to starboard. Since
Memphis was at the moment far down by the bow and up by the
stern, Commander Bennett had a unique close-range view of the
lower parts of her hull. He saw the three blades of the starboard
propeller completely out of water, and the entire starboard propeller shaft from the strut just forward of the propeller to where
it entered the hull of the cruiser. The propeller was revolving
slowly, he noted, and he marveled at the fact that he was able to
see rudder, starboard propeller, shafting, and a goodly section of
the keel all at the same time.

Then *Memphis'* stern dropped, the quarter-deck submerged,
and so did the after turret. Suddenly she appeared twice as far
away with all her after parts out of sight, and the tall mast at the
very tip of the visible stern made her look peculiarly truncated
and disproportioned. Simultaneously her bow rose, and the
whole broad expanse of her weather decks was exposed to Bennett's view from astern. As with the bow, the downward swoop of
Memphis' stern halted abruptly as she struck bottom once
more.

The timing of these events is not as firmly fixed as one might wish, since most of the participants had no watches on their persons and in any event there had been no foreseen necessity to syncronize timepieces. The fact that *Memphis'* starboard propeller was turning would place the time as 4:35 or later. By Commander Bennett's estimate it was somewhere between 4:30 and 4:45, and by Ensign Rockwell's it was "about fifteen minutes after the *Castine* had got under way," or 4:19. The fact that Bennett's log commented that, after clearing the lee of the *Memphis,* his ship was swept by "a number of the largest seas I have ever witnessed" and "we were set in again by large breaking seas, each one of which would shove the ship in on its crest a number of yards" would indicate that this was the same triple hammer that struck the *Memphis* at about 4:36.

On *Memphis'* topsides, everyone who could do so was watching the *Castine.* Several times she was completely buried by a breaking comber, so that only her masts and tall single smokestack were visible. She rolled violently, except that when the bathtub of her well deck was full of water, she would occasionally lie far over to one side for long moments until, winning free of the depressing weight, she would rebound like the gallant little cork that she was. The most spectacular sight of all was to see her take a big one head on, which she did several times in the near vicinity of the *Memphis.* As one man described it:

She seemed almost to jump out of the water. I could see light under her keel for more than half her length. Then her bow would plunge, exactly like a whaleboat in a surf, and her stern with its two little propellers spinning in the air would kick way up, and her bow and all the rest of her would be under. Twice she lay far over to port, masts and stacks almost flat on the water, and went completely under. None of us expected her to come up again.

Until the day of his death, Father never uttered the slightest criticism of his engineering department, or its actions on that fateful day. He frequently said that *Memphis* was the best-trained ship he had ever served in or had the privilege to command. Nevertheless the son, now writing the account of this event, must ask whether Father may not, once or twice within the secrecy of his own soul, bitterly have wondered why it was never reported that things were getting worse instead of better, that the fires under the four extra boilers, even though determined in advance as the best procedure in the event of bad weather, just were not able to take hold. Had he known this, if he had even as late as 4:15 directed that the two boilers he did have be forced to the utmost and had secured all other unnecessary machinery, it is conceivable that *Memphis* might have been able to get under way at 5 or 6 knots. There was less than a mile to go to the edge of the continental shelf. At 6 knots she could have reached it in ten minutes. The answer, of course, is that all such suppositions are pure hindsight. Everyone below did everything he could do, under the most extraordinary difficulties, in some cases unto death. Father never wavered in this attitude.

On the other hand, the possible need to get under way on minimum notice had been foreseen as much as it was possible to foresee any such cataclysmic occurrence. Had he actually gotten under way on only one-eighth of his boiler power, barring a conclusive report of the inability to raise steam on the others, he would have clearly been guilty of poor judgment. More power than this was essential to move this big ship! Besides, even though hurricanes were known to arise in very short order in the West Indies, and granting that August and September are indeed the hurricane months, under no condition had anyone envisaged a requirement to get under way in less than one hour. Under these circumstances, lighting the boilers which had been prepared for just this purpose was eminently proper. With six boilers going, the big cruiser would have had all her machinery fully capable and would have been fully maneuverable, with adequate steam for any demand.

But not only had they not had an hour to get the ship ready to get under way, she had been beset by heavy rolling almost from the outset. The motion of the ship greatly hindered the operations in the firerooms, and the frequent sprays of water which poured down the stacks constantly dampened the newly laid fires under the four just-lighted boilers. The result was that instead of having two boilers in top shape, making as much steam as they could make, at 4:30 *Memphis* had six boilers in poor shape, though the original two were far better off than the others. It had been necessary to detail firemen to carry some seventy scoop-shovels full of live coals from the two steaming boilers in number one fireroom—dropping in their haste countless bits of fire to form a glowing, red dotted trail—through firerooms three and five into number seven, and about half of them went one compartment further, into fireroom number eight on the port side. The high coamings of three low-overhead electrically operated "guillotine" doors and one ordinary watertight door had to be stepped across with the smoking shovels, the low transoms ducked through, while the direction of gravity shifted back and forth unpredictably through an arc of 90 degrees. After the ship's watertight doors were ordered closed and the electrical mechanism had operated, there was an additional impediment in that it was necessary to open and close each of the electric doors by the slow hand-raising mechanism provided. And all the while, water coming into the fireboxes kept the fires in the after boilers from building up as they normally would, kept depleting the strength of the fires under the forward boilers by creating a continual demand for more live coals, and in the end doused the forward fires also.

Steam pressure at 3:45 had been one hundred and seventy-five pounds per square inch; by 4:30 it had progressively dropped to ninety pounds.

From 4:00 o'clock on, Father several times asked the engine room when the ship would be ready to get under way, and was repeatedly informed that the engines would be ready at 4:35. Not once did engineering pride permit any hint of difficulty to escape from below, least of all any suggestion that the engines might not be ready as stated. All communications were by voice tube, there being no other means, and through this single link no discouraging news was allowed to pass. The unofficial code of the engineers—a holdover from the days of the independent Engineer Corps—forbade that they behave otherwise. It was not for them to bother the bridge with details. They would solve their own problems, down in their black holes below the water line, and they would, if humanly possible, be ready when they had said they would.

Until 4:35 Father had still harbored the vision of turning his big, dependable ship, sturdy engines racing, to face the oncoming wave. With 15 knots available he could steam into the sea and

over it, cutting into it, rising to it, breasting all its fury before
the wave had had a chance to concentrate its power upon his
ship. Now his only hope—a desperate one, but there was nothing
else—was that the boilers might be coming on fast, that they
might, in spite of not being fully ready, still be able to produce
enough steam to keep the engines going at reduced speed and
gradually build up to greater power. Even as Father gave the
order, however, he knew that he had waited too long. The great,
yellow wave was now so close that it would strike before his
ship could move. *Memphis* must withstand its onslaught at her
anchorage. Even then—could he but twist the ship to head more
directly into it, swing a little more to starboard, so that *Memphis'* bow pointed clear of Torrecilla Point—he might take the
sea head on and, as soon as the wave passed, go ahead on both
engines, slip the anchor from inside the chain locker, a move for
which preparation had already been made, and slowly win his way
clear through the inevitable following seas.

Had Father had but a little steam, this last-ditch measure
might have had success. But events quickly proved that even this
was to be denied, for the great wave was close at hand and
coming fast. The telltales on the bridge indicated that both engines had reached 30 r.p.m. in the ordered directions, but there
was little time for them to have any effect.

Suddenly, a deep hollow opened along the starboard side of
the ship, between it and the face of the wave now less than a
hundred yards distant. The oncoming rush of the sea slowed
perceptibly. It reared up in higher majesty, gathering up all the
water between it and the *Memphis,* and began to form its approaching face into the concave shape of a breaker. With a lurch
Memphis sank into the hollow, heeled far over to starboard, and
struck bottom. The steep, concave face of the wave rose nearly
vertically alongside, its crest reaching as high as the bridge, and
then as *Memphis* struggled to right herself in the onrushing
water, the sea flowed over her. There was no time for *Memphis* to
rise to it; she remained where she was while the water level rose,
precipitantly, some fifty feet or more. Father and those on the
bridge with him saw the main deck go under, then the turrets,
and then the boat deck, until only the four stacks, the two boat
cranes, and the two masts—the forward one carrying the bridge

—projected out of the sea. They could feel the surge of the ship returning to even keel and rising beneath them, but the broad flat surface of her decks resisted upward motion. A great turbulence was evident—water went simultaneously to port and starboard as *Memphis'* buoyant hull nevertheless drove upward.

"Thank God for Yancey's life lines!" thought Dad—he used to remember details like this—"and thank God for the fact that all hatches are shut and nearly everyone below!" He was also surprised, and thankful, that except for the surge of water caused by the rising of the hull beneath, there was relatively no motion to the sea other than its extraordinary elevation in level. As he expressed it, "The sea simply toppled aboard."

All hands on the boat deck were clinging desperately to the life lines. Those on the bridge, with less need, held equally strongly to the bridge railings. Lieutenant Withers calmly continued taking bearings of navigational landmarks, contriving to hang on at the same time to the steel pedestal on the port bridge wing upon which the bearing circle was mounted. Charged with knowing at all times the position of the ship, he had completely forgotten his illness, was alert to detect the first sign of a change in the bearings, which would indicate that the ship was dragging anchor.

It was an astonishing sensation, as Father later described it, to be standing on his own familiar bridge, only a few feet above a boiling maelstrom of churning yellow water, very much aware of the full extent of the broad decks of the ship beneath him and yet unable to see any of it! The sharpness of vision sometimes experienced at moments of unusual stress probably contributed to the clarity of his recollection of that suspended moment in time. It could not have lasted for more than a few seconds—perhaps a quarter of a minute—for there was much more to come.

Later descriptions of the tremendous wave which had overtaken the *Memphis* at this climactic moment in her life stressed, on several sides, that the wave was not smooth, or symmetrical, but instead in the form of three gigantic steps, the "risers" almost vertical, each surmounted with a plateaulike "tread," the whole racing shoreward with great speed. Its potential energy must have been enormous.

Memphis had only partially recovered from the first of the colossal watery steps—the top of her fore turret, with the range-finder and its tightly clamped turret captain's hatch, had just surfaced in a cascade of tumultuous water—when a warning shout galvanized everyone into a sudden grab for something solid. The second of the stepped mounds of yellow ocean water was at hand, towering above them. Subsurface water motion caused *Memphis* again to heel swiftly to starboard. Her tall masts swept through the still air and caused the Admiral's absentee pennant at the starboard yardarm and the square blue flag with twin white stars at the mainmast peak to flutter momentarily to port. The two plumes of smoke from her foremost and after-most stacks also streamed sharply to port, and the ship herself revealed her gray port side, framed in tumultuous white foam and yellowish red water. Water drained off rapidly from the sudden slant of her deck, and *Memphis* leaped bodily to the left as her submerged hull suddenly cleared itself of the weight of the sea.

Father's recollection of the next few minutes was as clear as anyone's, but not very clear at that. "In here!" somebody yelled. He felt someone—he never knew who—push him inside the cage of the foremast, that great work of steel lattice, sometimes derisively termed "an inverted wastebasket," which distinguished U. S. capital ships of the day. The bridge had been built around the forward portion of the broad base of the cage and, as a convenience, a section of the central portion of its deck had been extended into the interior. Now this arenalike enclosure, actually part of the navigating bridge, provided a refuge for Father and the men with him up there. The spaces between the interwoven strands of steel rod which formed the structure of the cage mast were large enough for a man to swing himself easily inside, yet they gave almost certain protection against being washed overboard.

It is fairly safe to say that at no time had the designers of the cage mast ever contemplated its possible usefulness in keeping the Captain and other bridge personnel from being washed overboard. Certainly they could not have conceived of such a danger existing forty feet above the sea. And yet this was the case, for the astounded bridge crew saw the yellow mountain of Caribbean water roll smoothly over the ship, over the turrets, over the lower bridge and, reaching high above the stacks, roll entirely over the navigating bridge as well! *Memphis'* bow plunged deeply, she rolled far to port and then to starboard, and then her bow rose valiantly and her stern went under.

All reports later attested to their surprise, likewise, at the temperature of the sea; as it first engulfed them it was colder than the normal temperature for that latitude, but shortly afterward it became noticeably warm, warm enough to become uncomfortable. Indelibly recorded in the memories of all hands also was the unprecedented fact that though it rolled irresistibly over the bridge, the water of this second wave had no driving force or velocity such as they expected. Its weight pressed upon them, holding them down on deck, clutching at their bodies, but it did not tear at them with any force of its own motion.

That the second great roller, like the first, did not sweep the decks in the accustomed manner of a great sea coming aboard a ship was partly due, no doubt, to the fact that *Memphis* was not herself under way; but part of it also stemmed from the nature of the roller, its source, and the phase of growth when it struck them. The navigator had indeed reported that the northern sides, or faces, of both first and second waves were considerably more perpendicular when they reached the ship than they had been only a few seconds earlier, and as they passed it was evident that the slope of the southern or back side of each was much flatter. Lieutenant Withers made note in his report that the three steps came almost one on top of the other, with virtually no trough or hollow between them, and struck the ship a triple blow in quick succession. He commented also that the first and second steps did not behave like breakers in the ordinary sense, but like huge rollers, and that the temperature of the water was peculiarly warm.

The third step or wave was entirely different. It foamed at the top as it suddenly stood beside the ship, rising stark, ever higher, towering above the suddenly tiny armored cruiser, bearing millions of tons of ocher-colored sea-water which had been swept upward from the shallow sea-bottom of the anchorage. Growing ever higher it paused, gathered its waters from ahead, formed a concave, nearly vertical face, consisting of an infinite number of shiny wavering yellow-green ribs, ranked side by side in perfect order. The face of this wave became a wall of solid water which extended for a mile ahead and a mile astern, and curved over at the top. Father's startled imagination later described it as though he were inside the rib-cage of a gigantic, dead, sea beast, lying on its back, its belly ripped open from neck to tail so that he had a quick glimpse of blue sky and a few white clouds between the foaming, closing, putrescent edges of the wound.

For a long second the huge breaker stood thus, at least sixty feet higher than the bridge of the ship. Smooth, clean, semi-translucent, backed by a thousand feet of solid water, its inner surface gave conflicting impressions of permanence and dreadful promise as it shimmered in the late afternoon sun.

Memphis had not had time to right herself, was still heeled far to starboard with bow and stern submerged. Great sheets of water were still cascading from her decks, as the curving, vertical side of the great wave stood upon her main deck, swept high above the people in the cage mast, curled immensely, and broke.

A million tons of seismicly driven sea struck *Memphis'* starboard side, flung her instantly far over to port, buried her deep, and slammed her full length hard against the rocky bottom. Her armored hull rang hollowly from the double blows of sea and stone. The light steel gun-port shutters around the starboard three-inch broadside guns bellied inward. One of them, badly supported by a stripped dogging bolt, was bent inward at the faulty corner. A stream of yellow-green water, two feet in width, burst into the enclosed casemate. Tons of water fell on the boat deck, flooded the ventilators, poured down the single watertight hatch which had been left open amidships for access below.

The port lifeboat, which half an hour previously had been filled with volunteers eager to go to the rescue of their shipmates in the swamped motor launch, filled instantly at its davits. It swung dangerously but, protected by the lee of the superstructure, this lifeboat and two others on the boat deck in the lee of the mainmast remained in place; all other boats, with griping lines parted or their pad-eyes stripped from the gunwales, were instantly swept over the side. All gear lockers, the "spud locker,"

other relatively loose or lightly secured equipment, went overboard also.

Charles Howard, the Warrant Officer's Steward, who had only
a short time ago been on watch in the Warrant Officers' messroom, had made the mistake of coming on deck and seeking
refuge under one of the launches. So had Fireman John J.
Sheehan. As the boat came alive in the onrush of water and tore
loose its fastenings from their cradles, Howard and Sheehan frantically tried to ward off its crushing drive. There was no one to
help. Their travail lasted only an instant. They lost their footing
in the sea which swept the deck, were borne irresistibly by the
sea. With a despairing shout, the two went overboard.

Most of the *Memphis'* crew were below decks and therefore
protected. All men still topside were on the boat deck and, seeing
their danger, had run to the port side. There they huddled in the
lee of whatever solid structure could be found and held desperately to the stack guys and life lines which had been rigged
there.

On the bridge, the sea bent the bridge railing, ripped its
painted canvas sides, even split the awning over it in its descent.
By coincidence the starboard-engine telegraph pedestal was
broken off by the pressure of the railing as it bent with the
pressure of the sea, just as on the bridge of the *Castine,* only a
few minutes earlier. Inside the cage mast, men were swept off
their feet for a second time, hurled against the latticelike sides of
the enclosure or flattened to the deck, pinned there by the pressure of the water for a long, lung-exhausting moment.

The highest man in the ship was Ensign Walker. Having been
relieved as O.O.D., he had contributed what assistance he could
to the preparations on deck and had then climbed to the top of
the port boat crane, some fifty feet above the water line. From
this advantageous perch he several times saw yellowish-green
water pour down the stacks as the ship rolled into the huge seas,
and twice in quick succession he had to wrap both arms around
the crane head, hold his breath, and concentrate on hanging on.
The first time he was badly scared for a moment, but was surprised to discover that except for the weight of the water he had
no difficulty. The second time he had the sensation of being
inside a breaker similar to those he had occasionally sought when

swimming on a beach—only much, much bigger. He was heavily buffeted in his exposed position and it was with some amazement that he recalled that only an hour earlier he had been calmly officiating at the dispatch of a boat to accommodate Commander Bennett of the *Castine*. Now, still wearing his best white service uniform, he was clinging to an exposed, elevated position and half-drowned.

As Walker recollected the scene, there was an appreciable moment when he was completely under water, and a far longer period during which the only portions of *Memphis* visible above the tumultuous uproar of water were the masts, the stacks, and his crane. It was fortunate that he had not chosen the starboard one, he thought. He could see great chunks of foam boiling around the stacks and twin clouds of black smoke, billowing out of numbers one and four, swept by the off-shore breeze, incongruously enough, in the direction whence came the sea—and he observed with concern the sudden cut-off of smoke when the ship rolled deep into an oncoming breaker and the tops of the stacks went under water.

Boiler designers are willing to accept the effects of even a heavy rain impinging on the open stack of a steaming boiler, for no rain can reach the fires against the hot counterflow of escaping gases of combustion. Continual rain could, however, harm non-steaming boilers by causing rust and scale on the tubes. Protection against this is afforded by drawing a canvas cover around the tops of unused stacks. Rain during start-up operations, when stack covers are off and fires weak, is simply ignored, since the wing fires under each boiler are not directly under the stack uptakes and would soon build up adequate updraft against the heaviest downpour. But no designer ever reckoned with the entry of salt sea-water in great volume at the top of a stack seventy feet high! A glimmering of the battle being waged below decks seeped into Walker's consciousness.

The young officer had a magnificent view of the chaos the sea had caused. The crash of the water on deck had smashed boats and equipment into junk and carried the broken parts everywhere. The normally neat and carefully tended deck was a mess of white foam, struggling men, loose boats, and other equipment. Number one motor launch, secured on the starboard side of the boat deck, was carried completely across the deck and over the side to port, taking two men over with it. Walker, high above, and Tom Wallace, doubled over a life line nearby, could only watch them go.

The ship-fitter's and boat-repair shop, a small, steel, slab-sided and flat-roofed building, was located on the boat deck between stacks number two and three, with entry door and portholes on each side. The doors and ports on the port side were closed, while those on the starboard side were open. Lying in chocks just before the open starboard door of the shop lay a whaleboat upon which some repairs had been in progress and the dinghy which had capsized an hour before. Instead of running to the port side of the boat deck with the others, Seaman Walter Henderson dodged around the boats and dived into the boat shop. As he later described his adventure, this move looked like an excellent idea at the time, but he had hardly gained entry when the whaleboat and dinghy were scooped up and smashed into kindling against the steel walls of the little building. Water poured into the room, compressing the air within it, flattening Henderson helplessly against the far side. As the ship rolled to port, a sudden increase in pressure, due as much to the momentum of the water as to the wave height above him, beat heavily upon his eardrums. For minutes, or so it seemed to him, he was held thus. Finally the water pressure eased as *Memphis* rolled back to starboard, and the dazed Henderson opened the port-side door of the little compartment so that, as he phrased it, the next time a wave like this came on board there would at least be somewhere for the water to go.

Lieutenant Withers, who was carefully keeping a check of the ship's position at about 4:20, noted a slight change in the motion of the bow of the cruiser, as she rose and fell in the already mountainous rollers. At 4:30 his observations of navigational marks convinced him that the ship was touching the bottom of the anchorage, and had started to drag her anchor. Both of these deductions were immediately reported. When the great combers came on board, at 4:35, he also had sought refuge in the cage mast and the first observations he was able to make thereafter confirmed that *Memphis* was now a hundred yards or more off her anchorage bearings.

Quartermaster Third Class Vincent Peltier by force of habit had noted the angle of roll as registered by the bridge inclinometer shortly before the wave struck; *Memphis* had been rolling 47 degrees to port and 45 degrees to starboard. When the comber reared up to its full stance and broke, the ship was thrown violently against the bottom of the bay and careened far over on her port side, some said as much as 90 degrees, or actually on her beam ends. Among the men who were washed overboard at this time was Melvin F. Frederick, the Captain's orderly, who had been standing alongside him on the bridge. In describing the incident to me, years after it had occurred, Dad commented several times that it might well have been his orderly (the lad was one of several who stood watches as Admirals' or Captains' orderly) who pushed him inside the cage mast and thereby saved his life. Though such a conclusion would be only conjecture, it is possible that this act of loyal duty cost Frederick his own chance of safety.

As *Memphis* came upright and floated off the bottom, the port engine was still going ahead, though slowly, and the starboard engine telltale showed that it was backing. Immediately evident to Captain and Navigator, however, as it had been a few minutes earlier to Commander Bennett on *Castine*'s bridge, was that the ship's bow had been flung so far to port that the only hope left was to back out.

"Port back full!" ordered the skipper. The port engine telltale showed that it was responding to the command. But no one who was not himself down below in the engineering spaces could possibly appreciate the problems the men of *Memphis'* Black Gang were facing. Out of their deep travail came a single entreaty, articulated in the standard phraseology of the Navy and shipboard communication: "Recommend answer bells on only one engine!"

Of all the personnel on the bridge, the Captain was the only one who fully sensed the real significance of this request, the deep and terrible trouble which could be its only cause. It was the second, and most conclusive, cry of distress from his men below. All his extensive engineering background sympathized with them, understood what the voice at the other end of the voice tube was trying to convey. He well knew that voice. I was that of a trusted subordinate, a professional friend of high esteem. "Very well," said Father. "Which engine do you want?"

"Starboard engine," said the voice tube.

"Port engine, stop!" Father ordered.

But the ship was dragging rapidly toward shore. As described by Lieutenant Withers:

Wave after wave followed at intervals of perhaps thirty to forty seconds. These waves were so large and their faces became so steep that they simply flowed over the ship. They flowed over our bridge many feet deep. They flowed over our stacks and flooded out our fires.

These waves were driven by no wind. They took the shape of breakers as they approached the shallow water, but they had very little driving force. Approaching they appeared irresistible, but if one held his breath, it required but little strength to hold on to the ship. Things around the decks were torn loose by the motion of the ship, especially after she began landing hard, but the waves seemed to have very little smashing power and did but little direct damage.

Father, in describing the situation many years afterward, used these words:

My noble ship had started to swing to starboard, and to starboard was the yellow mountain now filling the entire horizon and close at hand.

It struck the ship on her starboard broadside and it swept the upper decks clean. Boats, chests, awning stanchions, all sorts of tightly secured things were torn away. Light plating on the starboard side was bellied in from bow to stern.

And now—unbelievable as it may seem—the *Memphis* sank to the bottom of the Caribbean Sea. This was completely proved, for an American named Baxter, the general receiver of customs, standing on the bluff near the ship took a series of photographs at this time, and one of these showed only the ends of two masts projecting a few feet above the water. Water poured down the smokestacks and put out the fires in all the furnaces. Steam pressure dropped to fifteen pounds and now the boilers began to explode. Seven men were killed by these explosions. But for the drop in steam pressure from one hundred and seventy-five pounds to fifteen pounds the ship would have been blown to fragments.

Jones would not leave his post until all the firerooms were cleared. I have heard captains praised for being the last to leave a wrecked ship but what about the Chief Engineer who, standing in darkness, scalded by steam with boilers popping about him, is the last to leave his Hell?

As the mountain of water threw the ship on her beam ends, a hail of missiles filled between deck spaces. Mess tables and benches, pianos, practice shells, chests, human bodies hurtled through the air. Several men were killed by these flying objects.

Meanwhile I had jumped, or been thrown, from the bridge to the inside of the framework of the cage mast. The iron work of this mast provided a shelter that saved several lives; but my orderly, who stood beside me when we were overwhelmed, was never seen again. I was lying face down, flattened out with tons of water pressing upon me. But my ship, almost tight, had remaining buoyancy and struggled upwards. Soon we survivors were breathing air instead of water.

I think five following mountains of water struck us. Twice again we went under, but while burying us under water each huge wave picked up the vessel like a chip and hurled it towards the shore. Soon we were grinding on the rocks in shallow water. At 5:05 P.M. we had landed on a clump of rocks in twelve feet of water. There the ship is today, listing slightly to port, on an even keel fore and aft, not more than a hundred feet from the bluff. Much had happened in the preceding thirty minutes. Forty lives had been snuffed out. A great warship had been destroyed, but in her death agonies the noble *Memphis* had saved eight hundred and fifty lives. Sunk repeatedly, she rose repeatedly from the depths of the Caribbean Sea. Knocked over on her port beam, she righted herself. Though her boilers exploded she remained intact and preserved most of the lives in her keeping. With her outer bottom torn open in a hundred places, she still remained buoyant.

And her officers and men were worthy of her and of the Navy and of the country they served. As later investigation proved, while men and heavy objects were being hurled about decks (the distance from side to side was seventy-three feet), while boilers were exploding in the firerooms and with men being injured or killed all about the ship, there was no sign of panic, no demoralization.

Yancey Williams went from deck to deck inspiring officers and men with his own, glad, cheerful courage. Besides the killed, two hundred and four men had been badly injured. It was a badly battered Yancey when I next saw him. No matter how cheerful and courageous a man may be, he is likely to be hurt when catapulted seventy feet across the deck of a ship.

Up on the bridge I could only surmise what was happening below. The men about me were as steady and as quiet as if at church.

But during the wild convulsion we saw one heart-gladdening sight. The gunboat *Castine* was slowly creeping out. I saw her buried a dozen times and thought her sunk, but up she came. All honor to Bennett. By his fine seamanship, his correct judgment, his steady nerve, he saved his ship.

Dad, in his generous praise of the *Castine,* was wrong in one inference: She was not in the worst of the sea upheaval. She had gotten clear just before the great sea wave struck the still immobile *Memphis,* met the sea wave head on and rode through it. Commander Bennett's description of it as "a succession of the biggest seas I have ever seen," coincided with Father's.

At approximately 4:50, as nearly as it could be fixed by the clocks, there was a great gush of yellow smoke and vapor from the *Memphis'* engine-room hatches. Something, evidently a steam line, had carried away. At about the same moment white steam replaced the black smoke issuing from the foremost and aftermost funnels.

Memphis was dragging in a north-northwesterly direction, but at no time did she swing head on to the sea as might have been expected. Her anchor, after an initial massive jerk, slid rapidly along the bottom. No one could have survived on the forecastle long enough to have knocked loose the stopper holding the other anchor. Helplessly, Josh Carver, the ship's First Lieutenant, and his men watched for an opportunity, but the forecastle was practically constantly submerged under many feet of green water. The ship was carried in broadside, crashing onto the bottom, rolling far over from one side to the other and buried by each successive roller, surfacing only momentarily, with great cascades of water pouring fron her decks, only to go under again. Several sources state that she, like *Castine,* rolled her masts and stacks horizontal, and once it was feared that the next sea would roll her completely over, bottom up. But instead she came back, still staunch, righted herself, took the sea on her armored starboard side instead of her smashed and punctured bottom, and her terrible oscillations continued about her normal vertical axis.

Nothing more could be done for the *Memphis.* This was recognized by everyone. The saving of life was paramount from now on. All hands hung on where they were, hoping to save themselves from being thrown about inside the ship, or if on topside, from being flung overboard.

Yancey Williams in his own report made no mention of it, but others saw what happened to him. He was in the forward starboard side of the casemate when one of the deep rolls caught him unawares, smashed him head first into a steel bulkhead and knocked him unconscious. He would have been much more seriously injured had not several men leaped upon him, held him tightly against the wash of water sweeping the deck and with their own bodies protected him from the accompanying cascade of practice shells and other miscellaneous gear rolling and sliding about.

Recognizing that the ship's position was desperate, and knowing that some time previously the port anchor had been readied so that it could be dropped merely by the release of the stopper which gripped the chain, several men were eager to dash out on the forecastle whenever it momentarily appeared above the waves. Sometimes as long as a minute would intervene between inundations, but frequently the time intervals were much shorter; and the waves sometimes buried it as much as fifty feet beneath their crests. All that would have been necessary was a single blow of a sledge hammer to knock off the retaining keeper around the pelican beak of the stopper. Lieutenants Shonerd and Carver, Gunnery Officer and First Lieutenant respectively, were present with the forecastle anchor detail in the port forward section of the casemate, but although they had been directed to do all in their power to release the port anchor, they found themselves, instead, restraining their own men from what they were convinced would have been a suicidal attempt to go on the forecastle. The task was impossible. No one could have lived a minute in the seas coming aboard.

Boatswain Fred Plagemann was officially described as "indefatigable" in his efforts to release the anchor, but there was no opportunity until finally, timing the successive seas and seizing a moment when the deck was temporarily clear of water, Patrick Hayes, affectionately known by his shipmates as "Tubba," dashed out on the port side of the forecastle with a length of line tied around his waist. The ship's windlass and anchor engines were enclosed in a small solid structure known as the "windlass house," and to this Tubba hastily lashed himself. Dropping his sledge hammer in a sheltered angle on the lee side of the windlass house, he had barely finished knotting the line when another wave struck, burying him deeply in the warm water, forcing him to drop everything to hang on against the savage strength of the now sweeping sea. He had, however, given himself enough slack in the line to reach the port chain stopper, and as soon as the wave had roared past, he was once again on his feet, retrieved the hammer and ran the remaining few feet to the chain stopper.

Stopping swiftly, Hayes grabbed the tarred lanyard of the toggle pin which held the keeper in place, snatched the pin clear with a single mighty heave. Straightening up, he swung the sledge in golf-swing style and cleanly knocked the keeper free of the pelican-hook jaws of the stopper. The pelican-shaped jaws opened, instantly their grip on the chain was no more, and Hayes had the satisfaction of seeing the chain begin to run out. Then the next wave came aboard and swept him to the limit of his safety line in a broad arc which finally fetched him hard against one of the forecastle ventilators. He clung desperately to the hand-holds built on either side, as sea followed sea over the deck.

While in this position, he saw one of the forecastle seaman, a young fellow named Henry Mullaney, venture forth from the shelter of the casemate, evidently to come to his assistance.

"Go back, Mullaney!" shouted Hayes. "Go back! I'm all right! You can't make it."

Mullaney said nothing, but neither did he turn back. Seconds later another huge sea roared upon the forecastle, and when Hayes was able again to see above the water, Mullaney was gone. Hayes saw his head outlined for a moment in the tumult overside to port. A few seconds later, as another breaking wave reared alongside before dashing itself upon the ship, Hayes saw him again as the backlash swept him against *Memphis* armored side. He could hear—or imagined he could hear—the crunch of the broken bones.

But Hayes had no time to think of others, for this wave, larger than the rest, almost swept him from the ventilator. Had he not had his safety line to take some of the strain, his hold would have been broken, and he too would have gone overboard.

The effect of Hayes's effort was, however, very little. The anchor took hold, and the windlass brake was operated under Carver's direction from below decks. But *Memphis* by this time was already close inshore and driving closer every moment.

Ordinary Seaman Albert M. Barker had an experience typical of many. He was a "mess cook," that is, he was serving his three months' stint as a galley helper, setting up tables for meals for his division and clearing away afterward. Having finished up the noon-meal clean-up, he and other mess cooks washed some clothes and tied them to a clothesline which had been rigged on the forecastle. He and his mates were still there when word was passed to make preparations for getting under way, and they were promptly commandeered by Boatswain Plagemann to get in the clothesline and help furl the forecastle awning. The ship had already started to roll rather heavily, and Barker recalls standing on the highest wire of the life line around the side, stretching up to the limit of his reach, and undoing the lashings of the awning so that the heavy canvas could be rolled up. As the ship rolled, he and the other lads stood precariously, heels hooked over the life line, one moment in danger of falling on deck to possible injury among the anchor chain, capstan, and other forecastle gear, the next moment standing far out over the sea. "It was hard to hold on with one hand and let go clews with the other," said he, "but somehow or other, due to the effort of all of us, we got the awning rolled up in some fashion. Still no wind, but the swells were really getting large."

After furling the awning, Barker and the other mess cooks were called into the casemate under the boat deck and were there directed to close gun ports on both sides. He recalls helping to close the starboard gun ports, and that the seas were already high enough for water to pour into them before they could be fully closed. He was among those present when, with the rolling of the ship and the wash of water, the ship's piano broke loose and started to roll on its casters about the linoleum-covered deck. Barker found himself right in front of it, attempted to dodge quickly to get out of its way, slipped and fell on the slick linoleum. Ineffectually, he scrambled to get on his feet and at the same time to avoid the careening piano which, almost as though possessed with evil intent, followed him across the deck and through one of the openings between the stacks.

The ship's lurch was so heavy, the linoleum so slippery, that Barker was unable to regain his footing and skidded helplessly under a three-inch gun, striking and breaking his jaw on the metal as he did so. But the gun protected him from the careening piano, which a second later smashed into it, splintering wood in all directions. Then the ship began to roll the other way and the piano took off in another frantic gyration. Barker, semi-conscious, was also picked up by the reversed flow of water and washed halfway across the deck until he collided with a stanchion, which he still retained wit enough to grab.

A little later, someone—he never knew who it was—picked him up, swung him across his back, and carried him up to the lower bridge, where injured men were being collected and cared for.

C. R. Pinkerton, also an ordinary seaman, recalls that he was chipping paint on a searchlight platform on the mainmast and that as 4:00 approached, it became quitting time. He descended to the boat deck just as things began to happen.

Looking out to seaward he described the horizon as appearing like a low, long mountain.

I did not notice any motion at this time. It appeared to be a large amount of water suspended—our stacks began to belch smoke and the word was that instead of hoisting anchor they would slip a shackle on the anchor chain as we got underway. In due time I heard signals in the engineroom (my part of the ship was the boat deck) but instead of getting underway there was a large amount of steam gushing up through the escape hatches. In a few minutes there were mountains of water cascading down on us from the seaward side and you had to have a good hold on something substantial or be swept overboard. There was no panic, but lots of activity.

Many of us shed all our clothing and shoes except our skivvies and donned lifebelts. In shedding my trousers I forgot to remove my money so it was gone forever, but I learned a lesson. Thereafter every liberty party that I made I would manage to spend every cent before returning to the ship.

There was a small dog on board ship which if he was left on his own would surely be washed overboard. There was a hawser coiled and secured in an area expressly made for it with a heavy tarpaulin protecting it. I placed this little dog in the center of the coil hoping he would stay put.

The *Castine* had cleared out and we were slowly but surely being driven into the rocks broadside. Some of the firemen had managed to reach the topside. Some of them appeared to be in shock with the skin of their forearms and hands hanging very much as if they had full-length gloves pulled off inside out and still hanging at the fingers.

The ship's barber shop consisted of an area blocked off with a brass rail, midships on the main deck in the air castle. It held only a couple of gear lockers and three installed leather-upholstered barber chairs. The ship's barber, Alvion P. Mosier, was a man of small stature and combative disposition, who had never been known to admit that anything was too big for him to tackle. It was noted, however, that he invariably sought for his assistant a large, well-set-up individual, well suited to the task of lashing up or moving his heavy barber chairs for drill or heavy weather. Additionally, it might be opined, he chose with an eye to heavy weather of another kind, as might come his way ashore. Mosier's present assistant was Tom Wallace, today a rather unwilling one, since he had wanted to go ashore at 1:00 with the baseball and recreation party. There were, however, several members of the liberty party waiting for haircuts or shaves; so Mosier slyly asked Wallace to wait for the next boat, well knowing, as he later recounted it, that there would be no further shore-leave boats that day. Unsuspecting, Tom Wallace fell into the trap. When he discovered that he had been tricked, he called Mosier "all the names a Mississippi rebel could think of," but not long after was forced to admit that he was relieved not to have been in that particular recreation party.

Wallace states that when the ship began to roll heavily, he went topside to the boat deck and stood by the railing to watch the liberty boat returning. He was looking at it when it was swamped.

It rode the first wave, but failed to ride the second. After the wave I could only see the heads above the water. The next wave wrapped them up and I never saw them again. At that time the executive officer came running down the deck hollering, "Man the lifeboat!"—I was in the bow with my oar. By that time the boat crew was all ready and they were lowering the boat away. Before the boat touched the water Captain Beach hollered through a megaphone, "Do not lower that boat!"

The boat was secured again, and the boat's crew piled out. There being nothing further he could do topside, Wallace after a few minutes went below to see how the barber shop was getting along. There he found Mosier cursing him for being absent, busily lashing up his shop and at the same time trying to protect the chairs and himself from the loose drill shells, mess benches, and the piano which were already rolling or skidding around on deck as the ship rolled. As Wallace put it, "Everything that was loose was going from side to side."

Wallace's account continued:

"I was attracted by someone crying and I heard someone call the name, Mother. I turned and saw two men bringing an old, grey headed water tender up from the fireroom. He was scalded to death by steam by the main steamline pipe which had blown out. At the same time the lights went all went out and it was dark. When I took hold of the water tender's arm to help take him topside, the flesh all peeled off his arm. His tongue and eyeballs were white as cotton. I got him on my back and the other two men pushed us up the ladder to the topside. Then the ship submerged. I grabbed the railing around the top hatch and held on. But when the ship surfaced the water tender was gone. I never saw him again.

While I was hanging on to the rail around the hatch, number one sailing launch broke loose on the starboard side and came drifting across the deck. Two sailors were trying to hold it to keep it from going over the side. They were hollering for me to help them.

Gasping for breath, unnerved by having had an unconscious man torn from his arms and washed overboard, pinioned to his rail by the rush of water and shaken by the disaster he could see happening, Wallace could not move to render assistance. "I hung on to my rail," he wrote. "The two sailors went overboard with the boat."

Many acts of heroism survived in the memories of the *Mem-*

phis crew. Lieutenant Shea, whom Father had relieved of duty and confined to his room for twenty days for having remained overlong on shore following a party, disregarded his disciplinary restriction when the emergency burst upon the *Memphis* and reported to his regular duty station. There and elsewhere he was indefatigable in his efforts for those members of the ship's company who needed help. According to Wallace, when Shea arrived topside looking for a life preserver, there was none to be had. A young recruit, recently enlisted in the service, took off his life jacket and said, "Here, sir, take mine." Shea's response will always burn in the assistant barber's mind as it no doubt did in that of the man addressed: "No, sailor, I will not take your life jacket!"

Sam Worth and another young third-class electrician's mate by the name of Henry Kempka maintained a small repair shop in one of the firerooms where they were in charge of lights, forced-draft blowers, the fireroom clocks used for synchronizing the firing of boilers, and other electrical equipment in the engineering spaces. Worth was below decks when the ship began to roll heavily, and being off watch and of an inquisitive nature, he made his way topside to see what was going on. If the ship was getting under way, as he later said, he wanted a last look at the Island of Santo Domingo where, even if he appreciated little of what it was all about, he knew he had somehow participated in the making of history. Like many of the ship's company he wound up on the boat deck.

The big rollers hit the *Memphis* broadside, and the heavy seas came over the main deck and gun decks and high over the superstructure. By this time there was a lot of activity taking place aboard ship. I could not get back to my fireroom workshop nor to my general quarters station. I cannot remember all of the facts but I do remember a word was passed that Red Rudd, the chief machinist's mate, was in trouble and badly burnt and needed help. I helped to get him onto the quarterdeck and there was an urgent call to get a hammock to roll him in.

Each successive wave hurled the ship nearer to shore, depositing her squarely on the harbor bottom as it receded. Soon the *Memphis* was aground more of the time than she was afloat, but one beneficial result of this was that as the rollers came in and lifted the ship she was no longer, as previously, buried in what had been the hollow of the preceding wave. Consequently, although her bottom had already been ripped open in a number of places, she remained buoyant and lifted high with each successive wave, marching inshore in a series of staggering, crashing jolts across the harbor coral bottom, which, at times, was completely bare of water all about her. She still careened madly from side to side, more frequently to port than to starboard, and several times there were renewed fears that she might roll completely over. But in each case *Memphis* righted herself as the wave receded.

By this time, Father had only one concern, whether there would be great loss of life. Were *Memphis,* in one of her more violent movements, to remain poised on her side instead of coming back to an even keel as the water receded, the protection she could afford her crew would be greatly lessened and the loss of life correspondingly increased.

But *Memphis* was well and truly built, her design and construction embodying all that was best in our naval construction. Her side armor, installed to prevent entrance of enemy shellfire, held firm against the coral rocks against which it was hurled. Her protective deck, installed to prevent plunging shells from penetrating into the vital areas of the ship, added strength to her side and rigidity to her structure. The seventy-three-foot width of her hull added stability, and the honest workmanship of her Philadelphia builders caused her to hang together against stresses far in excess of those calculated by her designers when she was originally laid upon the drawing boards. A lesser ship, not built to take the fearsome pounding that ships of the battle line are designed for, would have been bilged and flooded, probably would not have been able to rise to the seas, would have lain supinely on her shattered side and given her crew to the elements.

The coral bluffs rimming the shoreline around Santo Domingo Harbor vary in height between twenty and forty feet above sea level. In the shallow water, the rollers were estimated to have reduced radically in size, but still they were in some cases two hundred yards from crest to crest, and in height they reached at least to the top of the bluff. In the maelstrom, still rolling violently and smashing her bottom against the coral beneath, *Memphis* pounded her way to within fifty feet of the shore, to perhaps a hundred feet from the upper edge of the bluff beyond. In the extremely shallow water each receding wave completely exposed the harbor bottom beneath the ship and then, hurling itself back, lifted her once more, drove her a few more feet to shoreward, and heartlessly dropped her upon the rocks again. Watchers on shore and the men topside on the *Memphis* both saw the entire hull of the ship at these moments completely out of water —a sight only seen when a ship is in drydock. As she rolled to seaward, those on the shore could see how badly smashed the bottom of her hull was, a view not given to those on board who had, however, been receiving for half an hour, in confinement-intensified force, the full benefit of the shrieks and groans elicited from the structure of their ship.

At about 5:00 *Memphis* reached her final resting place with a crunching smash which brought her up short and solid, immovable, within a hundred feet of the rocky bluff. For a short time she was intermittently lifted by the waves as they came boiling shoreward, still big enough to pour over her boat deck and cascade off in great sheets toward the shore. Froth and spray continued to reach high above the bridge, and some—no longer impeded by an updraft—still poured into the stacks and down into the now-sodden and completely dark furnaces. But this no longer mattered, for *Memphis* was a total wreck, her double-bottomed hull breached with large rocks into her vitals, her once-cared-for spaces now slowly filling through a hundred smashed plates in her skin.

Her entire travail, from the moment her skipper saw the first sign of anything out of the ordinary, had lasted only an hour and a half. She was destined to remain where she was for the next twenty-one years.

Chapter 13

The first alarm in Fort Ozama, that a U. S. Navy boat had swamped and its occupants were in danger, was sounded simultaneously by Captain Low and Lieutenant Case at about 4:15. A detail of marines was immediately sent out to the bluff a few hundred yards south of the fort to do what they could to assist anyone who might come ashore from the swamped motor launch. Lieutenant Peirce, with the remainder of the recreation party, arrived in the fort at about 4:30. Everything possible was being done for his men, he was assured. Still not aware of the full dimensions of the problems being faced by the men in the water and unable to appreciate the enormity of his own unwitting part in their tragedy, his only idea at the time was to write a message to the *Memphis* detailing the circumstances. When he left the ship he had not thought to bring with him a list of those who were in the shore party, however, so he could not give a list of the group he had put into the boat. Instead, he listed the names of those who were still ashore in the fort. By comparison with the recreation party list which Ensign Walker had in the quarter-deck log on board the *Memphis,* he reasoned, it would be possible to determine who had been thrown into the water.

A feeling of disquietude nevertheless concerned Peirce, for he anticipated embarrassing questions when he returned to the *Memphis.* Why had he not listed the men as they got in the boat? Why had he not personally inspected conditions at sea before permitting the boat to return? What had he done about Lindsay's report that it was getting rough? Again and again he berated the awful mischance that had prevented him from receiving the critically important message until just after the boat was beyond recall. Strangely, it did not occur to him that he ought, even at this late moment, to take personal interest in any rescue efforts which might be possible from shore.

It was while Peirce was laboriously working over each word of his message—knowing that there would be irritation at the need to put a lifeboat in the water and that, if anyone was drowned, his every move during the past half hour would be carefully looked into—that he suddenly heard a commotion. "The *Memphis* is coming in!" the voices said. "The *Memphis* is coming ashore!"

Forgotten was the message now. Peirce leaped to his feet, ran to the top of the ancient fort battlements.

Memphis, when he saw her, was obviously in distress. She was still broadside on, as she had been when he had last seen her, less than half an hour ago, but she was much closer to shore than before and was rolling almost to her beam ends with every sea, alternately showing him her decks and part of her bottom, obviously grinding on the rocks in the hollow of every wave and being picked up and hurled closer with every succeeding breaker. The combers were flowing completely over her decks, breaking over the bridge, foaming and splashing high above the stacks. Mingled white and black smoke poured forth from number one and four stacks, and a cloud of yellowish-white vapor was issuing from the engine-room ventilators on the boat deck.

From where he stood, he could see *Memphis'* bridge crowded with people, and her boat deck likewise. There was no one on the forecastle or quarter-deck—and for good and sufficient reason, since the successive waves would have buried them ten or fifteen feet deep in solid green water. Peirce subconsciously flexed his knees as if he could feel the crunch every time *Memphis* struck the coral bottom of the harbor, and as she rolled far over toward him or far away from him, he wondered if this time she would stay heeled on her side.

"Come on!" he yelled to his men down below in the fort. He dashed part way down the parapet steps. "Come on!" he yelled again. "The *Memphis* is wrecked!"

Followed by Kasburg and the twenty-five men remaining in his party, Peirce ran out the Fort Ozama entrance gates, turned sharply southward and raced down the unpaved road to the bluffs lining the shore.

A sizable crowd had already collected, conspicuous among them a number of women carrying black umbrellas. Conspicuous also were U. S. Marines in khaki-colored trousers, white underwear skivvy shirts, and broad-brimmed campaign hats.

The marines in particular, accompanied by groups of the heartier Dominican men, had ventured far out toward the edge of the bluff—as far as they dared, considering the seas which were constantly sweeping up to swirl white foam waist high about them. They had gathered in little groups in the least water-swept locations, some holding ropes and life preservers, some still carrying the blankets and first-aid kits with which they had been sent to succor the men in the swamped boat.

As Peirce ran out of the fort, he was aware that an alarm had been sounded. The results were soon evident as more and more marines continued to arrive on the bluff. Some of them, he noticed, drove up in great four-wheel-drive trucks, which lurched and careened across the uneven ground and then stopped, lined up hubcap to hubcap, like an impassive row of dour-visaged spectators upon the scene.

Memphis was coming in broadside to the shore, some distance to the westward of the mouth of the Ozama River. Here it was that the greatest number of spectators had congregated, and here Peirce raced with his men to join the groups of marines and more adventurous Dominicans.

But there was nothing to do—nothing anyone could do. Heedless of the splashing sea, or the rain which now began to fall, as it nearly always did in the early evening, all stood there helplessly, eyes fixed on the marine tragedy taking place.

American landing forces had been sent ashore on Santo
Domingo to preserve law and order and to administer the customs efficiently and honestly. The Dominican government had
officially welcomed the United States' assistance, but there were
those who insisted that this was under duress. Some local elements vociferously protested against what they termed an un-
warranted intrusion in their affairs, holding that even if the
Dominican Government was poorly run, their customs revenue
wasted in graft and corruption, this was certainly not any of the
business of the United States or anyone else. In any case, they
loudly claimed, this was preferable to the loss of political independence heralded by the arrival of foreign troops. The other
side of this argument was that "freedom" should be understood
to mean the freedom of the people, not the freedom of an incom-
petent political machine. The Dominican people had the right to
honest government and just administration of their national
revenues. Creditor nations had already indicated their intent to
foreclose upon their bankrupt exchequer by force of arms. Hence
U. S. intervention was a far more friendly act than they could
expect from any other power.

By consequence of all this, however, the Americans felt they
were on shore in the Republic of Santo Domingo on sufferance
only, and they had been instructed that they were in a poten-
tially hostile country. Shore leave, or "liberty," as it is normally
known, was not permitted. Fort Ozama was set aside for the
Marines for their encampment, as were certain other outposts,
and a recreation ground had been made available for them and
for sailors from the U. S. ships in the harbor. Otherwise they were
to stay out of trouble, not to mingle with the people, not to go
ashore in the town.

With the debacle in the harbor, however, these rules went by
the board. Ordinary Dominican citizens, U. S. Marines, American sailors, and high officials of the local government all stood
silently on the bluffs, looking out to sea.

People cheered when they saw the little *Castine* win her fight
and go on her way to safety. The few who had seen the motor
launch overturn ceaselessly explained to anyone who would listen just exactly how it happened, and how the *Castine,* by fear-
less seamanship, had attempted to rescue them, but had been

unable to do so. And now they all stood in awe and commiseration as the great battle cruiser which had lain off shore so many days—her very presence a force for stability and order—pounded and rolled and gashed her ruined body closer and closer to the piece of land on which they stood.

Corporals Flatten and Rogers had automatically joined the largest group, which was gathered nearest the *Memphis* where they could have a good view. The two marines stood for a time in the crowd, which rapidly enlarged as more Santo Dominicans came to watch the drama at sea, but after some minutes they left and proceeded along the shore to the westward, since it appeared that the men in the water were drifting in that direction. Flatten, having become separated from Rogers, came to a small inlet about forty yards across, one of many such eroded by the sea. There below him was a man in the water, and out beyond him was another. Standing on a ledge twelve or fifteen feet above the water line, Flatten shouted to the nearer man and pointed to an empty life belt which was floating nearby. According to Flatten, the man raised an arm in what might have been either a gesture of assent or a last desperate appeal. What he said, Flatten could not hear, but the marine noted the exhaustion evident in his face:

I had an urge to dive in to his rescue [related Flatten], but it would have been impossible to climb those walls even in a calm sea. Suddenly driven insane by the relentless lashings and with one decisive impulse he clasped both hands over his face then lunged backwards under the water. I was utterly dumbfounded to witness a suicide only twenty or thirty feet away, and the memory haunted me for many weeks.

In the few minutes that elapsed, while watching the man, I had failed to take any caution of the sea. Looking up I saw a mountainous wave coming toward me with the speed of an express train. I turned and ran a few steps and then was pitched headlong upon the reef. Frantically, desperately or instinctively, I grabbed onto something, anything, my hands clutching the jagged rock where I clung like a leech. I didn't dare to move because I knew the backwash would be almost as great as the inwash. Moreover I had previously observed that the greater volume of water went upward, I had estimated, about a hundred and fifty feet. I waited it seemed an interminable time when first the backwash rushed past me, then the downpour from above. I lay frozen to the rock. It seemed minutes. When the ton of water came down upon my back it felt more like a truckful of concrete. So oppressive was the weight that I was literally pinned to the rock. When I felt that all was clear, I returned to the rim of the bay to see if either of the two men were still there, but the water was now covered with two or more feet of foam and neither man was in sight.

Admiral Pond, seated in the front row of the Cathedral of Santo Domingo, was not at first aware that anyone had entered the building. He carefully read the message handed to him, pursed his lips. Then, raising his eyes to the marine waiting at the end of the pew, he nodded and indicated that the marine might leave. There was nothing directly alarming about the message, no action that he need take immediately, and he did not wish to appear abrupt or ungracious to his lecturer and hosts in the Cathedral. The time was shortly after 4:00 P.M. He remained perhaps ten minutes longer in the Cathedral, until the completion of the lecture, and then, expressing his appreciation to the Bishop of the Cathedral and to Consul von Zeilinski, he and the Russells, with the other members of the party, walked out to the street.

It was now about 4:10. It had been planned that following the lecture Admiral Pond would repair to the American Legation for his daily afternoon conference with Minister Russell. Automobiles were awaiting them outside the Cathedral, but upon coming outside it was immediately evident that there was excitement in the air. Numbers of people were hurrying through the streets, all headed southward to the waterfront. Excitedly, the Admiral's driver told him of the developments at sea in the harbor. A huge yellow sea wave had suddenly smashed into the anchorage, a boat had been capsized and all its crew drowned, and the *Castine* was also in the breakers and would shortly be wrecked. Admiral Pond and Captain Bootes, his extremely tall Marine aide, directed that the driver follow the crowds and take them immediately to the waterfront. Thus, from 4:15, Admiral Pond was an observer from shore, helpless to do anything to influence the course of events:

At the time I reached the foot of the street there were six or eight lines of heavy breakers outside the bluff at the west side of the mouth

of the river and about three lines outside of the *Castine*. These lines of
breakers were rapidly extending off shore and increasing in violence.
The *Castine* got her stern to the sea but was apparently unable, with
the increasing force of the breakers, to make more sea room and was
driven gradually to the westward and then began to make in shore.
While watching the *Castine* from my automobile on the Malecon, a
heavy sea swept over the bluff and completely crossed the Malecon,
completely covering the automobile, staving in the side towards the
sea and putting the machine out of commission. The bluff at this point
was about thirty or thirty-five feet high, the automobile about ninety
feet from the nearest point of the bluff, about one hundred and twenty
feet from the point of the bluff in the direction from which the sea
was coming. After being washed out of the machine I remained in the
vicinity about five minutes. The *Castine* at this time was so close that
I expected momentarily to see her strike bottom. She had a heavy list
to port and was apparently turning to port but was steadily coming in
toward the bluff.

I then walked toward the point where I expected the *Castine* to
fetch up against the bluff. A row of houses cut off all view of the sea
for a distance, and as soon as I got another view to seaward I saw
that the *Castine* had turned and was heading out. About this time the
Memphis was laboring violently. The seas were then beginning to
wash over her. Seeing that the *Castine* was heading towards safety, my
whole attention was turned toward the *Memphis,* which was by this
time beginning to drag. The *Memphis* was laboring violently and the
seas were washing completely over her. I remember remarking to
Captain Bootes, as the *Memphis* made one violent roll to starboard,
that she must have certainly dipped her smokestacks. From my position on the bluff it seemed at times as though the seas were even
sweeping over the tops of the stacks. These seas were not breakers in
the position the *Memphis* was in before the vessel started to drag, but
were evidently just on the point of breaking. I could see through every
crest, and remarked the light green color of the crests. The wind
during all this time was only a light gentle breeze, so there was very
little spray.

As the *Memphis* neared the beach and about the time I first felt
sure that she had struck bottom, I observed steam escaping from the
hatches aft and I then, for the first time, surmised that there was
something wrong below, although I had felt that from the violent
motions of the ship and the heavy seas that were constantly sweeping
over her that conditions below must have been very difficult. As the
vessel neared the beach I observed the crew gathered on the boat deck

and the Captain and others standing on the bridge. There appeared to be no disorder but, of course, at that time everyone was hanging on and looking out for himself. The ship struck at about five o'clock.

Captain James T. Bootes, U. S. Marine Corps, some six feet six inches in height, was Cruiser Force Marine Officer and had accompanied Admiral Pond ashore that afternoon. His account is a striking description of the scene witnessed by the watchers on shore:

A sea about six feet high above the Malecon Boulevard came all the way across that street breaking top of automobile, flooding it, putting engine out of action and drenching us thoroughly from head to feet, driving us out of car. The *Castine* was then apparently aground with her starboard side towards the shore, a perceptible list to port, and seas breaking all over her. We walked around the block for a better view and about 4:20 I saw the *Castine* turning to port and heading out, then passing slowly astern of the *Memphis*. Then my attention was attracted more particularly towards the *Memphis,* as the seas were getting higher every moment and seemed to come from farther south. The waves seemed to be huge walls of water of great height. The fartherest ones green, gradually increasing in height and of unusual length, until they reached the soundings of 7-½ and 8 fathoms, when they broke and became more irregular in length. While I was watching the *Memphis* I suddenly saw her bow thrown up so high by a large wall of water that I could see her bottom for some distance back from the stem and her after body plunged down deeply. I saw smoke coming from the first and fourth smoke stacks, but nothing from the second and third. Then the stern would be thrown up and the bow would dive down. These alternate movements continued, every one of them apparently making the *Memphis* leap sidewise towards the shore. I thought I could see the starboard cable standing out like a well-defined line while the *Memphis* bow was up with a sky background. The seas poured in torrents over the *Memphis,* at times over the forecastle, then the quarterdeck, then the boat deck. Many of these torrents were as high as the bridge forward and well up the smoke stacks farther aft, and one time when the *Memphis* was heeled over I saw a wall of water higher than the tops of the smoke stacks extend above all four of them and out both ways beyond the masts, and I thought the water from wave had surely put out of business all the boilers underneath. She must have struck bottom several times about 4:30 P.M., for her bow and stern did not seem to subside as formerly when the opposite end was cast up by the sea. I could see the water very clearly, sometimes brown and sometimes green, passing over the forecastle, quarterdeck, boat deck, splashing around the forward bridge, splashing around the smoke stacks and other obstructions on the boat deck, and when the highest sea came the splashing was so pronounced and the issue of smoke was changed so suddenly, I had no doubt that water had actually put out the fires and possibly done greater harm in causing something to explode down there.

Second Lieutenant Case, from a different point of view, also went on record with his observations, though to much lesser extent. He had spent some time searching for survivors of the swamped recreation party boat and, following that, had nothing else to do than observe the drama in the sea.

The *Memphis* commenced to come rapidly toward the beach, and I expected to see it go completely over. I did not see how it was possible for anyone to stay on the decks, I thought the only hope for them was to get inside. The ship did not roll to the starboard very often as the waves were hitting it so fast she did not get a chance to recover. I remember one instance when she did go to starboard, when a considerable amount of water must have gone down her stacks, unless they were plugged up, because the ends of the funnels were covered with water.

The Dominican newspaper *Listin Diario,* in its issue of August 30, 1916, contained a full account in Spanish of the catastrophe, the most dramatic news it had had in a decade:

Yesterday at 4:00 a steam launch with thirty sailors from the *Memphis* was on its way to the ship. As it headed out to sea the launch foundered in the furious swells which had arisen.

The *Castine,* which was anchored at Placer de los Estudios, attempted to help the victims of the wreck and went as far as throwing them life jackets, but the sea was so rough the *Castine* had to give up the attempt and look after itself for it, too, was in danger of foundering. When it headed out into the sea, its move was silently applauded by onlookers who had feared the *Castine* too would be lost. The ship had been covered by the waves several times and appeared as a veritable top spinning in the middle of the sea.

Of the thirty sailors in the small number two launch, only five survived in the vicinity of the slaughterhouse. A few others reached the reefs by the quay, but the moment they gained a foothold there, tremendous waves dashed them against the reefs. Bloody traces of their struggle could be seen later on that spot. The sight aroused the pity and compassion of the spectators who would have wanted to help the sailors in the terrible struggle which took their lives.

The cruiser *Memphis* which was also anchored at Placer de los Estudios intended likewise to fight the storm by putting out to sea. It was unable to do so, however, for it would have required the starting of at least ten of its sixteen boilers. The ship took blows from the sea on its side. Simultaneously one of the main boiler pipes broke. The explosion injured several enginemen, two of whom died last night in a hospital set up by the Americans on Jose Rez Street.

Powerless to fight the storm the ship was thrown on to the reefs behind the playground where it ran aground in such a manner that today it can hardly move. Once it was in this condition the disembarking of the crew began. It was accomplished rapidly with great order and with the help of some civilians and sailors of the Port Authority. The rescue began about 5:00 in the afternoon and ended at 8:30, Captain Beach being the last to disembark. The officers on board said the change in weather was so sudden that the barometer did not register it. Consequently they were unable to raise pressure for which they would have needed at least twenty-five minutes.

The disembarking was carried out under rain and wind. From that moment on there was a continuous drizzle which lasted well into the night. As the sailors came off the ship, they were taken by automobile and carriages to the *fortaleza*. The wounded were taken to the hospital.

The entire capital city, men, women and children, congregated on the quay from where it was possible to see all the operations.

About 7:00 P.M. the President of the Republic was requested to order all bars along San Pedro Street closed. This was done immediately and great order reigned throughout the night. The banquet which was to be held as a farewell to Count D'Arlot was cancelled because of the day's events.

At 4:15 P.M. the President of the Republic, Dr. Francisco Henrique y Carvajal, accompanied by the Secretary of Foreign Relations, Señor Jose Ma. Cabral y Baez, arrived at the location where an immense crowd watched the sad events. After a short drive along the shore the President, accompanied by Señor Cabral, stepped from his automobile on the grounds of the Plaza Colombia. At this moment the *Castine* was beginning to put out fighting desperately against the waves. The less fortunate *Memphis* was rapidly heading for the reefs where it was to run aground, which are directly in front of the Plaza Colombina.

The President hastened to dictate a few measures to help in the rescue of the American soldiers, but unfortunately very little could be done for those on board the *Memphis*. Their plight was desperate until they were able to throw a line from the ship to shore on which they descended one by one. There were no few Dominicans who lent their efficient help. Among those on shore the first injured was Ramon Elnanto, a Dominican, who was admitted to the First Aid station with a broken leg. Later a large contingent of American soldiers and sailors under the direction of Admiral Pond organized a rescue in an efficient manner.

After 5:30 the rescue was started by means of a line which had been thrown to shore from one of the ship's masts. When the first man descended on it with the help of a pulley the President of the Republic initiated a round of applause which was unanimously taken by the crowd in hopes of lending encouragement to those on board the ship.

For the third time in history, furious waves mercilessly swept the quay. Yesterday, part of the concrete fence near the sea, as well as piles, etc. were violently uprooted and thrown off. The playground, the slaughterhouse and the entire neighborhood were thronged by hundreds of people watching the rescue operations on the *Memphis*.

At 6:30 the President of the Republic left the Plaza de Colombia. By that time the rescue was perfectly organized and proceeding smoothly. As is customary under bad weather conditions, the electric light had been disconnected. The President gave orders to the Director of the Electric Plant, Señor Bulberes, to light up at least part of the city and especially to provide power for lighting up the scene of the catastrophe, making whatever arrangements were necessary on the spot. He also ordered that the telegraphic station be similarly notified.

Mr. Clarence H. Baxter, who had left his post as editor of the Patterson, New Jersey, *Guardian* to become the General Receiver of Dominican Customs at Santo Domingo, left a thrilling and rather emotional description of how the wreck of the *Memphis* looked to him. In a letter to the editor of his old newspaper, he wrote as follows:

At the end of a rather strenuous twenty-four hours I am going to take just a minute and tell you that it is not a pleasant sight to see a

United States battleship go on the rocks even if the sadness is miti-
gated more or less because of the fact that her companion ship, a
gunboat, made as gallant a fight against tremendous odds as was ever
witnessed by a human being and won out to sea. For three hours the
spectacle held the agonized attention of 15,000 human beings on the
shore, while only a few hundred yards distance away 900 men on the
battleship *Memphis,* and 200 on the gunboat *Castine,* were battling
for life with the grimness that comes only when the odds seem overwhelming. It is not pleasant to stand helpless in the face of such a
catastrophe, with a surf of tremendous power dashing against sharp
and cruel coral rocks, when you know that to be cast into such a sea
means sure death. And it is doubly hard when the battle is so close
that you can see the drawn faces of the men who are putting up the
fight for life. And the feeling of utter helplessness as you wait for the
end which seems so sure—the boats battling there within 200 yards of
the shore—so close that a strong man could throw a stone on board;
and with the knowledge that if we could only get a line on board, over
which the men might be sent to safety on shore, attended by our
acceptance of an utter impossibility in the face of the howling tempest
and the dashing waves.

We do not know yet just what it was. I got word from the Washington weather bureau at noon that a heavy tropical disturbance was
passing to the southward of us, but we had none of the usual accom-
paniment of such disturbances. We knew there was a hurricane off
there, but the sea here was calm and there was no great wind. The
Memphis was anchored about a mile off the mouth of the river, while
the *Castine* lay nearer the shore; both ships were on regular station,
with fires banked. Then about 3:00 o'clock it began to come—not in
the usual way, with plenty of advance warning, but suddenly and with
a sea of greater power that I have ever seen before. I was getting off
mail instead of taking a siesta. A squall came along and I walked out
on the balcony to take a look at the weather, and those ships were in
the midst of a smother of breakers and fighting to get out of it to
sea.

The *Castine* was seemingly trying to weather the point near the
river, but we learned later she was trying to save men in the waves
from one of the launches of the *Memphis,* which foundered in trying
to reach the ship. The men were all lost, and the gallant effort of the
Castine to pick them up came near proving the undoing of that ship.
She had got a little steam up, and with that she backed stern foremost
along the rocks, twice within a hundred yards of the shore—on this
coast you step from a coral cliff thirty feet high into deep water—and

for an hour she battled—every surge sweeping over and burying her deep—her captain and crew, lashed to life lines, but never giving up, while thousands looked on and wept and prayed for those who seemed doomed to sure destruction.

And when the *Castine*—she is only a little gunboat—seemingly very small indeed alongside her big sister, the *Memphis,* finally won out beyond the surf life and was out of immediate danger, what a cheer went up from those thousands on the shore. I never knew what a real cheer meant as an expression of pent-up emotion, and it certainly felt good. And then we looked around and the cheers ceased abruptly when we saw that the big *Memphis* was drifting in to shore; we had thought she had been standing by trying to aid the smaller boat; but as we looked in wonder to find such a big ship so close to the dangerous rocks, we saw that she was not moving; that she was out of control, that she was coming in broadside to the rocks. Then we knew that she was doomed, and the only hope was that she would continue broadside on and strike the rocks where the water would be deep enough to keep her on an even keel; where she would be close enough to the rocks to get life lines to the shore, over which the officers and crew might be sent to safety. And so for another hour we watched the *Memphis,* as we had watched the *Castine,* but not with the same hope; we knew the battleship was coming on the rocks, for we saw that she was helpless; we felt that only a miracle could save the lives of the hundreds of men who were in the sheltered places on her decks, to keep from being swept overboard by the big breakers that were breasting and breaking over her military mast sixty feet in the air and throwing tons of water on her decks with every surge. At first the thousands of onlookers shouted words of encouragement, in Spanish, to be sure; but the note of human sympathy was just as apparent as it was in the words of the mother tongue, as the marines and sailors on shore tried to send words of cheer to their comrades on the ships. But the warring voices of nature—the surge of the surf, the sweep of the wind and the roar of the rain made those human voices a whisper; the shouts of cheer were no more audible than the words of the silent women who knelt on the shore and with wringing hands and streaming eyes prayed for the human lives that were seemingly so near and close. They are an emotional people, the Dominicans, but their human sympathy in the face of the impending peril made them all brothers with the Americans who were with them on the shore.

And while we waited and hoped on the shore, everybody had been busy doing everything possible to be in readiness if what we hoped for came to pass. Life lines were made ready for casting to the ship after she went on the rocks, if she remained on an even keel. Along the rocks for hundreds of yards strong men were grouped to render aid if the expected happened, and the ship should be turned on her side and wave-swept; ready to snatch the men who would be swept to the face of the rocks. All the automobiles and coaches in the city were lined up ready to render service in caring for the dead, the wounded, or the living, as fate might have in store.

And then she struck, the stern of the ship first coming out of the smother so half of her propeller could be seen. And then the mighty surges broke clean over the ship, each mighty impulse sending her a little closer to the shore. With each wave we looked to see her break in two or go over on her side. But she held upright, in spite of the sea and its awful power. And as we saw her still standing staunch, a new impulse swept through those on shore; for the first time we realized that our hope had come to pass, and that it would be possible to get the men off the ship with life lines. And with each passing minute we grew more sure; we felt that a miracle had happened; that those men were going to win to shore in safety. The ship lay less than 200 feet away, breaking the waves so the marines and the sailors—and the Dominicans were right with them, shoulder to shoulder—could get on the outermost points of the rocks. So the life lines were cast from the shore, with life floats at the end, and finally one was caught from the water by an overcast line from the ship—and then once more the surge of the mighty cheer which comes when human effort succors men from the very jaws of the death. Then another line, and still another, while huge cables were first strung ashore to keep the ship from tipping over toward the sea. And then the life lines; it did not seem long now, because every one knew that the fight was won.

And then they began sending them ashore. First in canvas bags— the dead and the wounded—for we learned then for the first time that there had been an awful time on that ship when she had been caught in the sudden smother of the mighty waves that must have been caused by some submarine disturbance—bursting steampipes which left her engines powerless, and bursting boilers when the water reached the fireroom, where men were scalded and died like heroes. The injured were rushed to the hospital and the sea-drenched survivors to the fort; in two hours all were ashore, the captain the last to leave his ship.

The casualties will number about thirty-five. Most of these lives were lost when small boats attempting to reach the ships were swamped when the storm broke in its first fury. One launch put out to sea, and when she went down four men swam to shore several miles down the coast. It is too early yet to give details, but thankfulness is universal that it was not worse. They say the *Memphis* is a total loss;

that no one remained below, Father returned topside to super-intend the final abandonment.

Night had fallen. Rescuers and rescued alike began to shiver in the damp, salt-laden air. A light rain had begun and the wind had increased, blowing up to about twenty miles per hour from the land. Throughout the city the electricity had been turned off as a precaution when the tidal wave began to roll in, but as soon as he felt the city was safe from being inundated the President of the Dominican Republic himself ordered the electricity to be restored. At the same time, he directed that all bars and taverns be closed.

All automobiles in the city—trucks, taxicabs or private vehicles —had been brought to the bluff lining the spot where the *Memphis* was aground and, lined up as a backdrop to the area, provided lights for the rescuers. Two large fires were lighted on the bluffs to provide warmth for those who were wet and chilled. The skipper of the ancient Dominican Republic gunboat *Independencia* brought over her portable searchlight with batteries and this proved of considerable assistance because it could easily be directed wherever light was wanted.

But despite these efforts, to the men still aboard the *Memphis,* without lights except hand-held flashlights and a few battery-powered decklights, it was a night of blackness. Light was in the distance, and they were on its edge, looking inward, sending men into it two by two over the slender cobwebs of lines which led to the light source. In the warm glow of the light on the bluff, crowds of marines and Dominican citizens could be seen surging to and fro with the shore end of each line as *Memphis* rolled at the other end. As she rolled away, the seemingly fragile lines pulled the distant crowd of Lilliputian men toward her, and as she rolled toward the bluff, they ran backward rapidly to keep the lines taut.

And always, as the seas swept the now strangely disoriented and disordered decks, cascaded off into the frothy turmoil between the ship and the shore, the men went down the lines, two by two, held from going too fast by a preventer line tended from the *Memphis,* eagerly pulled shoreward by the growing groups of their shipmates who had preceded them.

Sick bay in the *Memphis* was located on the berth deck, two decks below the main deck and well forward on the port side. On this afternoon it held four men, three of whom were completely helpless. Two of them had sustained injuries from the events of that very afternoon. Chief Yeoman McCluggage had suffered a deep cut on one arm which had severed the femoral artery, and just before the watertight doors were closed, Leary, injured by the piano, was carried in by two shipmates. His rib cage had been smashed and he was in great pain, barely conscious. Half out of his head, he continued to murmur the same words he had said after the piano struck him: "Don't worry about me. Look out for the young guys." The third occupant of a sick-bay bed was a young boy who that morning had had the stitches removed from an appendicitis operation.

The only hale person present was Ira A. Majo, a hospital apprentice who had the afternoon watch. When the watertight doors were shut, he had followed instructions by closing the porthole in the ship's side and dogging down the "battle port," which excluded all light. They were isolated in their compartment, cut off from all communication, completely unaware of what was going on. After the electricity failed, there was neither light nor ventilation in the sick bay. In complete darkness the four men for half an hour felt their ship being hurled about, her hull crunching viciously against the bottom of the bay. Finally, with a series of heavy crashes, she came nearly to rest but continued rocking heavily from side to side. All this was accompanied by high-pitched creaking and squeaking from tortured substructure and bottom plating.

At about five thirty o'clock Hospital Apprentice Majo became concerned about how long they would be required to remain in the sick bay, and whether, indeed, anyone had remembered that there were people incarcerated in this somewhat out-of-the-way compartment. He knew there could be no egress through the watertight door. Everyone had heard the water sloshing about inside the ship, and it had become necessary to dog it down very tightly to prevent leakage around the gasket. The fact that this leakage existed at the top of the door as well as along the sides and the bottom was proof that the passageway outside was flooded.

The porthole might admit good air as well as light, but first it was necessary to see if this were feasible. The problem here was that the battle port, a heavy bronze cover, used the same set of dogs as the glass port. To remove the battle port required that the glass port be loosed; thus if the porthole were under water, water pressure, if any existed, would force the glass port in also. This might result in flooding the compartment, since Majo might not be able to reclose the port against the fire-hydrant flow of full sea pressure.

He tried to consult with the other men. Leary was in too great pain to be much help; the boy with the recent appendectomy was no better. The consensus, arrived at essentially between himself and McCluggage, was nevertheless to try the porthole. Possibly the dogs could be unscrewed part way so that, if the porthole were under water, this would become evident by water leaking in and they could be tightened again.

With great care, Majo applied the key-headed wrench, loosening the two dogs a little at a time on their screw threads, watching anxiously for the first evidence of water pressure against the outside of the port. None came. With growing confidence, he unscrewed the dogs the remainder of the way and opened the port entirely. It was out of water, well above the water line and, being on the landward side, was sheltered by the bulk of the ship from the leaping spray and the waves lashing her to starboard.

Poking his head out the now-open port, Majo was first astonished to see land only seventy-five feet away and, looking down at the water line, was equally astonished to see the ship largely out of water, perched upon glistening rocks and slimy coral growth. Not far aft, in the vicinity of the bridge, lines had already been passed to the people on land, and bulky coaling sacks were gingerly being eased ashore.

Water was still high on the other side of the watertight door which was the sick bay's only access; so there was nothing more to do but wait for rescue. There was, at least, a little more light than previously, since the darkness of the compartment was now alleviated, through the open port, by the waning light of day and the distant glare of the fires and light ashore. The dusk of the Caribbean night gathered. Majo remained at the porthole, reporting what he could see for the edification of his patients. It was not nearly so hard to wait now that they knew more fully what must have happened, and, more specifically, that there did not appear to be any further danger from the sea. The rolling of the ship, still quite extensive when the port was first opened, lessened perceptibly as Majo watched, and the noise of the grinding bottom plates subsided somewhat. A heavy surf still leaped along the water line, boiled and burbled among the rocks of the shore—or alternatively the water drew away entirely in great surging eddies around bow and stern and through crevices under the hull—but this too, seemed to be waning.

In an apparently short time there came a rap on the overhead, in the vicinity of a seldom-opened hatch which the thoughtful designers of the ship had provided. Grabbing the foot-long length of pipe which he had used for a dog wrench on the watertight door, Majo rapped back. The hatch could only be opened by someone on the deck above, and in a few minutes the cover was lifted off, ropes were passed down through the hole, and all hands in the sick bay were gently, though in some cases painfully, brought up to the boat deck and set ashore in boatswain's chairs.

Since Majo was uninjured, he and his first-aid kit were immediately pressed into service for those needing help as they came off the ship. Subsequently he was sent to the hospital in Santo Domingo to assist there, and his personal record indicates that he remained on duty for forty-eight hours before finally being able to get some rest.

There was also another story told about the last few minutes on board the ship, concerning the ship's magazines. The story apparently is authentic, though details at this distance in time are lacking.

It seems that when the watertight doors were shut, a number of men found themselves incarcerated in their duty station in the bowels of the ship, in her magazines. Modern smokeless powder, as furnished to our men-of-war, is made from TNT but is considered particularly stable insofar as accidental explosion is concerned. Its formulation is such that only the proper detonation procedure, or some tremendous shock such as another explosion, can set it off. Nevertheless, being cooped up with a hundred or more tons of smokeless powder near the keel of a ship whose bottom was being stove in was not productive of peace of mind.

When the ship began pounding on the rocks, many uneasy thoughts arose as to how much of a smashing the TNT could take before reaching the detonation point. If a large rock smashed up through the bottom and irresistibly compressed a rigidly confined stack of 10-inch powder bags in their steel tanks, would they or would they not explode?

Deep below the water line, in an airtight and watertight compartment, the men waited until nearly all motion on the ship ceased, except for some continued rolling and the noise of the rocks grating along her bottom. They knew from the action of the *Memphis* and the manner in which she came to rest, that she was hard aground. Now their fear was replaced by a new fear: that in the confusion of the past few moments they might have been forgotten in their infrequently visited compartment. The watertight doors, being shut, could be opened only from the outside. Since they were low in the ship, near the keel, the doors —indeed the entire magazine—might already be under water. They might be imprisoned here for days before someone came after them, and in the meantime the water level inside the hull might rise. Even if the magazine was not yet submerged, there was bound to be considerable leakage after the tremendous damage the ship had been taking. The worst thought was the virtual certainty that the air in their small compartment could not last very many hours. A hasty council reached the decision that waiting would increase the ultimate likelihood of drowning or being asphyxiated through lack of oxygen.

The Chief Gunner's Mate, the senior person in the party, was an explosives expert, who had participated in numerous experiments at the Naval Ordnance Proving Station. Now he put his experience to good use.

In every magazine is a little wooden rack containing a row of small glass bottles. In each bottle is a sample of one of the various types of gunpowder in the magazines, so displayed to facilitate maintaining the explosives under continuous observation. Any gunpowder has a tendency to deteriorate with age, and the precise time and manner this happens with any given batch can only be told by careful and constant inspection of samples.

The chief opened the bottles, gathered together all the sample granules of smokeless powder, crushed them between his fingers, placed them carefully on a black silk neckerchief, rolled them up. He now had an explosive rope which he wrapped tightly around the operating mechanism of the electrically operated watertight door which held them prisoner. Then, warning everyone to stay clear, he gingerly struck a match and lighted the end of the fabric.

Smokeless powder in its proper consistency—specially shaped granules—will burn at a rapid rate, but it will not explode unless a detonating charge is used. When granulated to a fine powder, however, it burns with an extremely rapid combustion which is, in effect, a low-order explosion. With a subdued *whoosh* the powder charge exploded, the watertight door was smashed, and the group in the magazine was freed. They climbed out into the handling room and proceeded from there to the topsides of the ship where they found the breeches buoy rescue effort in full swing.

The Reverend W. Angus Wiggins, of Daytona Beach, Florida, enlisted in the U. S. Navy in 1914 at the age of seventeen as a coal passer. Two years later he had become a blacksmith, but he still divided his day into three equal eight-hour parts, designated for work, study, and rest. Never having gone beyond the eighth grade, he regularly took correspondence courses and had the interested assistance of his division officers in his efforts to better himself. Newton George in particular he recalls as the officer who made available a small workshop over one of the firerooms for a place to study, and who spent many hours with him working out mathematical problems. The room was hardly the most comfortable study room inasmuch as it was prone to be very warm, not to say hot when the boilers beneath were in use—and, lacking ventilation, it was apt to be stuffy at all times. Nevertheless it provided what Wiggins needed most: a place where he could indulge his strange habit of studying correspondence courses in private. He was here, with his books, when the tidal wave came upon the ship. A shipmate, Herbert ("Red") Vallandingham, who was on the "binnacle list" with a severe inflammation of one of the fingers of his right hand, was also there. Neither youth heard the call to stations, and Wiggins, with understandable con-

Abandon Ship 247

fusion, at the kaleidoscopic rush of events, recalls his experience as follows:

I was in the shop when the first wave passed over the ship. The shop was in number three hatch, and the hatch cover had not yet been secured over it; so the place almost filled with water. The water slammed the door shut and jammed a workbench across it, so that it suddenly became impossible to escape and we feared we were headed for a watery grave. The two of us managed to get the door open before the second wave rolled over the ship. Red, with his hand out of commission, took cover in the uptake around number four stack while I went about the deck to help secure the gun ports. By this time there was so much water in the compartments that it would fill them to the overhead when the ship rolled far over to that side.

While I was doing this, some object rolled over my right big toe and cut off the end of it. The emergency we were in was so great that I did not realize that I was losing blood until I was so weak I had trouble holding on. . . .

We managed to secure the 3-inch gun ports, but the 6-inch ones we could not secure. Chief Warrant Machinist Thompson was almost drowned in the operation. He was caught under a blower housing, and being a rather heavy and awkward man, could not get free. I helped him to get out. . . . By this time I was so weak that even with the help of another sailor I could not secure the large piece of armor plate in the 6-inch port.

The word was passed for all hands to get life preservers and a blanket and stand by to abandon ship. I went topside to get a life preserver and blanket for myself and for Red. As I returned with them, the marine at the ladder refused to let me go below the main deck, and when I tried to argue with him he drew his .45 and ordered me to move on. Then I crossed to the starboard side, hoping the ladder on that side would not be guarded. Just as I arrived at the starboard ladder, a large section of lockers which the ship's band used to store their instruments in broke loose and lumbered across the deck. The guard was occupied with the lockers, so I made my way below to get Red. As we climbed the ladder on the way back, I had to pass the guard who had stopped me earlier. He put his hand on his gun and said, "I feel like giving you the works for disobeying orders!" I replied, "I saved my shipmate!" Somehow, it seemed easier for men to die together than separately. By this time I was so weak that I could hardly stand. Many times I fell down on the wet deck and could hardly get on my feet again. Everyone was bare-footed, as it was easier to hold one's footing without shoes.

As the crowds of men on deck thinned, the various breeches-buoy lines were abandoned until but one line was left, the original one, leading from the bridge. The last twenty-four men to leave the ship, twenty-two officers and two chief petty officers, left in couples on this last breeches buoy. The two chief petty officers were Chief Quartermaster Rose and Chief Electrician Erskine, both of whom had earned high praise for their steady bearing and valiant assistance during the entire period of the wreck. In Father's own words again:

At just 8:00 o'clock the breeches buoy made its last trip to the bluff. The New York papers said that, "Captain Beach was the last to leave the ship." This was not fully correct. It is certainly the Captain's duty to be the last to leave a wrecked ship, not a mere sentimental duty; but he also is honored for it. I felt that the crew of the *Memphis* had been so perfect in maintaining the Naval tradition that one of them should share this honor with me. Chief Electrician's Mate Erskine and I left the ship together on the last trip of the breeches buoy.

Chapter 15

When the *Memphis'* number two motor launch left the recreation dock and headed down the Ozama River on its ill-fated trip, it carried a total of thirty-one men. Four of them were the regular boat's crew—William B. Smith, Coxswain, R. G. Snell and M. A. McDermott, Seamen, and E. H. Drager, Oiler, who was the boat's engineer. In addition there was C. E. Taylor, Fireman Second Class, who was making the trip under instruction as relief engineer, and Ashton C. Lindsay, Boatswain's Mate Second Class, in the technical status of "passenger, in charge." Twenty-seven men had gotten into the boat, for a total of thirty-three. The last two to get in were John A. Barsuch, who had been playing left field, and H. E. Riedel, who had been in center field. They were among the last to arrive at the dock and they automatically stepped into the boat, not at the time realizing that Lieutenant Peirce had directed that only a certain number of men board it. They had seated themselves on the thwarts when Barsuch heard Lindsay say, "Sir, two more men got in the boat."

"You two men get out of the boat!" ordered Peirce. "I've

counted off twenty-five men and I don't want any more than that in the boat!" Barsuch rose to his feet and stepped out but, to his surprise, the man who got out with him was not Riedel, but W. C. Hull, alongside of whom Riedel had seated himself. Nothing was said. Peirce was perhaps unaware of the fateful exchange of position, and no one else felt called upon to point it out. The boat shoved off almost immediately.

Oiler E. H. Drager's story was similar to those of the five others who survived. From the dock, before starting out to return to the *Memphis,* he had observed the surf at the bar across the mouth of the Ozama River and had noted that it seemed to be getting somewhat rougher. It was not sufficiently rough, however, to give him any concern, and he made no complaint either to the coxswain of the boat or to any of the other men.

As the boat passed down the river the short half mile or so from the recreation landing to the mouth, he was seated on the right side of the engine, which he was tending, and therefore facing to port, away from Fort Ozama. So he did not himself notice anyone on the fort landing shout or wave to the boat, but he was aware from the reaction of some of the other men that someone had called to them from the fort side of the river. On the eastern bank some Dominican men waved to them, gesticulated some kind of warning which was not understood. The engine of the boat was making too much noise for anyone to distinguish the words that were said, and no one paid any attention.

At the mouth of the river the situation did not appear dangerous; the boat passed the bar without incident, breasting moderate rollers, and proceeded some distance out into the bay. It had arrived, in fact, almost abeam of the *Castine,* only some six hundred yards from the *Memphis,* when suddenly Drager realized that something was wrong.

Smith, Lindsay, and Snell were staring fixedly ahead. At Lindsay's motioned command, Snell had opened the boat's gear box under his seat and extricated the signal flags, but neither Lindsay nor Smith appeared to make any move to reverse course and return to the safety of the river. Although both must have been dismayed at the size of the wave they could see making in front of them, it is probable that they expected there would be but one, and that they would ride over it to find relatively clear water beyond. As the wave came closer, it took the form of a really big breaker, much farther off shore than breakers ought to be, and it then became apparent to Drager that to change course at this time would be the worst possible move, that the boat's only chance was to go through the breaker head on.

With ever-decreasing speed, engine laboring, the boat struggled up the increasing incline of the comber. Its forward motion had practically come to a stop and the boat, its bow high and partly out of the water, was actually flung backward a little as the wave crested. Then the boat slapped down on the comber's back side and its engine speeded up as the launch once more gained headway. But instead of encountering calmer water to seaward of the first breaker, they were beset at once with a second huge wave, and then with a third and fourth. The fifth comber broke right on top of the boat, filling it half full of water and drowning the engine so that it choked, sputtered, and stopped.

Vainly Drager engaged the starter. The starting motor turned the engine rapidly, but it would not fire. Snell frantically waved the signal flags to attract the mother ship's attention, and Smith kept the launch bow on to the next approaching breaker as long as it answered his rudder; but as the boat lost way through the water, he no longer had control, and it fell off to the right. The boat lay nearly broadside to the approaching breaker as the slanting sea rose under it, swept ever more steeply upward on its port side, poured over the now-low-lying and unresisting gunwale, crested in a ribbed curve above, and broke directly overhead.

The launch sank gently stern first, leaving its passengers floating in the water. As the weight of the engine carried its stern down, the water it had shipped flowed aft and the more buoyant wooden bow lifted higher, so that it appeared to leap rather suddenly part way above the surface upon the back of the breaker. It remained thus for some minutes as the little knot of doomed men struggled in the hungry sea, and gradually became separated from them as the group spread out and dispersed, each man working out his survival as best he could.

For a few minutes Drager paddled aimlessly. His life jacket kept him afloat, but he was completely disoriented. Land might have been in any direction, and a thousand miles away. Even when lifted up by a wave, knowing that but a few moments ago he had been standing on the recreation field dock, he was unable to see land. In a short time, close at hand, appeared another life preserver, which he clutched, and soon there were more life preservers than he could have used. Many of them, Drager noted, had *Castine* printed on them. He did not, however, at any time see the gunboat. The water was not very cold and, except for being lifted up and down rapidly as the huge seas rolled by, he was not uncomfortable.

Little by little the men drifted apart under the impetus of the waves dashing them about, and Drager soon had lost contact with all of his fellows. He heard the voices of Dugan and Teshack, evidently near by although he could not see them. They had apparently got hold of a piece of wood of some kind, were riding it together, and said something to the effect that they were having no trouble and could continue in this manner for some time. Then their voices were no longer to be heard. Shortly thereafter land could be seen on the occasions when a sea lifted Drager just right, and in about twenty minutes he noticed that he was approaching close to shore. He also saw that the surf was rising extremely high upon the rocky bluff.

If I hit there, I'm a goner. he thought. But he was fortunate. A larger than usual breaker carried him forward on its crest and desposited him gently nearly at the top of the bluff, forty feet above the normal water line. He clung desperately to his landing spot, which was fortunately high above the median height of the following waves, and before another extra large one could sweep him back into the maelstrom several marines and local people had reached him and carried him inshore to a place of safety.

Six men of the thirty-one in this boat were saved. Both newspaper accounts and the official reports mention a Dominican citizen by the name of Emeterio Sanchez as having been outstanding in his exertions and having personally, with great daring, rescued three of the six by entering the tumultuous surf and pulling them out.

Four of the six were injured, in some cases painfully, but none seriously. The exceptions were Drager, the only member of the boat's crew to survive, and a third-class Carpenter's Mate named Hicks. As might be expected, Hicks later related some details not mentioned or remembered by Drager. According to Hicks, who happened to be a strong swimmer, as the launch approached the mouth of the Ozama River, three men were seen in the fort signal tower, but none of these made any signal to them. A group of four marines on the fort boat landing tried to shout something, but the distance was too great and the noise of the boat engine too loud for the words to be distinguished. On the eastern side of the river there was a long dock a little farther downstream, parallel to the current, and here the boat ran sufficiently close for shouted warnings to be heard. There was a group of Dominican natives on the dock, and several of them ran along even with the boat as it passed downstream, waving and shouting. One of them could speak some broken English, and Hicks recalled that he shouted several times, "No go out!" and "Go back!" When his warning was not heeded, the last thing Hicks heard him yell sounded like *"Finish Americano!"*

Many of the men in the boat saw this exchange, but since there had been categorical orders to return to the ship, no one considered turning back. As the boat reached the mouth of the river, however, Smith, the coxswain, said, "Better take off your shoes, men. This might turn out to be a swimming party!" Even at this, and although everyone in the boat removed his shoes, the general consensus was that Smith was only anticipating taking water into the launch and getting their feet wet, and that for protection of their footgear it should be removed and placed on the thwarts. After the boat reached the mouth of the river it was seen that the water was pretty rough farther out, but no one had any doubts about their safety even then. The waves increased extraordinarily rapidly, but none of them broke for a time, and the motor launch rode over them safely at reduced speed. But suddenly one of the waves broke right over them, filling the boat to the level of the thwarts. Two men jumped out into the water.

"Stay in the boat!" shouted Smith. The men in the water had on life jackets and were only a few feet away, but Smith was powerless to return for them because the engine had stopped with a drowned ignition when the water came aboard. Everyone in the boat began to bail, and some busied themselves in casting loose the thwarts for additional flotation. Snell attempted to signal to the *Memphis*. The boat broached to and within a minute

another wave broke over it and filled it entirely. It sank gently
from beneath them, leaving the thwarts and other gear floating.
Everyone had something to assist him, and there was no panic;
but a third wave came over them and broke, knocking all of
them together and dislodging some of them from the thwarts to
which they were clinging. Hicks was struck on the head by one of
the thwarts, but received only a small swelling at the spot.

When *Castine* approached, it was at first thought she intended
to pick them up, but her motion was so great that it was patently
impossible, and the men swam away from her in concern that she
might come down upon them. Hicks went on:

About five minutes later I noticed St. Clair near me. He seemed, I
thought, all in and I asked him how he was making out and he told
me he did not have on a life preserver. So I told him to hold on to me,
which he did for about twenty minutes. But then the big breakers
would come and we submerged with the undercurrent, which was so
strong that he finally lost his hold and we were separated. I looked
back about a hundred feet and saw him just barely able to stay up. I
turned around and started to work my way back but another wave came
and that is the last I saw of him. As it was useless to exert yourself in
trying to swim, I just drifted and in about forty-five minutes after I had
been in the water I noticed that the beach was only a few yards from
me. A large wave caught me, pushing me on toward the beach. I got in
a big whirlpool which took me under, judging from the undercurrents
which took me in four or five different directions, and while submerged
I felt a rock which I clung to and waited a few seconds, then my head
appeared above the water and when the water rolled out I was high
and dry. I immediately got up and walked up on the top of the bank,
removed my life preserver and was taken to the hospital by two marines.

In the same category as the story about the men trapped in
Memphis' magazines—a tale which has always been believed as
true but for which no substantiation can be found—is the story
of the unknown survivor of the launch. All members of the surviving ship's company attest to its truth, but rumor alone seems
to be the source. For this yarn to be accepted there must have
been one more man in the boat, for all six survivors' stories have
been checked, and, unless what follows is a time-garbled version
of Hicks' experience, it could not have been any one of these. At

any rate, this man was not wearing a life preserver and gratefully put on one of the *Castine*'s. As he did so, he noticed that most of the group in the water had obtained some sort of flotation equipment and were apparently not in immediate trouble. The water was not cold. The real danger lay in the menacing rock-strewn coast and the heavy surf dashing upon it. This man, a strong swimmer, swam with his life preserver for some time toward shore, but then felt that it was retarding his progress through the water. He had also become concerned about handling himself with this encumbrance close inshore. For this reason he discarded it, but he continued to make progress toward the shore, conserving his strength by riding the seas, surfboard fashion, whenever possible. Periodically, however, the seas would curl and break over him, forcing him underwater and usually down to the bottom of the bay. In his youth he had learned how to take care of himself in the surf, though admittedly this was bigger than any surf he had ever been in. He would take a deep breath, clasp his hands over his knees, and hold himself in a knee-chest position until, after rolling for some time along the bottom of the bay, he was in due course swirled again to the surface.

Apparently a number of men in the recreation party succeeded in reaching the beach, but there met their deaths upon the jagged rock and coral formations, or were perhaps drowned and cast ashore later. For several days searching parties scoured the beaches to recover their bodies. This man, however, more fortunate or perhaps more skillful—perhaps a little of both—had the good luck to pick up an extremely large sea dashing toward the beach at a point where it was rimmed by a coral shelf only fifteen to twenty feet high. Having had some experience at this sort of thing, he swam violently, as hard as he could, stayed on the crest of the breaker and in fact surfed in with it as it swept above the dangerous coral shelf and inland quite some distance from the shoreline. There it dumped him, unhurt. Exhausted, unable to come to his feet, he rolled over and over to get farther away from the shoreline and the sea and then lay panting for some minutes.

After resting for a short time, he pulled himself together and began to walk toward the city, not too far to the eastward. It was at first slow going on the rocky land, but soon he came upon a road skirting the shore, and trudged along the road with the half-formed thought of perhaps being in time to catch the second boat, either to return in it to the *Memphis* if conditions were better, or possibly, by his warning, dissuade it from making the attempt. If it had already headed back, as was most likely, he would find someone in the fort to whom he could report. As he passed a turn in the shoreline, however, he suddenly saw the *Memphis,* close inshore, obviously aground, being heavily battered by gigantic seas sweeping completely over her. His own recent experience suddenly lost all importance. He hurried forward to join the group on the bluff opposite the ship—marines, sailors, and Dominican natives, who were preparing to rig a breeches buoy. No one had yet come ashore from the ship, though some lines had already been gotten over, and he immediately recognized Lieutenant Peirce in charge of a group of men handling their shore ends.

His initial impulse was to report his safety to Lieutenant Peirce and he approached the officer with this intention. But as he came nearer to the group of Navy men, all of whom he recognized as having been in the recreation party, someone handed him the end of a line from the ship, and he promptly became submerged and indistinguishable among the group of American sailors trying to lend a hand to their imperiled shipmates not many yards away.

When the *Memphis* number three motor launch, which had been directed to follow its mate to the recreation landing for the second portion of the recreation party, had completed picking up equipment floating in the water from the capsized dinghy, it reported alongside *Memphis'* port gangway. The time was about 3:35. Yeoman Second Class J. W. Thorner, the ship's mail orderly, had been awaiting an opportunity to go ashore to make his afternoon mail run. Ensign Walker granted him permission to go in this boat with the understanding that the launch would leave him at the Fort Ozama landing on the way in and that he must be waiting on the dock when the boat returned from the recreation field.

Before permitting the number three launch to begin its trip to shore, Ensign Walker first directed it to "lie off" awaiting orders, while he sought out the Executive Officer for permission to dispatch it. As Officer-of-the-Deck he could have done this on his own, but events of the past fifteen minutes suggested the advisability of giving his superiors an opportunity to revalidate their previous instructions. *Memphis* was rolling perceptibly more—the end of the port boat boom had just touched the water. It was the first time Walker had ever seen this happen. He reached the starboard side of the quarter-deck, reported the boat ready, and for the first time really appreciated that something very out of the ordinary must be going on. The Captain an Executive were both staring fixidly to seaward, the Captain through binoculars, and alternating this with careful inspection of the shoreline. Williams was so preoccupied that he hardly acknowledged Walker's report. For several long seconds the young officer stood silently, while his superiors conferred. It was evident that the rollers in the bay had become far too big for safe boating. The trip to the recreation landing was canceled, a signal was sent to the fort to hold the one boat already enroute, and Ensign Walker was directed by Commander Williams to get all boats ready for hoisting aboard. The time was then just 3:40.

Before it was possible to carry out the last order, the ground swells had further increased to such a degree that it appeared unsafe to bring any boats under the boat booms and cranes of the now heavily rolling *Memphis*. Therefore, at about 3:45, the executive officer directed that the coxswains of the two boats—the steam launch which had just returned from taking Commander Bennett to the *Castine* and the motor launch with the mail orderly—be directed to proceed to sea and await arrival of the *Memphis*. They would be picked up out there in the smoother water. Obediently, both boats headed south, riding easily over the long, undulating rollers, taking mail orderly Thorner on an entirely unexpected cruise.

In a short time it was noticed that a motor launch belonging to the *Castine* had cast loose from that ship and was also proceeding to sea. At a little after 4:00 o'clock all three boats were seen lying-to in a little group, well clear of the anchorage and riding easily in long even swells beyond the deep water line.

None of the fourteen men in the three boats had any real

appreciation of what was going on in the harbor. They had left
before things had become really serious and had every reason to
expect their ships would be out to fetch them later on. As the day
waned, however, the sky became overcast, and darkness came a
little sooner than usual. Visibility—never very good from a low-
lying boat in a seaway—became very poor. At about 6:30 it
began to rain and Thorner requested transfer from the motor
launch, which had no protection from the weather, to Memphis'
steam launch which had a canvas canopy. This was accomplished
without difficulty, the two boats easily holding themselves alongside each other long enough, despite the swell, for the mail orderly to transfer his sack and himself to the larger boat.

All three craft remained in contact with each other until it
became quite dark. The men in the two open boats were the
most uncomfortable, but all of them were hungry, thirsty, bored
with the hard seats, the ceaseless, jerky motion and the lack of
activity. The engineer of the steam launch became concerned
over his dwindling supply of coal. They could not understand
why the Memphis had not come after them, as promised, and
they were completely unable to comprehend the Castine's actions. The gunboat had stood out of the anchorage around 4:45
and had gone out of sight to the southeast but, surprisingly,
appeared not to see them.

The sea rose considerably after dusk, thus further increasing
the discomfort of their situation. Soon the only evidence that
they were not at sea in a completely deserted ocean, in a world
that had forgotten they existed, was the blinking lighthouse of
Santo Domingo, some miles due north of their position.

Commander Bennett had assumed that the men in the boats
would appreciate the advantages of being off shore instead of in
the surf and would simply wait the eventual arrival of the Castine next day. He did not realize that the boats' crews might not
have been able to see the events in the anchorage and therefore
would not understand why no one had come out for them. Next
day they might even expect to be asked, with some disbelief and
possibly even disapproval, why they had stayed out all night and
why, with the rain and increasing heavy seas offshore, they had
not proceeded closer inshore to the protection of the land. It is
undoubtedly true that, had they any realization of the real state

of affairs, they would happily have endured the discomforts of a night at sea.

This was not, however, the decision they made. At some time prior to 8:00 all three boats turned and headed for the lighthouse, keeping together in a more or less undisciplined fashion until, because of the condition of the sea and the reduced visibility, they lost sight of each other. The steamer made it all the way to the coast, about two and a half miles west of the lighthouse, where it was smashed on the rocks at about 8:30. Three of the seven men aboard, J. Schocklin, the coxswain, J. J. Harrington, the engineer, and J. W. Thorner were battered to death by the surf.

Number three motor launch was swamped and sunk about a mile from shore and only two of the four men in the boat survived. W. C. Diehl, the coxswain, and L. L. Crosier, its engineer, were never seen alive again.

The *Castine* motor launch was least fortunate of all. None of its crew of three survived, and consequently there is no information as to precisely the nature of their deaths. The *Castine* launch had remained in company with the *Memphis* motor launch most of the way in toward the lighthouse, and it is probable that the two boats were swamped at or nearly the same time, possibly by the same big sea.

Of the total of thirty-one men in the *Memphis* number two motor launch when it left the recreation dock, twenty-five died and six were rescued. Six out of fourteen men in three other boats which had been sent to sea for safety survived the ill-considered decision to return shoreward. A total of thirty-three men lost their lives when their boats either swamped or were smashed to pieces against the rocky coast.

Chapter 16

THE END OF THE MEMPHIS

Next morning all was quiet. Shortly after dawn, a glum crew gathered on the bluff opposite their ship, now looking so disheveled and beaten. *Memphis* was down by the bow and listed slightly to port, her ruined appearance the very antithesis of the pride they had heretofore had in her. The sea was calm again, the weather balmy. It was as though the great wave had never arrived, that they had not been in danger of their lives only half a day ago. But the *Memphis* effectively dispelled that illusion. Something had indeed swept the harbor the previous day and now she lay firmly wedged on the rocks, less than a hundred feet from the nearest point of dry land. One of the boatswain's chairs which had been used the night before was still where it had been left, and Quartermaster Third Class Vince Peltier went aboard via this means to carry out the ceremony of morning colors.

From the shore it could be seen that the union jack on the jack staff was still flying from the bow, having been left there all night, but the national colors which normally flew from the stern while in port were missing. Inspecting further, Peltier found that the flagstaff on the stern of the ship had been broken in its socket by the action of the seas. Both the flag and the flagstaff now lay in the quiet water gurgling around *Memphis'* stern, attached to the ship by the halyards that had hoisted the ensign at morning colors the day before. Peltier hauled in on the halyards (the upper one had parted) and brought staff and flag and all on deck. Then he detached the flag and carried it up to the boat deck, where he spread it upon one of the engine-room hatches to dry. The previous afternoon there had been another flag prepared for hoisting to the mainmast gaff, where under-way colors were normally flown. This ensign, a smaller one, was still where it had been left, bent on to the halyards but still tucked away, unraised. Thus, morning colors on 30 August, 1916, was made with the "steaming colors" prepared for the day before, hoisted to the under-way steaming position at the gaff of the main-mast.

As Peltier relates the story, shortly he had carried out these duties Captain Beach returned aboard and ordered Peltier to half-mast both the union jack on the bow and the colors at the gaff in respect for those of the ship's company who had lost their lives the day before. Peltier did so; and then, returning to the place where he had laid out the wet flag of the day of disaster, he could not find it. Someone had taken it, and he realized that he would probably never see it again.

In the meantime, the men on shore had begun to fashion a more convenient means of access to the ship and in a short time had completed what they called a "swing bridge," a walking platform between two lines so arranged that a person could work his way on board by walking gingerly on planks suspended between two swaying cables, while holding firmly to a third line for safety.

It was immediately apparent that the *Memphis* would be a total loss. Her bottom was stove in in a number of places, her main engines had been forced out of line by rocks coming in through the bottom, other rocks had driven through into the firerooms, compressing the boilers against the overheads, smashing the tubing and breaking crossboxes, fireboxes, and other component parts, and the lower decks were flooded almost to the water line. Soundings were taken in several places, and it was discovered that *Memphis,* a ship drawing 27 to 29 feet in normal condition, was resting in twelve feet of water. Both propellers and the rudder were partly exposed. That she appeared much nearer to her normal water line, when seen from the shore, was due to the battering her bottom had taken. Damaged, wounded, destroyed, *Memphis* lay there, in mute but eloquent testimony to the power of the elements. As Father surveyed the wreckage of his ship, he was heard to comment that it was difficult indeed to appreciate that all this damage could have been suffered in the space of one half hour.

Late that afternoon the *Castine* chugged slowly into Santo Domingo and proceeded immediately to the dock in the Ozama River which she had occupied during a previous visit there. She looked, as one eyewitness put it, as though she had just been through a battle, and "perhaps indeed she had." Her deck had been swept absolutely clean of all equipment, paraphernalia, and boats. She had great dents in her port bow where her anchor, which they had been unable to secure properly, had been banging against the side until fear that it might smash through the thin side plating had prompted a decision to jettison it in the deep Caribbean.

But the officers and sailors of the *Castine* themselves stared with astonishment at the fate which had befallen their great consort. Their own trials, they realized, had been small compared to those she had suffered.

Of the remaining history of the *Memphis* there is very little to tell. The *New Hampshire,* a battleship a few years older and somewhat smaller than the *Memphis,* was sent to Santo Domingo to remove her guns, salvageable machinery, and whatever other equipment might be worth saving. Then the *New Hampshire* left her there to await the ship-breakers. Thus she remained, a sorrowful spectacle upon the unfortunate coast of Santo Domingo, prey to the lash of storms and the harpies of the land, gutted but still strong, the cynosure of curious eyes. She was to be proof against any further destruction by the sea, against any hurricane spewed forth from the mother of storms, and against the uplifted hand of man as well, for twenty-one long years.

Her ship's bell, dismounted from its position on the foremast, was desired by the Church of Las Mercedes of Santo Domingo and was gladly given in appreciation of the assistance rendered by Emeterio Sanchez and others of the Dominican Republic on the day of the disaster. This bell has been used by the church ever since. In 1930 it was discovered to have cracked, and it was therefore sent to Spain to be recast. It has since been returned to the church and hangs there today, now bearing a Spanish inscription which, rendered into English, reads: "The Bell, which is called Our Lady of Mercies, was re-founded in the year 1930, when the Superior of the Franciscan Mission was the Very Reverend Father Leopoldo Ubrique."

Lieutenant Jones, Machinist Willey, and Chief Machinist's Mate Rudd, the latter posthumously, received Congressional Medals of Honor. Numerous other awards and commendations were awarded to other members of the ship's company.

Lieutenant Peirce was exonerated by the Court of Inquiry held to determine cause and blame attaching to the deaths of twenty-five men in the Naval Service, but he shortly became aware that criticism was nevertheless growing against him for having sent a launch back to the ship loaded with the members of a ship's recreation party without having made adequate check of the weather. That sending it back was a piece of very bad business was proved by what had happened to it; Peirce's explanations of his action were not as good conversation topics as the tragedy to the boat. There were rumors that Lindsay had begged him not to send them back, but that he had stubbornly insisted upon doing so because the Memphis had had a recall flag flying at one time. This signal, intended to recall Lindsay before he reached the shore, had been ordered but was never flown. It was canceled when the motor launch passed the Ozama River bar. It was flown for the first time a little later, when the launch was swamped, with the idea of having one of the boats which had been sent to sea come back to help; but this, of course, could not have affected Peirce's decision and in any case the flag was quickly hauled down.

Another story was that one of the men had refused to go into the boat, and that Peirce had threatened to shoot him if he did not carry out the orders. No substantiation was ever found for this story, but it was nevertheless averred that the man said, "Go ahead and shoot me if you want, but I ain't going out there to be drowned." No one has ever discovered who this man was, or if the exchange actually took place. Possibly the reference is rooted in Teshack's abortive attempt to leave the boat just before it shoved off from the recreation-field dock.

None of the facts of the investigation or the reports of any of the witnesses bears out these stories, and it is probable that, like many such, they are simply versions which developed in after years as memories dimmed and discussions waxed. In any event Peirce never recovered from the shock of being the instrument by which twenty-five men died, of being criticized for not having kept the boat's crew a little while longer, or, indeed for the misfortune wrought by the sequence of circumstances by which the message to hold them arrived moments too late. By chance he once met one of his old *Memphis* shipmates, years later, in a shop in France, approached pleasantly with the query, "Haven't I met you somewhere before?" Upon discovering that the association had been on board the *Memphis,* poor Peirce turned without another word and strode out of the store.

And there is one other loose end to tie up before the story is entirely put to rest. It is possible—though again it is only rumor —that the actual loss of life from this boat was only twenty-three instead of twenty-five. The circumstances are these:

It will be remembered that after Drager had been dumped in the water from the swamped number two motor launch, he saw Teshack and Dugan floating on a piece of wood, a thwart or something that *Castine* had thrown over, and heard them say that they were all right and having no trouble. He never saw them again. There is no specific record of what actually happened to them. In testimony before the Court of Inquiry, however, almost every witness who was asked whom he could positively certify as having been in the ill-fated recreation party boat mentioned first Teshack and Dugan. Even Drager remembered their names before those of the boat crew, who might be expected to be far better known to him. Logically, Drager might have been expected to recall first the names of the men with whom he had been all day long.

Other incidents are still more puzzling. After the disaster, in order to prevent pilferage of the ship's equipment, a guard was set up in tents on the bluff nearby, and every few hours a sentry patrolled the ship. It was customary for this sentry to go into the galley when relieved and bring back "night rations" for the guard personnel ashore in the tents. Chief Boatswain's Mate Mielke one night had the midnight sentry duty on board the *Memphis* and was starting to enter the galley when suddenly, to his consternation, there before him was the shape of a man. Slowly, slowly, the apparition wheeled. Two deep sunken eyes glared at Mielke. Its shrunken skin stretched tightly across the drying facial bones as it made a ghostly grimace of death and foreboding, and after a long moment its rotting vocal chords uttered a deep silent moan. Mielke was terror-struck. Despite the changes which death had brought, he would have known that face anywhere! It was that of one of the dead men, the Indian, Teshack! The gaunt figure made as if to reach for Mielke, and this was more than that otherwise steady individual could stand. He turned and ran from the galley.

From that time on, sentry visits to the darkened portions of the ship were always made with the brightest flashlight it was possible to get, and an extra man customarily went aboard with the relieving sentry at midnight to assist in bringing back the few tins of food which the early morning gourmets required. It was held, at least, that the incident explained one phenomenon they had noted, that someone had been pilfering their store of food supplies in the galley. And it also went a long way to substantiate the theory, held by some, that ghosts did eat, after all, despite their supernatural status. That Teshack's ghostly attitude toward his erstwhile shipmates could not be of the friendliest was accepted by all. Of Indian heritage, taciturn and withdrawn by nature, possessed of no friends on board with the single exception of his buddy, Dugan, an equally tough and hard-to-handle customer, no one wanted to put his infrequent good nature to the test now that he had assumed the spectral form. Teshack's ghost, all agreed, was not to be monkeyed with, any more than Teshack himself had been while still alive.

A few years later two members of *Memphis'* old crew, then serving aboard the *North Dakota*, were talking over old times. "Guess who I saw last weekend in Baltimore," said one.

"Who?"

"Dugan! I was in a beer hall, and all of the sudden there he was, so we sat and talked for a while."

"I thought he went down with that motor launch!"

"That's what I asked him, of course. 'In a pig's eye,' he told me. He and Teshack got a hold of an old door that was thrown overboard from the *Castine* and they drifted about four miles down the coast before they finally found a little cove where the sea wasn't very rough, and they just walked ashore. Some natives took care of them and they decided not to come back. This was too good a chance to miss. Besides, they liked it there. Dugan said that the Dominican natives were all very friendly, and there were a couple of girls there who were especially nice. Teshack and Dugan had both tried to go over the hill a couple of times already. Why should they come back now?"

"So neither one of them drowned! They're deserters?"

"Neither one, and I guess they're deserters, all right. But, as a matter of fact they did come back once. They sneaked aboard the *Memphis* one night and spent about three days there hiding out—you know they knew more places to hide to get out of work than anyone else on board; they weren't the only ones who used to work that dodge, either—and then they shoved off again the same way they came.

"Dugan told me they worked their way to Colombia, where they started a gold mine up in the hills, and every year one of them takes off to come back to the states for a while."

"Well, I'll be damned," said the other. "It figures though. Those guys always were tough, and bad actors besides. But anyway, I hope they struck it real rich!"

To which the first speaker nodded his agreement.

In justice to these two men, it must be pointed out that although the conversation here related did take place, there has never been any factual proof of the authenticity of the yarn. Teshack and Dugan are both still officially listed as "missing and presumed dead" as a result of the events of 29 August, 1916.

Among the crew which returned to the ship in that first group next morning was C. R. Pinkerton, who had scooped up the terror-stricken little dog the day before, placed him inside a coil of rope and then stretched the tarpaulin back over him so he could not get out. Pinkerton relates that his first move upon returning to the ship was to go where he had left the dog, remove the lashings and lift the tarpaulin, and "there he was in his little nest, tickled to death to see somebody."

Early in 1917, Corporal Flatten suggested to his friend, Corporal Rogers, that they pay a visit to the old ship.

As Flatten describes it, perhaps his visit came from only a morbid curiosity, but he preferred to call it a last tribute to the ship in which he had once served. She had once been the flagship of her division, hostess to the President of the United States and other government officials, the pride of the U. S. Navy. Now she rocked slowly from starboard to port—a monotonous, restless cadence—day and night, weeks and months, never ceasing. His description of his visit is imaginative:

An eerie feeling came over us as we approached her. Once she had been a living, pulsating monster of steel, immaculate from stem to stern. Now she was, by contrast, dead, a useless hulk of eroding metal. There seemed to be a spectre of death hovering over her. The sides once glistening gray were now covered with rust. Two gaping holes in her forward turret where her 10-inch guns had been removed stared skyways like a giant skull. The empty gunports along her side yawned hideously like toothless cadavers. We found her deck dirty and disheveled just as the salvage crew had left it, with a few patches of white paint on her bulkheads being all that remained of the painstaking hours which had kept her so shipshape.

There was a nauseating stench drifting up from her hatchways, so foul that it seemed almost visible as it rose from the stagnant water trapped in her hold these many months under the tropical sun. We had been aboard but a few moments when we were startled by a sudden tremor that shook the ship as she began to roll to starboard. First there was a hollow rumble from deep below as her eighteen thousand tons ground into the rocks upon which she rested. It became louder and higher in tone to a groan then a howl, higher and higher in pitch until it reached a piercing scream like that of a woman in distress, but amplified a hundred times. Curiously, the sound of grating steel upon rock coming up through several feet of water modulated the tone into the simulation of a human voice. As she continued to heel over the sound subsided lower and lower until the ship came to a stop with a convulsive shudder. After a period this was repeated as she began to roll to port.

Our curiosity led us below to the gun deck where the secondary batteries were once mounted. It was empty, divested of all the familiar gear. Our voices sounded dull and far away. Sea scum and rust encrusted her deck and bulkheads as we wandered through passageways from bow to stern. It was the same depressing atmosphere when we decided to go below to another deck, defying the stench that had become even more rank, more debilitating. It was much darker. The passageways disappeared into tunnels of total darkness below.

All the while there were those intermittent rumbles, groans, howls and hellish screams that chased each other's echoes through those black chasms that honeycombed her interior, now amplified to a sounding box of reverberation. Still, we attempted to go below another deck, but were stopped halfway down the ladder by water. Our eyes had become adjusted to the darkness so in the immediate area of the hatchway we could see a few yards beyond the smooth, purple black slime that lay below, oozing slowly from side to side with the roll of the ship.

We returned to the topside for fresh air and returned to shore. We left her behind, but ground into my memory were those strange impressions. With poetic imagination I can hear her suppliant cries, as though calling her crew back to quarters to carry on while she struggles ceaselessly, day and night, from starboard to port, as if by her own efforts she could free herself from the coral reef that held her fast. Those fiendish wails and cries might have been interpreted by a credulous person to be the voices of those men drowned, scalded in her engineroom, or who were drowned in the motor launch.

Many years passed before I met an ex-Marine officer who had been in Santo Domingo several months later than I. Our conversation turned to the *Memphis* and he informed me that no one could go aboard her any more, as the suspended gangway across the forty feet of water between her and the shore had been cut down. He explained that it was because the ship had become a too frequent rendezvous for suicides, no less than three or four had occurred on board.

Flatten insists that the ship actually rolled from side to side while he was aboard and that the sound effects were about as he described them. One would have imagined that by this time, with the hulk filled with water up to the level of the sea, it would have no further buoyancy; and that without buoyancy there could not be any rolling motion such as he has described. The fact that he so definitely remembered this led to a search for corroboration, which was found in the report of a salvage engineer who inspected the hulk. He, too, noted the rolling motion. One therefore envisages the hull still basically tight, although flooded, so placed on the ledge of rock that an incoming roller could add just enough buoyancy to rock her on her twisted, armored keel and quicken the ruined body with the appearance of life. No doubt this would be accompanied by much bending and wracking of rusting bottom plating. Such could have been a possible explanation of the motion and the noises. Doubtless they continued for only a few months or so, until some permanent deformation of hull or rock stabilized the wreck and eliminated what semblance of life it still retained.

Chapter 17

Captain Beach's first act, upon returning to the deck of his ruined ship the morning after the wreck, was to direct Peltier to half-mast the colors. Then, with grief in his heart but outward demeanor unperturbed, he inspected everywhere it was possible to reach. *Memphis* was flooded to the level of the sea outside, was listed 5 degrees or so to port, and was down by the bow in conformity with the slant of the ledge upon which she rested. All was calm and peaceful, but she rolled uneasily, with creaking bottom, as the rising and subsiding undulations of the nearly calm sea imparted momentary buoyancy to her shattered hull. Soundings by lead line on both sides of the ship at the bow, amidships and astern showed depths of water averaging 12 feet to port and 15 feet to starboard. She lay upon a ledge of rock and coral extending her entire length. Doubtless there had been considerable displacement of the relatively porous coral as *Memphis'* heavily reinforced keel and battleship bottom plating drove into it; but the conditions of the decks below the armored deck, and the bulkheads supporting them, showed that there had been a corresponding crushing of the ship's bottom. Above the water line there was no evidence of damage; her armored sides had held firm. But below the armor belt it was evident that her hull had been badly smashed, and generally stove in, by the force of the successive collisions with the rocky bottom of the anchorage.

All naval officers are to some extent, by avocation, constructors and designers of ships, even though only a few are members of the specially educated corps of Naval Constructors. Father, because of his earlier engineering background and experience, was especially of this bent. His careful inspection could lead his trained mind to but a single conclusion. There was nothing that could be done for the *Memphis*. It would be next to impossible to lighten her enough to float her off, and likewise, while it might be technically possible to make her hull watertight enough for the long tow back to a repair yard, it would then be necessary to rebuild the entire hull below the armor belt. In the process, this would involve removing, realigning, and replacing all machinery. The effort involved would have been prodigious. It would be easier, and doubtless cheaper, to build an entirely new and more modern ship.

Forward and aft, wherever he could go, hastily improvised lashings on loose gear, water-torn hatch covers, disarranged or not properly arranged heavy-weather battens, smashed boats, broken stanchions and light deck structures, bent ventilators, ripped canvas on the bridge and elsewhere, piles of debris here and there, left either by the seas or by his crew in clearing working space for themselves—all testified to the suddenness of the attack from the sea and the battle put up by his men. On the decks which so short a time ago had been neat and organized, as properly befits a man-of-war, nothing but a jumbled confusion met his eyes. The starboard side gave clear evidence of the power of the sea in the bent and driven-in gun ports and the sundered boat-gripings and holding-down tackle. *Memphis* looked like what she was, a total wreck.

In his own cabin, last seen when he and Commander Bennett had left for the quarter-deck on that once lazy afternoon, seemingly so long ago, a fresh and deeply personal disaster awaited him. Unaccountably the ports around the three-inch gun located in the main section of the Captain's suite had not been properly closed. Every sea had had free access to pour into and back out of his private quarters, and the force of the water had, in its repeated bursting intrusions, destroyed everything, broken everything, swept everything away. The entire space was a shambles. The only thing that remained was the three-inch gun itself, whose rigid mounting, designed to withstand the shock of firing, had stood proof against the sea. Not a vestige of his clothes, his papers, any of his personal belongings, had been spared. Gone were the photographs and mementos of Lucy, whom he had buried in Boston less than a year ago; gone were his books, and the bookcase in which they had stood. Gone, with the chest in which it had been kept, was the medal for his service in the Battle of Manila Bay. The furniture, once so familiar, where he had entertained Secretary McAdoo and the International High Commission, was now foreign to him. What had been bolted to the deck was broken off at the mountings. Everything was smashed into unrecognizable sticks, covered with mud and dried salt, discolored. The only thing he was able to salvage was his Navy dress sword, its scabbard battered by repeated blows from some heavy object, the gilt tarnished and salt-encrusted. It was a depressing sight. He took his sword and left the compartment, never to return.

But he had an urgent duty to perform, and he needed somewhere to do it. He found the place under the bridge, in the bare, sparsely furnished sea cabin in which he always slept while the ship was under way. The room contained only a bunk and a tiny locker, and had no desk. In dimensions it was 10 feet by about 6; but all its fixtures, at least, were still there. Yeoman Third Class Ernest Button, a bright young lad of nineteen whose regular assignment was in the pay office, reported to him in these familiar surroundings to take dictation.

From Commanding Officer, USS *Memphis,*" dictated Father. "To Secretary of the Navy, via Commander, Cruiser Force. Subject, *Memphis*—loss of. Paragraph one. I have to report that yesterday afternoon, at about 5:00 P.M., the USS *Memphis* was, by heavy seas, driven from her anchorage off the city of Santo Domingo . . ."

It is not generally given to enlisted men to have an insight into the inner thoughts of Navy captains, but of those who occasionally do, most are yeomen, whose duties bring them into contact with them on more intimate terms than do the duties of others. Ernest Button, moreover, was not a usual type of person, as might perhaps have been suggested by his history up to that time had anyone known it. His name, first of all, was fictitious. Buttons' real name was Leslie Kidwell. He had run away from home in rebellion at his father's announced plan to educate only his older brother, Alvin, and confine the younger son, Leslie, to the life of an uneducated farm drudge. Fearful of being returned to his father's control if discovered, he had given both false name and false age upon enlisting in the Navy in 1914. The ideal of a proper education was never far from his mind and he studied correspondence courses his entire naval service, during the course of which he rose to the rating of Chief Yeoman. Thirteen years after his discharge he was commissioned a Lieutenant (Supply Corps) in the Naval Reserve, and some time later he was also commissioned a Colonel of the State of Kentucky. It is from Colonel Kidwell, now a retired Chicago businessman and incidentally the brother of the senior State Senator of Kentucky (his father was at least correct in his assessment of the older boy's potential), that the author of this book has obtained much objective detail of how events affected the persons aboard the *Memphis* that fateful day.

Colonel Kidwell recalls marveling at Father's ability, this next day after the catastrophe to his ship, to remain objective as he described her destruction. The trauma of the previous day seemed not to have affected him at all, except for perhaps a more somber mien than was his normal habit. He dictated carefully and precisely, with gradually increasing speed as he found that the correspondence courses which his young stenographer had been taking had given him the capability to keep up, and he waxed eloquent only when rendering praise to the officers and men whose deportment in the emergency had come to his special notice. The letter, when complete, was nine pages long, single-spaced, and Kidwell still recalls with pride that Captain Beach signed the initial draft when he presented it, correct the first time.

Among the passages transcribed by Kidwell in this report to the
Navy Secretary can be found the following:

I invite particular attention to the conduct of Lieutenant C. A.
Jones, Machinist Willey and Machinist George, and such men of the
Engineer's force who were with them. These men stood at their post
with scalding steam enveloping them, with thousands of tons of water
coming down on top of them through hatches and ventilators, and
remained there as long as the engines would turn. I know of nothing
finer; I can conceive of no finer conduct than that exhibited by these
men.

Elsewhere in the letter he wrote:

I cannot forbear from referring to the excellent conduct of enlisted
men, Chief Quartermaster Rose, Chief Electrician Erskine, and others. These were leaders of men. The attitude of all was characterized
by coolness, unselfishness, courage, hopefulness and fearlessness.
    At about the time the ship reached her present position, the Execu-
tive Officer, Lieutanant Commander Williams, was knocked senseless
by a heavy sea and badly battered, as he was carried, charged and
jammed about the decks by the sea. I did not know how badly he was
injured and so, although he had by this time recovered sufficiently to
protest urgently against going, I directed that he be sent ashore. On
reaching shore, bruised and battered as he was, he took charge of the
men as they came ashore. When I got ashore, about 8:15, I found
that Mr. Williams had seen about having sentries stationed about the
ship and patrol parties organized. He had taken means to house all of
the men and to provide them with dry clothes and blankets. For this
splendid officer I shall have enduring admiration, gratitude and affec-
tion.

Of the *Castine,* Father dictated:

It is probable that a more magnificent spectacle has never been
presented than Commander Bennett's management of the *Castine* at a
time when she was in imminent danger of foundering. His subsequent
handling of the *Castine,* with, as I have since learned, a disabled
steering engine, is conclusive proof that he embodies in his character
the highest type of manhood and the highest qualities of a Naval
Officer.

And finally, referring to the loss of life in the boats, Kidwell transcribed these words:

> The full responsibility for sending the motor sailer for the recreation party and sending another motor sailer and a steam launch to what was believed to be a place of safety, belongs to, and must remain with, the Commanding Officer.

The captain of a ship of the Navy assumes entire responsibility for everything connected with her. He is held to the highest standards of performance and leadership, his ship to the most exacting criteria of efficiency and effectiveness. His is the general credit for success, a credit which tradition requires he share with his subordinates, and his is the blame for whatever goes wrong—a blame which tradition holds cannot be passed along to anyone else. A captain who loses his ship during war as the result of enemy action need only fear that somehow his handling of her in combat might be open to criticism; but a captain whose ship is lost or damaged from any other cause, or from any cause whatever in time of peace, must expect that he will at the very least suffer a most searching Court of Inquiry, as the legally constituted investigating body is called, in which his every move and order will be inspected for its complete and perfect adequacy, his every action under the stress of emergency inquired into at leisure and at length, the full benefit of hindsight brought to bear upon it. A Court of Inquiry would soon meet upon the case of the *Memphis,* and the Captain's words in his official report were intended to show only that he knew and intended to abide by the rules of the profession by which he lived.

Of the strenuous and soul-crushing months which followed, his manuscript autobiography has only this to say:

> Within ten days a Court of Inquiry met at Santo Domingo to investigate everything connected with the disaster. They were there two or more weeks and then proceeded to Norfolk. It took them thirty days to complete their inquiry. My court-martial followed, which took three days. All of this time was necessary for complete investigation. If there was anything not thoroughly looked into by the Inquiry and the Court-Martial, I do not know what it was. The guidance of the Navy has been built up by the work of these courts. I know of nothing

more thorough, more unprejudiced. The facts ascertained by such investigation serve to guide officers for the future.

He neglected to mention that there was not one inquiry but three, counting the Board of Inquest into the deaths of those men whose bodies were recovered and a more general Court of Inquiry into the death or disappearance of forty-three members of the Naval Service. All three of these courts met during the first weeks of September, and before all three of them Father was required to repeat, in detail, the story of the travail of his ship and crew during the late afternoon and evening of the twenty-ninth of August. The Board of Inquest and one of the Courts of Inquiry were, however, concerned only with establishing facts as to the loss of life. Both of these were completed by mid-September. The third court had been instructed to conduct a most searching investigation as to the responsibility for the accident, and it sat for eighteen days in Santo Domingo, took a recess for a ten-day period during which the transport *Hancock* carried members, witnesses, and all parties to the Inquiry north to Norfolk, and then sat in the Naval Base there for twelve days more. This court held a preliminary and perfunctory session on board USS *Hancock* on the twelfth of September and then adjourned to meet again on the quarter-deck of the listing, broken *Memphis*.

All surviving officers and men of the *Memphis,* with the exception of those who were still under treatment for their injuries, were mustered. The President of the Court of Inquiry, in a few clearly enunciated words, explained the purpose of the proceedings and the rights of all parties present. The setting was that of a stage play, except that the assembled crew of the *Memphis* were the players and the four members of the Court, including its Judge Advocate, a legal officer, were the audience. Still in the same carrying voice, the President asked, "Captain Beach, do you have the official report made by you on the loss of this ship?"

This was part of the play. "No, sir!" Father's answer was equally clearly heard.

"I hand you herewith a copy of a document certified by the Commander, Cruiser Force as a copy of said report. If you recognize it as a true copy, will you so state?"

"It is."

"What disposition was made of your original report, Captain?"

"The original of this report was delivered to the Commander, Cruiser Force, for further forwarding to the Secretary of the Navy."

The President of the Court, a Captain Hood, was a crusty old shellback of a seadog, about to retire after many years of service. He did not, however, lack a sense of the dramatic. He paused just long enough. "The Judge Advocate will read the official report aloud," he ordered.

And so, with his entire ship's company assembled before him, on his own listing quarter-deck, Father was forced to hear his deeply felt report of the destruction of his ship read by an unknown voice, devoid of feeling, unimpressed by the dimensions of the cataclysm against which they had fought, impressed only by the extent of the damage which he and his crew had somehow allowed to occur to a first-line ship of the Navy. When the Judge Advocate, who was to be the investigative prosecutor during the proceedings of the Court, had finally finished reading, the President asked his next *pro-forma* question: "Is the narrative just read to the Court a true statement of the grounding and loss of the *Memphis?*"

"Yes," said Father.

"Have you any complaint to make against any of the officers or men of said vessel on said occasion?"

"No!"

"Officers and men of the *Memphis,*" said the President of the Court, "I shall ask you the same question. If anyone has anything to say in connection with this question, he will please step to the front." He paused. The ranked men and officers, their count depleted by the absence of those dead or injured, now numbered a little over seven hundred. They stood impassive, resentful at having to participate in this assault upon the integrity of their disaster, this travesty upon the injuries suffered by their shipmates, this incipient deprecation of the worth of their own efforts to prevent it.

The President of the Court was fully aware of the effect of his words, allowed plenty of time for them to sink in before he spoke again. "Officers and men of the *Memphis,* have you any objection to make to the narrative just read, or have you anything to lay to the charge of any officer or man concerning the grounding and loss of the USS *Memphis* on August 29, 1916?"

The ranks stood mute, impassive. The ship's officers, in the front rank, responded first. "No!" they said. Then, like a slowly welling ground swell, a resentful murmur came forth from the serried ranks behind them, an emotion-laden, deep-throated growl of refusal: "No!" The rows of men stood stock-still, each man afraid that his slightest movement might be erroneously interpreted as a breaking of the just-consecrated faith. For a long moment the men of the *Memphis* stood, in agitated hostility, facing the men ordained by officialdom to be their tormentors, facing also, because of the arrangement of places, the man who had been their Captain, who was still their Captain and who, everyone knew, was to be sacrificed for the greater good of the Naval Service at large. This too was preordained, for no captain lost a ship and came out of it unscathed. But they would not be a party to officialdom's intention to add to his torment. Whatever might later be laid to their door in terms of omission or commission on the day of the wreck, in this they would not be faulted.

The record of the Court of Inquiry consists of 482 pages of testimony and opinions, plus two hundred more pages of individual statements and special exhibits. Altogether, it fills a binder five inches thick. For a total of eighteen days the Court sat in the wardroom of the *Hancock,* an ex-Army transport now commissioned in the Navy, which had brought them from Norfolk, Virginia. On the tenth of October it reconvened in Norfolk, having taken all the testimony which it was possible to obtain in Santo Domingo. "Interested parties," by which is meant those persons against whom the evidence might point and who therefore have a right to be present to hear all the testimony, be represented by counsel and question witnesses in their own behalf, were Jones, Williams, and Father. Claud Jones, of course, could not be present since he had been invalided home as quickly as possible and remained under treatment for his burns and steam inhalation for several weeks longer.

On the eighteenth of October, having heard testimony from Lieutenant Jones and Machinist Willey, both of whom were reluctantly released from the hospital for just the time it took for them to appear, the Court of Inquiry rendered its judgment.

Captain Beach had sensed that the decision was going against him and at the end of the proceedings, but before the rendering of the findings, he attempted by means of a carefully considered statement once more to describe the extraordinary circumstances with which he and his crew had been confronted, and the pitiless rapidity with which they had arisen. Even as he read this into the record he knew that, so far as he himself was concerned, this could achieve but little. But there was one thing he might be able to bring off. Tradition, in the Navy, is important and tradition dictated that except under the most unusual circumstances he, the Captain, must stand trial and, unless his every action and every preparation were adjudicated perfect, must suffer some punishment. Even though they had to do their duty and could not let friendship or prior association influence them, there was no member of the Court of Inquiry who did not fully appreciate that he, in the same situation, might have fared no better. Dad's own fight was lost, but he might perhaps even yet salvage the service lives of his trusted subordinates and fellow "interested parties." The traditions of the service did allow him this, and Father therefore concluded his statement with these words:

I believe it has been shown that the senior engineer officer obeyed every order he received with skill, intelligence, and dispatch; that efficiency and fine spirit marked his deportment; that courage and character marked his own spirit and inspired the officers and men with him, and that in standing by his post nobly and heroically he carried out the finest traditions of the Naval Service.

I desire to record my conviction that Lieutenant Commander Williams and Lieutenant Jones each did everything that he should have done; that they did nothing that they should not have done; that neither of these officers in any way or in any degree is responsible for the disaster to the *Memphis,* nor the attending circumstances. Further, it is my conviction that if responsibility in any respect or degree attaches to any officer, it is to the commanding officer and to him solely.

The reaction of the members of the Court is nowhere recorded. That they recognized the statement as essentially the right of

every captain, is probable. Their action, in any case, was in conformity with the tradition.

In accordance with the regulations governing Navy Courts and
Boards, the findings of the Court of Inquiry were divided into
findings of fact, findings as to causes, and recommendations. As
prescribed, they were entirely written by hand and in ink by the
Judge Advocate of the Court, and they fill twenty-four pages of
the long legal-size paper the Court used.

Significant among the findings of fact is the statement that
between 4:20 and 4:30 the *Memphis* was rolling so heavily that
"spray" went above the stacks and "some of it" went down the
stacks—this in the face of evidence by a dozen witnesses, both on
the topside of the ship and on shore, who saw green seas go
higher than the tops of the funnels so that as *Memphis* rolled
deeply to starboard those open tops entered solid water. It was
evident then, and is still clear today, that none of the experienced officers who made up the Court could conceive of a state of
affairs such as had been adduced to them; no ship had ever rolled
so deeply, had ever been beset by seas so great and coming so
close together that as she rolled into the trough of one sea the
oncoming wave front of the next would break upon her with
sufficient height to engulf the tops of her stacks, that the abrupt
cut-off of the flow of black smoke at such times could only have
resulted from the complex blockage of an exit passage and that
this, in turn, could only have happened if the tops of the funnels
were covered entirely.

Also significant is the finding that a tropical disturbance
passed south of Santo Domingo during the night hours and was
estimated as having a force, in squalls, of 10 by the seaman's
Beaufort Scale. This equates to a wind velocity of 48 to 55 knots
and is generally described as a "whole gale." It is worthy of note
that this wind velocity was described as "in squalls" and that the
Court recognized that the wind strength was otherwise considerably lower; but it is of more note that as the *Castine* rode
through this disturbance, with her rudder out of commission and
much water in the ship which her crew was in the process of
bailing and pumping out, her log, which might have been excused for reading things on the high side, estimated the wind as
being generally force 5 ("fresh breeze") and 7 ("high wind") in

squalls. Nevertheless the Court found as a finding of fact that this tropical disturbance, even though there was neither wind nor other indication of weather at Santo Domingo, "produced the heavy swells which, coming in from the deep water to the shallow water of Santo Domingo City anchorage, caused the high seas and heavy surf that eventually dragged and wrecked the *Memphis.*" Disregarding professional testimony from certain officers who had made a lifetime study of oceanography, the dedicated professional Navy men of the Court could not conceive of any other source for the waves than what they had either experienced themselves or studied during the course of their naval careers. Neither the sight of the forlorn hulk of the *Memphis,* lying in twelve feet of water with her bottom crushed and partly torn out, nor eyewitness testimony that the waves had reached an estimated height of sixty feet and completely covered both *Castine* and *Memphis* at their anchorages, could convince these gentlemen that, contrary to all their experience and their years of service in the Navy, something more than a tropical disturbance of minor quality must have taken place on the twenty-ninth of August.

As to causes of the loss of the ship, the Court found that Father should have ordered steam raised sooner, a tautology with which it would be difficult to disagree; that he had anchored his ship in an unsafe anchorage, which was certainly true since all of the Santo Domingo anchorage was exposed to the sea and therefore unsafe; that he had failed to recognize the existence of an emergency soon enough to take adequate action to save his ship. This last was indubitably true, as established by the fact of the wreck itself. Whether Father had reacted "as soon as he should have" was obviously purely a matter of basic subjective opinion on the parts of whoever might have to sit in judgment. No one was held responsible for the loss of life, though in the findings of fact there is mention of Lieutenant Peirce's failure to ascertain the condition of the sea in the bay before sending off the recreation party.

The recommendations of the Court were in a sense a victory for Dad, in that they conformed to the unwritten law that only the Captain has to go down with his ship, and that by doing so he expiates all other sins. For the faults cited in the findings, the

Court recommended that Captain Beach be tried by General Court-martial, but it made no other recommendations regarding anyone else. In simple justice, it would hardly have been possible for the Court to have recommended otherwise so far as the Captain of the *Memphis* was concerned, whatever the private feelings of its members; and in any event they could salve their consciences by reflecting that their decision was not a conviction, but only a recommendation that other proceedings be held, before a completely different tribunal. But it did mean that the interminable administration of naval justice—which in this case meant the pitiless inquisition, over a period of months, of every action taken during *Memphis'* hour of struggle—would have to turn through yet another cycle.

The Navy of course carefully considered the findings and recommendations of the Court of Inquiry. Paramount among the questions to be decided was whether or not a Court-martial, as recommended, should be held. The Secretary of the Navy, mindful of the previous services of Captain Beach in a position of high responsibility, and doubtless particularly sensitive to the fluctuations of fortune as they might pertain to a political career —and therefore to a naval one as well—felt that the cause of justice had already been achieved by the fine grinding of the several courts already convened. Others, and certainly Admiral Caperton in the Pacific, would have expressed a similar opinion had they been asked. But most held the view that no captain can be exonerated of blame by administrative process. A capital ship of the U.S. Navy had been stranded and lost. The processes laid down for such cases must take place.

Late in October the order for a General Court-martial was given. The senior legal officer of the Navy, the Judge Advocate General, was directed to draw up charges, and Father was ordered under arrest awaiting trial. The "arrest," of course, while not a pleasant status, was a formality which meant only that he could perform no other duty while awaiting his trial.

The office of the Judge Advocate General was thorough in its preparation of the charges upon which the final judgment of Father was to be made. He read them with growing concern. How, he thought, could he defend himself against the impenetrable and obscure legalisms which reiterated the same criticisms over and over again, in different guise? The charges were:

Improperly hazarding the *Memphis,* on two counts: not promptly securing for heavy weather, and not keeping sufficient steam up to get underway on short notice.

Inattention and negligence, on three counts: neglecting to keep enough steam up to get underway on short notice, not immediately securing for heavy weather, and not promptly closing gun ports.

Culpable inefficiency in the performance of duty, on three counts: not ordering fires lighted on more boilers, not keeping himself informed of weather conditions, and not choosing a safe anchorage.

Formally and impeccably typewritten on legal document stock, the charges were delivered in mid-December. Father had a few days to obtain counsel and prepare himself for trial, and on the twenty-first of December, 1916, the General Court-martial convened in the wardroom of USS *Connecticut,* the same ship which had led the round-the-world cruise only nine years earlier, now lying obsolete and in reserve in the Philadelphia navy yard.

The initial formalities over, Father was arraigned on each of the charges and on each of the specifications. To all he pleaded not guilty, and the trial began. His counsel was Commander Crosley, skipper of the *Prairie,* a repair ship which had many times been anchored exactly where *Memphis* had been on the twenty-ninth of August. Yancey Williams was present as associate counsel, as was a long time friend from civilian life, a lawyer named John Blair. Yancey Williams, Claud Jones, Newton George, and Charles Willey were among the many witnesses brought forth either by prosecution or defense.

A certain amount of prearrangement of the trial had been allowed by mutual consent. It was at first necessary to get all the facts in the record, and Lieutenant Commander Williams, as executive officer, was the first witness the prosecution called.

"What is your name and rank?" asked the Judge Advocate.

"Yancey S. Williams, Lieutenant Commander," he answered.

"Do you recognize the accused—if so, state as whom."

"I do, as Captain Edward L. Beach, U.S. Navy."

"What duty were you performing on August 29, 1916?"

Several more *pro-forma* questions were propounded, with

Yancey Williams alert to avoid any trap into which he might unwittingly fall to the detriment of his friend and former skipper. This was, so far, only the routine questioning undergone by every witness to establish on the record his competence to give testimony.

"Did anything unusual happen on board the *Memphis* on the afternoon of August 29, 1916?"

"Yes."

"Please state what it was."

This was what both sides had been preparing for.

Choosing his words carefully, Yancey Williams began, once more, to relate the terribly long and distressing story. "At about 3:15 in the afternoon it was reported to me that a dinghy had been swamped alongside the ship. I went on deck . . ."

Yancey Williams' testimony covered page after page in the court-martial record and was followed by page after page of questions. Questions on the ship's organization, her procedure for rigging for heavy weather, the provisions for installing gun-port shutters, for shutting and battening down hatches.

"Were all hands called?" the Judge Advocate, Commander Carter, asked.

"Yes, all hands were called," said Yancey Williams.

"And was the usual call sounded or any alarm sounded?"

"No alarms were sounded at first. Word was passed for all hands by word of mouth."

"What is the most important thing to do by way of securing ship for heavy weather?"

Williams explained the procedures and responsibilities for securing ship, pointing out some of the things that had to be done.

"Did men who were stationed at the six-inch guns go to furl awnings before they went to secure the gun shutters?"

Carter's question was delivered in a rising inflection, a slightly incredulous tone, as though to point out to the Court that men might have been ineffectively employed, or diverted from more important duties.

"No. Some of the men in the ship's company were in the recreation party at this time; some were in the liberty party at this time; some were furling awnings; some were putting in gun ports; some were putting in gun shutters; some were putting down hatches; some were securing the boats for sea; some were securing chests, tables and other articles, and furniture which was not secured at all times for heavy weather. In other words, every man in the ship's company was busy doing something as the necessity for doing all these things came at the same time."

"How long did it take, ordinarily, to put in all the gun shutters on the gun deck and secure the gun shutters of the six-inch and three-inch battery?"

"Under the best conditions it takes about twenty-five minutes to put in the four sections of a six-inch shutter and secure it properly for heavy weather."

The Judge Advocate tried a new tack: "How many boilers was it necessary to have steam on in order to move the *Memphis?*"

"The *Memphis* in the best conditions could be moved with steam on four boilers, but I consider it advisable to have steam on at least six boilers to move a ship of the *Memphis* class."

"How many boilers were under steam on the afternoon of August twenty-ninth?"

"Two, previous to the time that steam was ordered on four additional boilers."

"The two were not sufficient to get under way at short notice?"

"I don't think that the two boilers were sufficient to get under way on any notice."

"Then the *Memphis* was not prepared to get under way on short notice?"

"Yes, she was," stated Yancey Williams firmly.

"Explain what you mean by short notice, if she was prepared to get under way on short notice."

"The *Memphis* was prepared to get under way in forty-five minutes, and the only known danger to be prepared for at the anchorage off Santo Domingo City was from the West Indian or Caribbean cyclonic storms or hurricanes, and as all known storms, so far as I am aware, previous to August 29, 1916, had given more than forty-five minutes notice of their approach, it was my opinion, and still is, that the *Memphis* was ready to get under way at short notice."

It is significant that nowhere in the record of proceedings is there testimony by the Cruiser Force Commander as to why *Mem-*

phis had steam on only two boilers. Nowhere was it brought out that her commander had protested this order, or that previous policy had been to keep four steaming. So far as the evidence placed before the Court shows, this was purely the Commanding Officer's decision.

The reason for this seeming lack must partly be surmised. Father never alluded to it, but John Blair was less reticent. The defense had asked Admiral Pond to testify, and was very disappointed when he asked to be excused. Dad would not countenance Blair's proposal to invoke the statutory right of calling him, and refused to permit the evidence to be presented otherwise.

There were a great number of other questions related to the conditions of the sea, the possibility of the waves being merely from a local blow off shore, whether or not weather warnings had been received. (They had not.) Then the witness was turned over to the defense for cross-examination. Inasmuch as Yancey Williams was an associate counsel for the accused, this examination was also purely to put more facts in the record.

"You have testified as to waves passing over the bridges of the *Memphis*. What did you observe as to the temperature of the water?"

"The temperature of the water changed with the waves coming over; that is, the temperature increased enough to warm up the body while the wave was passing over. I noticed this personally at the time, and in order to see if anyone else had noticed the same thing, I spoke to probably half an dozen or more men of the ship, and to one officer that I remember."

When Lieutenant Withers appeared, many questions were asked him concerning the anchorage and the bearings of navigational markers. He testified, as had Williams, that the ship struck bottom at her anchorage before dragging her anchor. Then the President of the Court, showing his seaman's incredulity at the facts presented, asked, "You testified that the sea passed over you on the bridge. Did you mean to tell the Court that this sea was a solid green sea that passed over you, or was it spray?"

"No, sir," said Withers, "it was a green sea, in which it was necessary to hold one's breath. There were several times that I did not hold my breath and got full of salt water, and the weight of the water, as the wave ran off the ship, would sometimes knock me down."

Lieutenant Jones, when he appeared, answered the same perfunctory questions at first as had all the others. The attention of Commander Carter was, however, quickly directed to the basic issues. "Were two boilers sufficient to move the *Memphis?*" he asked.

In a sense, the answer to this question was crucial to the entire case. Could it be shown that good judgment would have gotten *Memphis* under way on only two boilers—only one-eighth of her total engine power—as recommended in some quarters, then, conclusively, this should have been done. But the question of how many boilers were actually needed to move the ship was itself a matter of judgment, apart from the larger question as to whether, or when, Father should have ordered her under way on the boilers which had been steaming, without waiting for the other four to come on the line. Had the anchor been hove up, or slipped, and *Memphis* been unable, because of low power, to hold her head to the rollers as they swept in from the sea, then assuredly this would have been a serious error. Holding on at anchor to await the availability of greater power, which was also expected momentarily, might have been—and indeed proved to be—inadequate to avert the disaster. But by what criterion should a captain make this judgment? Should it be done on the basis of all previous experience, on everything he knew or had studied about hurricanes in the West Indies, or should he make a new and untried decision based only on the as yet only partially evaluated situation of the instant?

As events turned out, there had not been sufficient time to await more steam. The *Memphis* might have wound up no worse off had she made the effort with two boilers—but she might, also, have been no better off.

Lieutenant Jones did not believe that two boilers could be adequate under any circumstances, no matter what the unnamed engineer officer who wrote a pamphlet advocating the idea might have thought. This, a matter of judgment, was assuredly not his judgment. "No, sir," he tersely answered.

"How many boilers would be necessary to get the ship under way?"

"Four boilers," said the Chief Engineer.

In cross-examination by defense counsel, Jones conclusively confirmed that although some water might have entered fire-rooms by coming down through the ventilators, this could not have gotten into the vicinity of the fires, and that the only water which could have had any effect on the fires was what came down through the tall funnels of the ship. At 4:20, he said, he had every expectation of having plenty of steam at 4:35; but from then on the conditions had deteriorated rapidly.

Lieutenant Shonerd, called as witness, testified to the orders given and action taken to secure the gun decks and main deck. It was evident from his account that a growing feeling of urgency possessed him and all his men, but that while they were able to get the gun-port shutters into position and thus keep out the major portion of the water welling up against them as the *Memphis* rolled and the swells rose, it was impossible to get the dog nuts on the threads and make the heavy steel shutters completely tight. The shutter on number nine three-inch gun, in the Captain's cabin, could not be closed at all. The three-inch gun ports, considerably smaller than the openings required for the much larger six-inch guns, had single-piece shutters which swung outward and down upon hinges along their bottom edges. When raised into position and their dogs set, a circular cut-out fit tightly around the protruding muzzle of the relatively diminuitive three-inch gun. The awkward angle at which the weight of the steel plate had to be attached from within the cabin dictated that a man had to be sent topside with a piece of line to raise it from a position of greater leverage. But this had not been possible since the quarter-deck, from which the line would have had to be worked, was periodically inundated by water over twenty feet deep and anyone venturing out upon it would have instantly been swept away.

Newton George and Charles Willey both testified as to the sequence of events in the engineering spaces, and the futile struggle they and their men had waged to get their ship under way. Brought out was the fact that the main engines had been made ready, that firerooms were on the point of developing steam in adequate amounts, had been developing normally, in fact, hindered only by the extraordinary rolling, until approximately 4:30 when large quantities of water entered the furnaces from somewhere above, in the vicinity of the furnace uptakes, and came down inside to splash upon the fires and drown them. Some time around 5:00 P.M.—when it was evident that there was nothing more that could be done, that the engines could no longer turn and that escaping steam was endangering the lives of all those who remained in the engineering spaces—both fire-rooms and engine rooms had been abandoned.

The engine room reported that an order to put the starboard engine full speed ahead had been received at about 4:45. Testimony from Captain Beach and from other bridge personnel, specifically from Chief Quartermaster Rose, Quartermaster Sheil who kept the "quartermaster's notebook" and Yeoman Second Class John Kernan who was stationed at the bridge annunciators, was to the effect that no order other than "back full" was ever sent to the starboard engine. A little after 4:40, as nearly as can be determined from the accounts, a heavy sea came on the bridge and broke the starboard annunciator short off near where the pedestal was bolted to the deck. The deduction must be made that this casualty simultaneously caused an erroneous order to be transmitted to the engine. There was no inference that this in any way contributed to the loss of the ship; but the very fact that the bridge annunciators were damaged in this way gives some indication of the conditions under which the *Memphis* and her crew were laboring at the time.

Permission had been granted for the Court-martial not to sit on Christmas day. The day following, at 11:00 A.M., the Court met again. The proceedings were taken up almost entirely by an oral argument from Mr. Blair. It is here, perhaps, that the son, from the vantage of fifty years, must fault his father. A navy general court-martial is very different, in many ways, from the civilian courts to which Mr. Blair was accustomed. One of the more subtle differences is that civilian courts customarily judge against a standard of what might be expected of the average citizen, whereas the naval court-martial judges against a standard of perfection in the absolute sense. In civilian courts counsel may use emotion in their arguments before a jury composed of laymen with generally only a rudimentary knowledge of law, it being the duty of the trial judge, a qualified lawyer, to determine the limits of propriety to which such argument may go. Naval courts have no jury. Usually the Judge Advocate is the only trained lawman present, but all—Judge Advocate, members of the Court, the accused, his counsel—are trained in the same profession. Members of the Court sit as both judge and jury, and they pride themselves at being as fair and objective as it is possible to be. They will allow no preventable emotion to affect their judgment. While they will, of course, allow an accused person every latitude to present his case, it is also true that, being only human, they subconsciously tend to hold an accused brother officer to standards which they know they themselves could not have met had they been placed in the same circumstances.

Generally untrained in law, but perfectionists all in a demanding profession and essentially idealists in their outlook, the members of a naval court view their duties with distaste but with one emotion only: the greatest good of the naval service. They do not like outsiders to attempt to tell them how to administer naval justice, no matter how modestly and clearly stated their arguments.

There was no doubt of Father's right to introduce civilian counsel, nor of the precedent therefor. Naval law specifically provides for this. But in a case so directly revolving upon a matter of professional performance there is much room for consideration of whether this was a wise move. Naval officers, professionals in matters of the sea and their organization—the United States Navy—can be excused for developing a little professionalism themselves. The reaction of the court to Mr. Blair can only be guessed. That its members were fundamentally antagonistic to his presence cannot but be surmised; and I, the son who has borne his father's name in the same profession, am the only one with the right to say this.

Father once admitted to me that John Blair, when he learned of the trouble his old friend was in, insisted upon coming to Philadelphia to help in his defense and, after sitting through the entire trial, actively sought the opportunity to make his final argument for him. Mr. Blair, whom I have always known as "Uncle John," died but a few years ago and was always most close and affectionate in his relations with me. Once, in a reflective mood, he told me that he, too, has since felt that he did not correctly evaluate the difference between the positions in judgment of the members of the Court and the members of the civilian juries with whom he most frequently dealt. It would be entirely wrong to aver, in any way, that the Court was influenced against Father by hearing Mr. Blair's argument; but it has since been John Blair's conviction that neither did they permit themselves to be moved in his favor.

Mr. Blair opened his argument objectively enough, pointing out that orders to begin rigging ship for heavy weather, to light fires under four additional boilers and to prepare to get the ship under way were issued within seven minutes of the first inkling of an unusual situation. He also well disposed of the allegation as to the inadequacy of Father's preparations for being able to take *Memphis* to sea on short notice. As he correctly summed up, the whole argument revolved around the definition of "short notice," under the circumstances in which *Memphis* found herself.

Of the total of eight counts in seven specifications upon which the three charges were based, one count was stated twice and one three times. Blair pointed out that all had been disproved. The accused had promptly secured for heavy weather and ordered gun ports closed, if seven minutes could qualify as "prompt" for a big ship at a peaceful anchorage with part of her crew ashore. He had made arrangements to get up more steam if needed, and by actual test this could be done in forty-five minutes. He had used all available means of getting information about weather conditions, more so than had any other captain who had had cause to anchor his ship in Santo Domingo, and he had chosen that anchorage in the roadstead which, by all testimony, was the best one for a large ship like *Memphis*.

The entire decision of the Court as to guilt or innocence, said Mr. Blair, depended upon two determinations: whether seven minutes for the evaluation of the developing situation could be considered dilatory, and, most specifically, exactly what should be considered to be "short notice."

In all this, my father's good friend was on safe ground. Whatever the collective opinion of the members of the Court regarding the presentation of these arguments by a member of the civilian bar rather than an officer of the Navy, the points made were cogent to the case. But then Mr. Blair expanded upon the

subjective judgment required to render opinion on these two
matters and related this to his experience in civil law. Perhaps
the court was not favorably impressed by the subtle challenge to
its competency; perhaps it was. At any rate, the eloquence of
John Blair's words, spoken directly from the heart in the defense
of his friend, my father, ring as true today as the day he uttered
them, half a century ago. They deserved a better audience:

We have listened for three days to what I think is the most dramatic
recital that it has ever been my privilege to hear, more dramatic by far
to me because of the quiet, the studious thoughtfulness, the measured
words, the conservative utterance, in which various witnesses have
recounted it. There have been no disputes on questions of law, no
wrangles over facts, no opportunity or occasion for interjections of
lawyers; without a break, one after another, slowly, carefully, each
man with the obvious weight of his oath upon his conscience, mindful
of his duty as an officer of this service, charged to his lips with the
tense seriousness of the occasion, has told us a story, and, commencing in calm, tropic, summer afternoon, hurrying with ever-increasing
sweep through billows and seas, the maintainance of the ship, and life,
amid crashing water and blackness without light, escaping steam,
death and destruction—all in one half hour. The witnesses who testified have been scalded with live steam, buried under twenty feet of
solid waters, driven across deck and knocked unconscious What else
was transpiring we can only guess. The fact, the all-important fact, the
all-impressive fact is that under these circumstances, with water pouring
into the ship through the smoke stacks and lights going out and steam
weakening and the sea overwhelming, the organization continued;
men were not on dress parade, with vacant spaces in the ranks to
mark their absent fellows, but the things which their drill and knowledge and constant enforcement of duty led them to know had to be
done, were done; and when a man found a spot at a gun port he filled
the spot, or the boatswain's mate put him to it; and that thing has
been held up, not before this court, but it has been held up, that the
siren was not sounded because of imminent collision. Collision with
what? Does an earthquake produce collision? If the floor of the sea
rises or the sea itself separates and the ship drops to the bottom, it is
perhaps a collision, but would the siren being sounded prevent that
or would a collision mat meet that situation? Would any call conceivable by naval regulations meet such a situation?
If there was one thing which human hands, guided by human brain,

could have done to save the *Memphis,* let the accused pay the penalty for his dereliction. It was his duty to do everything human to nerve his personnel to their duty and guide their arms to its performance. But if the requirements of the case were superhuman, if it was the Omnipotent reaching into the sea and crushing that ship that caused her destruction, shall the penalty fall upon one man?

It has seemed to me while sitting here, with this novel experience—novel in its occasion for silence on my part as well as in many other particulars, that there was no need for a lawyer; had we known what testimony was to be offered by the prosecution, what answers were to be given by witnesses, what was to be the atmosphere of the trial, I at least of counsel for the defense, should have strongly recommended that there be no civil counsel present, as there was no necessity for it; but we did not know. Occasion might have arisen, and my friend of more than twenty-five years' intimacy was at the crucial moment of his life, and I had to be here.

I came here to help in the defence, if I could. But the facts speak for themselves. I have remained without ability to help but with power to admire, as I have admired, not only the character of the accused as developed by the evidence, but the character of the service which has developed such men as I have heard testify here, men who could and did comport themselves in an awful cataclysm of nature, as we have heard them recite. I leave here now in the firm belief that the verdict of this Court is going to be, not acquittal—we do not ask simply acquittal—but most full and honorable acquittal. The accused has not been found guilty; there is no proof upon which he can be found guilty, but "not guilty" is not enough. Character, self-respect, reputation among his fellow officers, all things that a man of honor holds dear, demand now that this stain which has been held toward him be waved aside and the one wholly cleansing and repurifying power possible be placed in its stead—a verdict of most full and honorable acquittal.

Commander Carter, Judge Advocate of the Court, listening, can have had but one thought. The hour was late, the trial was done. The members of the Court were anxious to arrive at a decision and be freed of the black duty of judging their follow naval officer. He submitted his case without remarks of any kind. The President of the Court ordered the courtroom cleared. Everyone except the members of the Court left the wardroom of the old battleship.

Two hours passed, and the Judge Advocate was recalled.

To Father, waiting with John Blair, Yancey Williams, Commander Crosley and other friends in a stateroom of the *Connecticut* which had been set aside for them, this intimated an adverse decision. Had the verdict been a most full and honorable acquittal, as Blair had demanded and Father had hoped for, there would have been an opening of the Court and a friendly reading of the verdict. Still he waited; Carter's recall might have been only to explain some obscure point of naval law. But as the minutes dragged, he knew what the signs portended.

Half an hour passed. Then a stirring of chairs and opening of doors gave news that the trial was over. Crosley said, "Let me see what I can find out," and left the room. He was back in a few minutes, solemn-faced.

"I'm terribly sorry, Beach," he said, deliberately employing the friendly salutation despite his inferior rank. "They've hung you on not being able to get under way immediately. Carter wouldn't tell me the sentence, but it's not too bad. And they did make a recommendation for clemency."

Father tried to swallow, could not. His eyes hurt. It had been a terribly long ordeal. Within a year he had lost his wife, then his ship, and now his reputation as a competent, successful officer of the Navy. For four months he had been subjected to the deepest mental torture, buoyed always by the conviction that he had behaved properly, carried out the traditions of the Navy as he knew them, had knowingly done his best at all times. Now the last blow had fallen. In his own mind his conscience was clear, his faith and confidence in himself and his professional ability as great as ever. But could that avail him anything, any more? He would have to go away somewhere. He would ask for leave. Perhaps he could spend some time with his niece and her husband, in Saratoga Springs, where the warmth of their loving hospitality could bring some balm to his burning soul. He would have to think over his next step carefully. Leave, to leave this place of disgrace, was the thing. Unconsciously, he bowed his head. Maybe he should retire from the service. It could hold no more for him.

"Ned," a voice said. He looked up. It was Carlo Brittain, tall and beefy, a classmate and close friend, who had been a member of the Court. Brittain's hand was outstretched. "Ned, old friend, you don't know how sorry I am! There's not a man on the Court who didn't realize that had he been in your shoes he'd have been caught just as you were." His handclasp was almost brutally hard. "I wish I could talk more, but you know I can't. But keep your faith in the Navy!" Then Brittain, a professional success, soon to wear a rear admiral's stars, was gone.

Father hardly knew how to take this final comment, was too choked up to respond to his friend's effort. He mumbled something inane, sat down again. It was John Blair who rose to the occasion, for the others, also depressed, were of far more recent acquaintance. "Come on, Ned," said Blair. "Let's go over to my hotel. I have something in my suitcase that should relax both of us, and then we'll go somewhere and have a good dinner!"

The record shows that the Court found Father guilty on only one count, that of not having enough steam available to get under way on short notice. All other counts were disproved, but since this specification had been laid under two charges, even though the other specifications under these same charges were not proved, he was automatically found guilty of both charges. He was sentenced to lose twenty numbers in his rank of captain on the lineal list of the Navy. The Court also placed upon the record of proceedings, on the page immediately following those containing the finding and sentence, its unanimous recommendation for clemency in execution of the punishment prescribed:

In view of his previous excellent record; and in view of the fact that he took extra precautions which in his judgment would have met the requirements of any contingency; and in view of the fact that the extraordinary conditions that arose so quickly were not only unprecedented but could not be foreseen and came with only slight warning; that apart from the fact that he did not have steam in sufficient boilers to get underway immediately he took every measure which could be taken to ensure the safety of his vessel, we recommend the accused in this case to the clemency of the revising authority.

In February, 1917, the Secretary of the Navy affixed his signature to what at the time purported to be the final action upon this case:

> The Department has given careful consideration not only to the record of the foregoing trial of Captain Edward L. Beach, United States Navy, but also to the unusual circumstances out of which this trial arose (the wrecking of the USS *Memphis* off Santo Domingo City on August 29, 1916).
>
> The only portion of the specifications found proved by the court consists in the allegation that Captain Beach failed to keep sufficient steam on his vessel to get underway "on short notice."
>
> The records of the Department show that Captain Beach has served in the Navy for over thirty-two years, during which time he has maintained a spotless record. His reports on fitness are conspicuous on account of the zeal and careful and efficient manner in which he has always performed his duty. The efficient manner in which he has done so has always met the highest approval of the various distinguished officers under whom he has served.
>
> As shown by the recommendation to clemency, his actions on the occasion of the disaster were sufficient to impress the members of the court-martial which tried him and inspire them to spread upon the record the above quoted impelling and unanimous recommendation for clemency.
>
> The proceedings, findings, and sentence in the foregoing case of Captain Edward L. Beach, United States Navy, are approved, but in view of the recommendation to clemency and the previous excellent record of Captain Beach, the loss of numbers is reduced to the loss of five numbers in his grade.

The loss of five numbers on the list of captains—which only meant that five captains who had been Father's juniors were now advanced over him to become his seniors—was insignificant; the real punishment, one by no means lost on the members of the naval fraternity, was the fact of punishment itself. It meant that there could be no hope of future promotion. He was at the end of the line.

Chapter 18

In Father's unpublished autobiography, written years after the events related so far in these pages, the following appears:

The big comforting fact, the fact that has made me glad, was that in a convulsion of nature rarely experienced in world's history, my noble, splendid ship, *Memphis,* in the face of overwhelming, destroying force, though herself destroyed, yet by the soul of the United States Navy which built her and which had guided and controlled her on the day of her destruction, saved all but fifteen of the eight hundred and fifty lives on board at the time. Twenty-five of the lives lost were in the liberty boat returning to the ship

I do not use the term 'the soul of the United States Navy' lightly. I use it seriously and earnestly. Naval officers had designed that ship; had ordered every rivet that was driven; had made the drawings of every detail of machinery and hull; and the ship had been built under the immediate supervision of naval officers. The officers and men had been trained for their duties by officers of the Navy under Navy Department direction. These officers had inherited the traditions and the experiences of our Navy from its beginning in the year 1775. The men on board the *Memphis* on August 29, 1916, had maintained by their own conduct and actions these traditions. Therefore I believe I am justified in stating that the *Memphis* on that sad day represented, structurally and personally, the soul of the Navy.

Of course I knew that I was finished so far as any future naval career was concerned, and so, naturally, great was my surprise when, a few weeks later, I was ordered to command the Naval Torpedo Station, one of our most important naval stations.

I hurried there. On arrival I telephoned the Commandant of the district, Admiral Sims, that I had been ordered to report to him for this duty, but that I was minus the necessary reporting uniform—that it had been destroyed with the *Memphis*.

"Hell, Beach," replied Sims over the telephone, "come over in your undershirt and drawers!"

Which was quite like Sims.

Father was in this post for a year and a half, during the course of which he earned the thanks of the City of Newport, Rhode Island, for preventing a disastrous munitions explosion by his forethought and early precautions. He also sought out and married Alice Fouché, a descendant of Jean Jacques Fouché of French Revolution infamy. She, the French girl whose family he had protected in Haiti years before, had come to New York to complete her studies.

In September, 1918, he reported to Scapa Flow to take command of the battleship *New York,* then flagship of the American Battle Squadron in the British Grand Fleet. He felt immediately at home. The *New York* was exactly like the *Memphis,* except that she was a one-third larger edition and carried bigger guns arranged in five twin turrets instead of two. Below decks and in the engineering plant she was virtually the same. The engines were identical.

Everyone at Scapa Flow was sure that, sooner or later, the German High Seas Fleet would venture forth once more, and this time, with the dashing Admiral Beatty in command, the unjustified slurs upon the Grand Fleet because of the indecisive outcome of the Battle of Jutland would be avenged. One day, while the Grand Fleet was on maneuvers, word was received that the High Seas Fleet had finally come out. Beatty instantly reversed the Grand Fleet's course and steamed to intercept. The American squadron, steaming last in the formation, suddenly found itself in the van, leading the British Fleet into action; and the lead ship of the entire fleet, destined to be the first to exchange salvos with the enemy, was the fast-shooting, hard-hitting *New York*. For a time spirits ran high, but this greatest sea fight of the battleships never took place. The German fleet got wind of the Allied move and just as quickly returned to port. The next time the High Seas Fleet sallied forth it was to surrender.

Early in 1919 Dad brought his big battle wagon back to our own country and anchored her in the Hudson River. Among the happy visitors who thronged aboard was a diminuitive French girl with a joyous, piquant face. She had wanted to bring the baby, she told the *New York*'s Captain, but had been unsure how she would manage the transition from boat to gangway, and so had left him home. Besides, he had grown so heavy to carry!

In July the following letter was received at the office of the Commandant, Mare Island Navy Yard:

27 June, 1919

From:—Secretary of the Navy
To: The Chief of the Bureau of Navigation
Subject:—*Beach, Edward L.,* Captain, U.S.N.; restoration of loss of five numbers in grade as result of sentence of General Court Martial approved 13 February, 1917.

1. In view of the recommendation for clemency spread upon the record of the General Court Martial in the case of Captain E. L. Beach, U.S.N.; inasmuch as the storm which occasioned the loss of Captain Beach's vessel was of volcanic origin and of such unusual severity that it may properly be considered an act of God which it was humanly impracticable to foresee and to make adequate preparation to meet, and further, [since] the record of Captain E. L. Beach during the war has been most excellent; all of which has been frequently and carefully considered from time to time by the Secretary of the Navy, with the result that I have arrived at the decision that now is the time to take the action clearly indicated in this case and to remit the numbers lost by Captain Beach as the result of the Court Martial above referred to. Therefore, the unexecuted portion of the sentence of general court-martial approved 13 February, 1917, in the case of Captain Edward L. Beach, involving the loss of five numbers, is hereby remitted and the Naval Register will be corrected accordingly.

JOSEPHUS DANIELS

The Secretary of the Navy had not forgotten the Navy captain who, with his cruiser and her complement of sailors and marines, brought order, peace and tranquility to a tiny nearby country beset by internal strife and thereby added to the luster of the accomplishments of our Naval Service, and those who are a part thereof.

Today, fifty years after the wreck of the armored cruiser *Memphis,* it is that baby son, the same who had grown too big for his mother to carry on board the battleship in the Hudson River, who with the help of those members of his father's old crew who still survive has pieced together the story of that epic disaster. Many are the lost details which have come to light in someone's scrapbook, or somewhere in the recesses of his memory. They have been faithfully set down here, and, making allowances for the faults of fading memories and the absence of some who could have added much more had this project been started sooner, they draw an accurate picture of what occurred. The purpose of this book is to tell how Father and his crew were worthy of their ship, and how that ship, staunch and truly built, was worthy of them, and of her naval heritage.

In 1937 a man named Robert McClintock, who later earned the right to prefix his name with "The Honorable" by virtue of attaining the rank of United States Ambassador, was a member of the U.S. Embassy staff at Santo Domingo. In that year he published an article in the U.S. Naval Institute Proceedings in which he gave further details of the final disposition of the wreck of the *Memphis.* Staunch the old ship had stood for a generation, while the son of her captain grew up and in his turn went to the U.S. Naval Academy at Annapolis, and salvage company after company unsuccessfully undertook contracts to break her up. Even after years under salt water and tropic sun, *Memphis'* protective deck and her side armor, wrote McClintock, had withstood the corrosion of time and were nearly as strong as they were the day her builders at Cramp in Philadelphia had put her together. One ship-breaker after another found that his equipment and crews were not equal to the task of cutting through those still shiny plates of special steel. In 1937, however, beginning fittingly enough on the anniversary of the day the old ship went ashore, new modern equipment finally began to bite into the rugged hull. By the end of 1938 there was nothing more to be seen of the remains of what had once been one of the finest ships in the U.S. Navy.

Once a year, on the twenty-ninth of August, the Survivors' Association of the Armored Cruiser *Memphis* meets in some city for a night of reminiscence. Their numbers are dwindling, but the spirit of the Old Navy still glows brightly. Ceremoniously they hoist a somewhat threadbare old flag—the same one which Vince Peltier found gone from the place where he had laid it out to dry—and the same bugler who sounded officers' call on the day of the wreck intones "attention to the colors," on the same bugle, while the same quartermaster who lost it then hoists it now.

How the flag was discovered once more bears repeating. Fireman Second Class Stanley P. Moran had surreptitiously purloined it for a souvenir from the engine-room hatch on the boat deck where Peltier had left it, and it had gone ashore safely and unknown, and back to the States, in his sea-bag. When he learned of the formation of the Survivors' Association, he sent the flag to Les Kidwell, with a letter explaining how it had come into his possession. I first saw it on August 29, 1959, and borrowed it for a while early in 1960, as has already been related.

All that is left of the *Memphis* today are the scrapbooks kept by some of her crew, the undimmed memories of her sponsor who still keeps the broken bit of champagne bottle which she smashed upon her receding bow that December day in 1904, now mounted on a silver base, and a bronze plaque in the city of Memphis, Tennessee, commemorating the loss of life and the heroism of the men who served in her. Her recast bell, now disguised with a new inscription, still hangs in the belfry of the Church de las Mercedes, where the notes to which it has become accustomed have a cadence very different from the quick military striking of a ship's bell; but they are the same clear notes the *Memphis* once heard, and they carry out far beyond the old ship's last resting place and will continue to do so long after all those interested in remembering her have gone from the ken of men.

And, of course, the flag under which she served.

Acknowledgments

At Philadelphia, Pennsylvania, on 29 August, 1959, there came into being the Survivors' Association of the United States Armored Cruiser *Memphis*. Included among its members are the crew of the *Castine,* also in Santo Domingo on August 29, 1916, and certain personnel of the U.S. Marine Corps who were billeted in Fort Ozama. On the anniversary of the disaster, forty-eight years later, at the Memphis Museum in the City of Memphis, Tennessee, the Association dedicated a memorial plaque to their old ship and shipmates in the presence of the mayor of the city and other dignitaries. Emblazoned thereon is a rendition of the ship in the throes of her calamity, the names of those who lost their lives, and the names of Jones, Rudd, and Willey, the three who received the Congressional Medal of Honor.

In the course of the dedication ceremony, the names of those who died were read aloud, accompanied by a roll of drums from a detachment of a Navy Guard of Honor, and with trembling hands and misty eyes, each one of these long-departed dead was reported present at muster by one of his old shipmates, who accompanied the sometimes inarticulate words with a salute in proud memory.

The plaque was unveiled jointly by Mrs. Keith Frazier Somerville, now a great-grandmother, who had christened *Tennessee* sixty years before, and myself, acting for her last skipper. It will someday be joined by the flag which was flying at the time of the wreck, when the Survivors' Association will have ceased to meet.

In preparation of this manuscript, I have been particularly indebted to the following persons:

Mrs. Somerville, still surprisingly like the youthful photograph of herself taken so many years ago on the launching platform of the Tennessee, who loaned me her scrapbook of the clippings related to that cold December day in 1904. She is probably best remembered by the Navy for founding the Society of Sponsors of U.S. Men-of-War, a

303

social group of ladies who have christened the ships in which we serve. In answer to my questions she responded, "Yes, I did launch the ship with champagne," and "Yes, I broke the bottle on the first try. I was told by Mr. Grove just when to hit it a second time, and did it just as the ship was starting down the ways, and I most certainly did say, 'I christen you *Tennessee*—God speed you,' and I was *not* too excited to do that properly!" The fifteen-year-old daughter of the Governor of Tennessee still harbors the thrilling memory of that day. Not only did she launch a great warship—she also received her first proposal of marriage!

Leslie B. Kidwell, ex-yeoman, U. S. Navy, now a retired business-man of Chicago, who prepared Father's official report of the destruc-tion of his ship and first made me aware of the existence of so many of the survivors.

Sam and Alice Worth, of Cleveland, Ohio, who have for years made a hobby of his memories of the *Memphis* and have faithfully collected all the information they could obtain about the ship. It was largely through Sam Worth's efforts that the first reunion took place in 1959, and he has been its moving spirit ever since—aided and abetted by Alice!

Lieutenant Commander Newton R. George, U.S.N. (retired), who provided a veritable treasure of information, all meticulously neat and organized, like everything he has ever done.

Vince Peltier, who was at the time a third class quartermaster, who aided mightily with his clear memories of both the *Memphis* and the *Castine.*

The Reverend W. Angus Wiggins, who was a blacksmith's appren-tice and part-time coal passer in 1916.

Captain Kenneth C. McIntosh, supply corps, who nearly forty years ago wrote an article about the catastrophe in the *Atlantic Monthly* which was of much value.

Machinist Charles H. Willey, who passed on his private papers and a copy of the citation for his Congressional Medal of Honor.

Captain J. Hobart Rockwell, who has been most helpful with con-structive comments and by criticism of this manuscript.

Raymond M. Pennell, who provided a thoughtful review of these written words from the point of view of the port engine room, so long ago.

Captain George W. Davis (SC), U.S.N. (retired) who through his long service with my father in USS *Washington* provided many details of great interest and value.

And the members of the Survivors' Association, listed on the following pages, who have been so generous with the information which they possess and so willing to send me anything and everything which could be of benefit to this effort. It has not been possible to single out each one for the special contributions he or she has made, but I hope that the effect thereof will be evident between the pages of this book, and that those who can identify where their influence has been felt will be pleased with the result.

Everyone who has been in any way associated with USS *Memphis* is living proof that old sailors never die, and that service in the United States Navy, one of the finest organizations of men that has ever existed anywhere, provides a tie that binds forever.

1916–1966
"TO KEEP US TOGETHER"

I submit to you as complete a roster as was possible to obtain, of all known shipmates of the crews of the U. S. Armored Cruiser *Memphis* (*Tennessee*); U. S. Gunboat *Castine;* U. S. Marines who aided in the rescue—wives—widows and several of our most interested friends.

SAM WORTH

January 1, 1966   *Ship's Writer*

† indicates deceased members

A

Robert W. Anderson
    24 Hendrick St.
    Schenectady, New York
Loy R. Andrews (Sarah)
    1905 Burk Street
    Tampa, Florida 33604
Mrs. James Angus (Ruth)
    140 West Walts Ave.
    Deland, Florida 32720
William P. Arrowsmith (Bertye)
    2635 - 66th Terrace, So.
    St. Petersburg, Florida 33712
Merton E. Aspinwall (Elizabeth)
    15 Searle Avenue
    Brookline, Massachusetts 02146

B

Evald Backstrom (Ola)
    2115 Grandy Avenue
    Norfolk, Virginia 23504
Oliver H. Bagnal, Sr. (Grace)
    #7 Elm Street
    Aynor, South Carolina 29511
Taylor M. Baird (Gabrielle)
    25 Circuit Drive
    Waveham, Mass.
Charles Baldwin (Mary)
    11-09 - 150th Street
    Whitestone, New York 11357
John B. Baranski
    1710 East 6th Street
    Long Beach, California 90812
Albert Barker (Louise)
    60 Spear Street
    Melrose, Massachusetts 02176

John A. Barsuch (Mary)
    214 East 10th Street
    Oswego, New York 13126
Captain Edward L. Beach (Ingrid)
    3716 Cardiff Court
    Chevy Chase, Maryland 20015
Mrs. Edward L. Beach, Sr. (Alice)
    1883 Park Blvd.
    Palo Alto, California 94306
Charles E. Beckman
    137 Midway Drive
    Batavia, Illinois 60510
Mrs. Victor Bergstrom
                (Louise Colleran)
    1305 N.W. 58th Avenue
    Margate, Florida 33063
Clay Bernichon (Esta)
    Winter:
    Lot 142, Sunshine Trailer Court
    7403 - 46th Avenue, No.
    St. Petersburg, Florida 33709
    Summer:
    51 Araca Road - #15
    Babylon, Long Island, New York
                                            11702
Lieut. Louis Bertol (Lydia)
    502 N. Norwood Street
    Arlington, Virginia 22203
Thomas J. Betka (Pelagia)
    3479 McShaneway
    Dundalk, Maryland 21222
John E. Birney
    10 West Drumbed Road
    Villas, New Jersey 08251
Ben Blaine (Anna)
    1245 S. Carolina Avenue, S.E.
    Washington, D. C. 20003

Mrs. Otto Blum (Esther)
  87-56 Francis Lewis Blvd.
  Hollis, New York 11423
Lee Bowles (Edythe)
  4753 French Street
  Jacksonville, Florida 32205
Sidney M. Bright (Elise)
  1025 Casa Calvo Street
  New Orleans, Louisiana 70114
Anthony H. Brinkhaus (Bertha)
  10524 Thomas Avenue, So.
  Minneapolis, Minnesota 55431
George H. Broyl (Marion)
  1233 Congress Street
  New Orleans, Louisiana 70117
Harry Burgess
  243 Sunset Lane
  Lakewood, New Jersey 08701
William P. Busse (Phyllis)
  1950 Kenneth Road
  Glendale, California 91201
William Butler (Nellie)
  520 Portsmouth Blvd.
  Portsmouth, Virginia 23704

C

William L. Carlberg (Theresa)
  Route 1 - Box 946
  Bonita Springs, Florida 33923
Andrew Carlisle (Grace)
  2720 Frenchman Street
  New Orleans, Louisiana 70119
William J. Carr (Helen)
  Red Bank & Lincoln Avenue
  Thorofare, New Jersey
Mrs. Alvin Carter (Georgina)
  1514 Behrman Avenue
  New Orleans, Louisiana 70114
Capt. Wilbur J. Carver (Henrietta)
  1926 Collier Avenue
  P. O. Box 22
  Fort Myers, Florida 33902
Mrs. William Chapman (Leona)
  60 Clover Drive #60
  Pittsburgh, Pennsylvania 15236
Mrs. Ben J. Clift (Mary Lillian)
  893 Brookwood Court, So.
  St. Petersburg, Florida
Glenn W. Coate (Mary)
  6146 S. Menard Avenue
  Chicago, Illinois 60638

Alfred F. Cole (Miriam)
  24 Darrow Street
  New London, Connecticut 06320
William H. Cousins (Ruby)
  8519 Philbin Avenue
  Arlington, California
Claudelle M. Cox (Elizabeth)
  100 Kingston Avenue
  Rome, Georgia
Donald M. Cozzens (Elizabeth-Ann)
  P. O. Box 71 Cedarville,
  Michigan 49719
Francis M. Criste, Sr.
  1735 Lexington Avenue
  San Mateo, California
Mrs. Harvey R. Crowell (Ruth)
  1039 North Street
  Pittsfield, Massachusetts 01201
Marshall K. Crowell (Rose)
  2909 White Avenue
  Baltimore, Maryland 21214
Karl R. Crusilla (Irene)
  426 East 163rd Street
  Bronx, New York 10451
Edward J. Cullen (Anna)
  48 Westchester Square
  Bronx, New York 10461
Mrs. James Cunningham (Mabel)
  1328 North Street
  Daytona Beach, Florida 32014
John L. Cunningham (Louise)
  3 South Gilmor Street
  Baltimore, Maryland 21223
William J. Curley
  89-09 - 162nd Street
  Jamaica, New York 11432

D

Lieut. F. G. Darby (Gladys)
  P. O. Box 87
  Oklawaha, Florida 32679
Lt. Cdr. R. T. Darrow
  France Apts. #206
  Stuart, Florida 33494
Rear Admiral Benton W. Decker
  (Edwina)
  1086 Bangor Street
  San Diego, California 92106
Albert DePrez (Nellie)
  R. D. #1
  Thomasville, Pennsylvania 13764

George Dessin (Sarah)
  145 Pinehurst Drive
  R. D. 3 - Box 35
  Mays Landing, New Jersey
Edward Doerwang (Catherine)
  42 Gurley Road
  Nixon, New Jersey
Mrs. James J. Doran (Helen)
  Rt. 2 - Box 293
  Tampa, Florida 33610
Elmer K. Douglas (Gladys)
  4105 N.E. 42nd Avenue
  Portland, Oregon 97218
Henry Dutton (Liddie)
  P. O. Box 8952
  Albuquerque, New Mexico 87108

E

Joseph E. Ellis (Myrtle)
  1230 Redbank Avenue
  R. D. 2 - Box 276
  Thorofare, New Jersey 08086
Mrs. John P. Ernst (Anne)
  2326 S. Bancroft Street
  Philadelphia, Pennsylvania 19145
Mrs. Gus Erzmoneit (Jessie)
  16 Brower Avenue
  Clifton, New Jersey
Al R. Eselhorst (Anna Mae)
  19 Eastship Road
  Dundalk, Maryland 21222
Mrs. Roy Ezzell (Corinne)
  11709 Sussex Avenue
  Detroit 27, Michigan

F

Joseph W. Farrell (Albina)
  1510 East Susquehanna Ave.
  Philadelphia, Pennsylvania 19125
Mrs. John R. Fernald (Lorraine)
  Box 68
  Greenland, New Hampshire 03840
Fred L. Finch (Irma)
  2830 N. Tonti Street
  New Orleans, Louisiana 70117
Alfred H. Fink
  P. O. Box 2564
  Cleveland, Ohio 44112
James J. Fitzsimmons (Pearl)
  21 W. McKinley Dr.
  Poland, Ohio 44514

Louis N. Flatten
  648 Northeast Avenue
  Tallmadge, Ohio 44278
Harold T. Flavell
  17 Chapin Street
  Hartford, Connecticut 06114
George H. Freda (Bertha)
  94 Luddington Avenue
  Clifton, New Jersey
Mrs. Ada Frybarger
  1213 Fairfield Woods Road
  Fairfield, Connecticut 06432

G

Mrs. D. C. Gaines (Ruth)
  5646 Heiskell Street
  Philadelphia, Pennsylvania 19144
Robert J. Ganley (Alice)
  1885 Shore Drive, So. #527
  St. Petersburg, Florida 33707
Mrs. Henry R. George (Gladys)
  305 Severn Avenue
  Metairie, Louisiana 70001
Newton R. George (Ellen)
  4515 North Woodburn Street
  Milwaukee, Wisconsin 53211
Julius Goldsmith (Beatrice)
  627 West 164th Street, Apt. 31-A
  New York, New York 10032
Bertram R. Graham (Mary)
  85 Heard Street
  Chelsea 50, Massachusetts
Mrs. George Guerin (Mary)
  24-42 - 33rd Street
  Astoria 2, New York 11102
Howard Guerin (Blanche)
  Coloma Road
  Rt. 4 - Box 19
  Placerville, California

H

Charles H. Hadley
  8 McKinley Street
  Concord, New Hampshire 03301
Clifton O. Hall (Blanche)
  73 Government Street
  Kittery, Maine 03904
Mrs. Albert Hanson (Olga)
  3011 Humboldt Avenue, No.
  Minneapolis, Minnesota 55411
Mrs. Arthur Harder (Anna)
  1060 - 65th Street, So.
  St. Petersburg, Florida 33707

Patrick Hayes †
557 - 56th Street
Brooklyn, New York 11220
John W. Hayner †
196 McKinley Drive
Mastic Beach
Long Island, New York 11951
Walter E. Henderson (Fairy)
4953 West 12th Street
Indianapolis, Indiana 46224
Millard W. Hessler
20 W. Hazel Avenue
Orlando, Florida 32804
Mrs. Edwin L. Hoffman, Sr. (Della)
205 Hughes Street
Berwick, Pennsylvania 18603
John Hoffman (Mary)
345 North 9th Street
Philadelphia, Pennsylvania 19107
William Hogan (Jean)
2290 N.E 126 Terrace
N. Miami, Fla.
Henry H. Holland (Elizabeth)
14 East Palmer Avenue
Collingswood, New Jersey 08108
Frank Horan (Marcelle)
7736 West 14th Avenue
Palm Springs Lakes
Hialeah, Florida 33012
Mrs. Frank C. Huntoon (Frances)
3727 South Braeswood Blvd.
Houston, Texas 77025

I
Diamond L. Iannetta (Adeline)
2427 South Iseminger Street
Philadelphia, Pennsylvania 19148
Mrs. Albert H. Ison (Annie)
842 Virginia Avenue
Hapeville, Georgia

J
J. Walter Jones (Regina)
2915 Garnet Road
Baltimore, Maryland 21234
Mrs. Claud A. Jones (Margaret)
640 Holley Road
Charleston, West Virginia 25314
Thomas Dewey Jones
1623 - 26th Avenue
Hueytown, Alabama

Ernest Judson
1213 Fairfield Woods Road
Fairfield, Connecticut 06432
Charles Junius
3120 N. Romero Road, #26
Tucson, Arizona 85705

K
Harry L. Kaplan
c/o Commodore Hotel
11325 Euclid Avenue
Cleveland, Ohio 44106
Joseph Keehen (Lillian)
811 Locust Avenue
Long Beach, California 90813
Joseph A. Kennedy (Maxie)
76 E. Wesley Road N. E. #3
Atlanta, Georgia 30305
Les B. Kidwell (Betty)
1003 North East Avenue
Oak Park, Illinois 60302
Mrs. John Klein (Bessie)
4717 Prince Georges Avenue
Beltsville, Maryland 20705
Mrs. Fred W. Kleps (Phoebe)
631 Park Avenue
Amherst, Ohio
William J. B. Knokey, Sr. (Mildred)
455 Park Street
York, Pennsylvania 17404
Carl Kraft (Violet)
3511 College Avenue
San Diego, California 92115
Adolf Kronemeyer
753 Warren Avenue
c/o F. Schneider
Thornwood, New York 10594
Anthony L. Kuchta (Mary)
3556 So. 15th Street
Milwaukee, Wisconsin 53221

L
Earl F. LaBrague (Julia)
123 Henshaw Avenue
Space 218
Chico, California 95926
Earl Clayton Lee
3237 Fairmount Avenue
San Diego, California 92105
Commander Chester E. Lewis
19 South Gate Avenue
Annapolis, Maryland

Fred F. Lindemuth (Myrtle)
2114 Donald Street
Ft. Pierce, Florida
Clarence Lindenberg (Loretta)
Chasha,
Minnesota
Cdr. Stephen A. Loftus
5147 - 33rd St. N.
Arlington, Va. 22207
Grover Long
#8 Riche Manor
Georgetown, Illinois 61846
Mrs. William W. Long (Tillie)
2145 - 11th Street
Bremerton, Washington
Theodore M. Losch (Dorothea)
2203 West Morse Avenue
Chicago, Illinois 60645
Mrs. William Luckock (Mary)
#11 French St.
N. Quincy Mass.
Harry M. Ludwig
899 Lafayette Avenue
Union, New Jersey 07083
Carl E. Lundgren
135 Eldridge Street
Cranston, Rhode Island 02910

M

Ira A. Majo (Theresa)
Cape Vincent,
New York 13618
Arthur McCormick (Sadie)
46 - 8th Avenue
Brooklyn, New York 11217
Clyde H. McCormick (Orrie)
P. O. Box 62
Jasper, Florida 32052
Frank O. McNaughton †
2210 So. 75th Street
Milwaukee, Wisconsin 53219
Mrs. Charles J. Mongan (Mae)
118 Hancock Street
Cambridge 39, Massachusetts
Mrs. Stanley Moran (Stella)
1401 Maryland Avenue Apt. 6C
Wilmington, Delaware 19805
Capt. Tom Moran
2325 "S" Street - N. W.
Washington, D. C. 20008
Alvion P. Mosier (Anna)
611 Rector Street
Philadelphia, Pennsylvania 19128

Robert R. Myers (Viola)
458 Platt Street
Long Beach, California 90805

N

Charles Nelson
c/o Naval Home
24th Street & Grays Ferry Road
Philadelphia, Pennsylvania
Walter J. Nobles
Rt. 4 - Box 460
Ft. Worth, Texas 76112

O

John W. Ostrom (Lillian)
224 S. Bruce Street
Baltimore, Maryland 21223

P

Major Andrew J. Pancoe (Gertrude)
70-35 - 72nd Street
Glendale, New York 11227
Donald Parmenter
12612 Rose Avenue
Los Angeles, California 90066
Vince Peltier (Vena)
5350 East 21st Street
Tulsa, Oklahoma 74114
Raymond M. Pennell (Henriette)
Millrift,
Pennsylvania 18340
Harold Pheasey (Mamie)
13717 Woodward Blvd.
Cleveland, Ohio 44125
Fred Pickard (Ruth)
McGregor Groves
1438 Charles Road
Fort Myers, Florida
Capt. Nathaniel M. Pigman (Juliette)
2505 N. E. 43rd Avenue
Portland, Oregon 97213
Charles R. Pinkerton (Mary)
R. D. 1
2923 E. Emig Road
Comins, Michigan 48619
Capt. Arthur R. Ponto (Marjorie)
254 Mira Mar Avenue
Long Beach, California 90803
Henry B. Power
P. O. Box 422
Walhalla, South Carolina 29691

Howard S. Pryor (Lillian)
Star Motel
Rt. 1 - Box 2890
Port Richey, Florida 33568
Theodore B. Purvis (Ellen)
P. O. Box 133
Dover, Florida 33527

Q

Harry Querry (Faith)
Pinettes
Belfast Post Office
Prince Edward Island
Canada

R

Mrs. Francis A. Rachiell (Elizabeth)
2865 Lake Avenue
Baltimore, Maryland 21213
Mrs. Harry Rash (Eva)
207 No. 12th Street
Independence, Kansas 67301
Mrs. Thomas Reed (Anna)
135 Lynn Avenue
Hampton Bays, Long Island
New York 11946
Mrs. Caroline B. Renne
3 Oak Street
North Aurora, Illinois 60542
Mrs. Forest A. Rennick (Dorothy)
3742 Campbell Street
Riverside, California 92509
Mrs. Walter A. Reynolds (Florence)
6330 - 30th Street, So.
St. Petersburg, Florida 33712
Reuben J. Roberts (Clara)
2135 White Street
Dubuque, Iowa
Irvin E. Robinson (Mildred)
109 S. Main Street
Champlain, New York 12919
Capt. J. Hobart Rockwell (Mary)
232 Stonewood Avenue
Rochester, New York 14616
Mrs. Fred F. Rogers (Winifred)
63 Ayrault Street
Newport, Rhode Island 02840
Col. Joseph A. Rossell
c/o The Roosevelt
2101 - 16th Street, N. W.
Washington, D. C. 20009

Mrs. Fred Russell (Eva)
Rt. 2 - Box 59
Bradenton, Florida 33505

S

Charles C. Savage
2109 No. Spruce
Wilmington, Delaware 19805
Leo A. Schario (Esther)
15 Park Street
Danville, Illinois 61832
Mrs. Walter Schneider (Frances)
753 Warren Avenue
Thornwood, New York 10594
Rear Admiral Roscoe E. Schuirmann
(Hardinia)
3315 "N" Street N. W.
Washington, D. C. 20007
John T. Shanahan (Elizabeth)
3108 Chesterfield Avenue
Baltimore, Maryland 21213
Mrs. Edward R. Sharp (Elvira)
17877 Lake Road
Cleveland, Ohio 44107
Cdr. Henry Shonerd, Jr. (Mildred)
8257 Rensselaer Way
Sacramento, California 95826
William E. Small (Elizabeth)
1401 Desire Street
New Orleans, Louisiana 70117
Lawrence J. Smith (Letty)
1410 E. Florida Street
Long Beach, California 90812
Thomas Snyder
26 Schemerhorn Street
Brooklyn, New York 11201
Mrs. Keith Frazier Somerville
517 S. Victoria Avenue
Cleveland, Mississippi 38732
John Spencer (Ethel)
208 Franklin Street
Cape May, New Jersey
Joseph F. Stein (Anna)
190 Tate Avenue
Buchanan, New York
Page Steiner (Viola)
153 Galveston Place, S. W.
Washington, D. C. 20032
Mrs. Max Stone (Martha)
9 Dean Road
Milton, Massachusetts 02186

Herman Struck (Helen)
4351 Shamrock Avenue
Baltimore, Maryland 21206
Thomas W. Stubbs, Sr. (Mabel)
Route 1 - Box 14
Helena, Alabama 35080
Frederick Sturm (Helen)
17 Lincoln Avenue
Lehigh Acres, Florida 33936
Nestor J. P. Sullivan
40 Florence Avenue
Creskill, New Jersey 07626
Frank B. Sumner (Ivy)
200 Chesapeake Avenue
Portsmouth, Virginia 23704
Earl E. Sutton (Rose)
4021 Paula Street
LaMesa, California 92041
Hugh G. Swaney
Smithville,
Missouri 64089
Charles Swartley
3186 Maine Street
Long Beach, California

T

Bert Taylor
c/o New Amsterdam Hotel
2142 Euclid Avenue
Cleveland, Ohio 44115
Mrs. Elbert Terhune (Pauline) †
2726 Bridgeport Road
Indianapolis, Indiana 46231
E. R. Tomlinson
#142 St. Lucie Crescent
Stuart, Florida 33494

V

Harry Vortriede (Helen)
2737 So. 12th Street
Philadelphia, Pennsylvania 19148

W

Mrs. John A. Walker (Marie)
2101 Hildarose Drive - #102
Silver Spring, Maryland
Mrs. James L. Wallace (Velma)
2510 Tulane Avenue, Apt. B
New Orleans, Louisiana 70119

Tom Wallace (Belva)
4304 W. Capitol
Jackson 9, Mississippi 39209
Mrs. Harry Warshaw (Pearl)
2730 Collins Avenue
Miami Beach, Florida
Carl W. Wass (Rachel)
630 West Vale View Drive
Vista, California 92083
Arthur H. Watson (Rose)
735 Washington Avenue
Charleroi, Pennsylvania 15022
Major Steve L. Watts (Ruth Virginia)
P. O. Box 226
Front Royal, Virginia 22630
William D. Weise (Bertha)
1412 Morling Avenue
Baltimore, Maryland 21211
James Wells
Rt. 1 - Box 154
Big Stone Gap, Virginia
Roy Whitlock (Lucille)
2656 W. Milton Road
Tucson, Arizona 85706
Rev. W. Angus Wiggins (Marjorie)
535 S. Seneca Blvd.
Daytona Beach, Florida 32014
Charles H. Willey (Rose)
R. F. D. #7
Lake View Drive
Penacook, New Hampshire 03303
Daniel Williams
c/o Naval Home
24th Street & Grays Ferry Road
Philadelphia, Pennsylvania
Mrs. John Guy Wilson (Thelma)
114 Wedgewood Drive
Lafayette, Louisiana 70501
Franklin L. Woodruff
1721 Centre Avenue
Reading, Pennsylvania 19601
Sam C. Worth (Alice)
4019 Stilmore Road
Cleveland, Ohio 44121

Z

Mrs. William J. Zimmerlund (Anna)
843 N. Oxford St.
Indianapolis, Indiana 46201

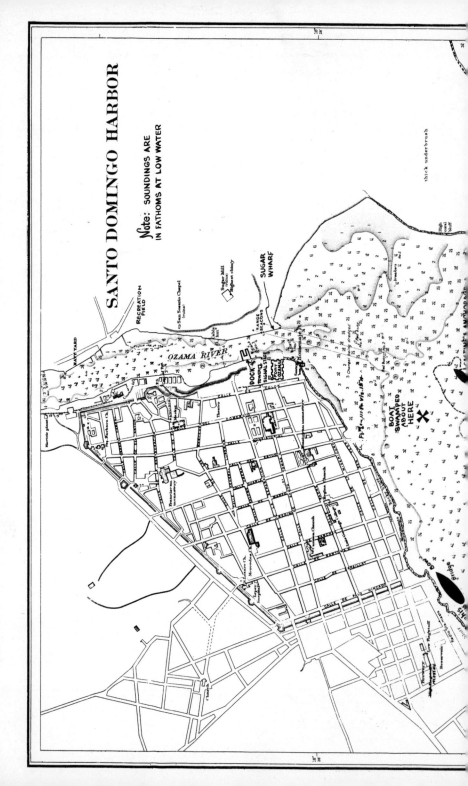

SANTO DOMINGO HARBOR

Note: SOUNDINGS ARE IN FATHOMS AT LOW WATER